# Endorsements for *Lonely No More*

"*Lonely No More* offers a clear path to healing your false beliefs and learning to love yourself. Margaret Paul shares a surprisingly powerful process that shows you how you can meet your innermost needs, and as a result, be able to deeply connect with others. This book is not to be missed."

—MARCI SHIMOFF, #1 *New York Times* bestselling author,
*Happy for No Reason* and *Chicken Soup for the Woman's Soul*

"Margaret Paul's book, *Lonely No More*, offers a powerful process for learning to love yourself, take responsibility for all your feelings, and learn to fill yourself with love to share with others. An important book for these tumultuous times."

—JOHN GRAY, Phd, best-selling author of
*Men are From Mars, Women are From Venus*

"The greatest gift we will ever give ourselves is the gift of true and soulful self-discovery. It is the foundation of sustainable freedom and joy in health, in relationships, and in life. Dr. Margaret Paul's work is an accessible, skillful process of guiding anyone who wants to learn to see with their heart, their true magnificence, receive that gift, and create a life they love. Thank you Margaret, you've done it again!"

—DR. SUE MORTER, Best Selling author of *The Energy Codes: The Seven Step System to Awaken Your Spirit, Heal Your Body and Live Your Best Life*, Creator of BodyAwake Yoga, Developer of LiveAwake Life Mastery Training

"*Lonely No More* guides us in a loving and compassionate way toward healing the wounds and resistance that lead to anxiety, depression, anger, addictions, and the many social problems of our time. Margaret Paul provides a clear transformative pathway to connect with yourself, others, and your intuitive guidance."

—JUDITH ORLOFF, MD, *New York Times* best-selling author
of *The Genius of Empathy* and *The Empath's Survival Guide*

"Margaret Paul has been a true leader in the field of helping people work through the pain of their traumas and return to loving themselves. Her process has always been empowering, brilliant, and down to earth. Now, in *Lonely No More*, Margaret takes us on a spiritual journey of deep and permanent personal transformation.

"*Lonely No More* provides an abundance of help for those of us who are tired of living a life filled with blocking beliefs dissolving our true desires and our dreams of what we wish to create in this life. These blocking beliefs keep us disconnected from ourselves and life and also create a lonely life.

"*Lonely No More* is filled with a wealth of spiritual tools and practices to move readers back into connection with life, joy, and to bringing in the goodness of life. This book is a treasure and Margaret Paul gives us so many gems to inspire us to live a life of joy and connection to all. I am so happy for all who get to read this book and now have the opportunity to create the life they want."

—SANDRA INGERMAN, MA, award winning of author of thirteen
books including her newly released book *Walking Through Darkness:
A Nature Based Path to Navigating Suffering and Loss*

"*Lonely No More* guides the reader in a loving and compassionate way toward healing the woundedness and resistance that lead to anxiety, depression, anger, addictions, and the many social problems of our time. The always brilliant and profoundly insightful author, Margaret Paul provides a clear path for you to connect not only with yourself and others, but with your higher guidance. This book will change your life."

—DEBRA PONEMAN, bestselling author and
founder of Yes to Success and Ageless Seminars

"*Lonely No More* is a beautiful offering meant to help us more deeply connect with ourselves and others. It will support anyone who has suffered with feelings of separation and loneliness to learn the inner practices of loving themselves as the foundation of loving others. Written by a masterful practitioner of the art of self-love, this soulful book goes straight to the heart of the matter."

—KATHERINE WOODWARD THOMAS, *New York Times* bestselling
author of *Calling in "The One"* and *Conscious Uncoupling*

"With compassion, simplicity, and mind-bending wisdom, Dr. Paul captures our greatest existential pain and shows the path to personal joy, love and meaning. I don't say this lightly; this stunning book is bursting with transcendent yet deeply accessible wisdom.

"Step by step, Dr. Paul teaches us how to heal the ache of aloneness and the pain of self-criticism by developing a living, joyful relationship with our own healing inner guidance. This book is a bible for self-love and self-understanding. It's a map for creating a better world, and a life rich with joy and love. I'm in awe of the life-changing wisdom in this book. I urge you to welcome it into your life."

—KEN PAGE, LCSW, Psychotherapist, bestselling author of *Deeper Dating*, and host of the Deeper Dating Podcast

"*Lonely No More* is a treasure chest full of gifts to provide you with the tools you need in today's world to rise above fear and into the love and compassion for ourselves and each other that we need to heal our planet. A wonderful book!"

—CHARLOTTE REZNICK, PhD, author of *The Power of Your Child's Imagination: How to Transform Stress and Anxiety into Joy and Success*

"Dr. Margaret Paul's brilliance once again shines a powerful light on our Divine connection and a profound sense of Oneness with all of life. *Lonely No More* takes you on a journey of self and spiritual connection that leads to the end of ever feeling alone or lonely once and for all. Essential reading for today's connected, yet seemingly disconnected world."

—ELIZABETH HAMILTON-GUARINO, bestselling author of *The Change Guidebook* and Founder of BestEverYou.com

"In *Lonely No More* you will learn an incredibly powerful process for healing pain and moving into peace, joy, and loving relationships. This practice of Inner Bonding, taught by Margaret Paul, one of our true sages, is a simple yet powerful process that is life-changing and much needed for all of us."

—ANAT BANIEL, founder Anat Baniel Method®NeuroMovement®, author of *Kids Beyond Limits, Move Into Life*

"The current mental health epidemic stems from millions of people feeling lonely and isolated. Margaret Paul brilliantly shares the antidote in *Lonely No More*. The Inner Bonding process presented to the reader cultivates self-love, acceptance, and healing, putting them in touch with the Oneness that connects us all. The personal transformation that *Lonely No More* provides is the foundation for becoming a well-adjusted, happy, and fulfilled citizen of the world."

—ORNA & MATTHEW WALTERS, founders of Creating Love On Purpose

# LONELY NO MORE

## The Astonishing Power of Inner Bonding

MARGARET PAUL, PhD

WITH DR. ERIKA CHOPICH

MEDIA

Published 2024 by Gildan Media LLC
aka G&D Media
www.GandDmedia.com

Front cover design by David Rheinhardt of Pyrographx

Interior design by Meghan Day Healey of Story Horse, LLC

Library of Congress Cataloging-in-Publication Data is available upon request

ISBN: 978-1-7225-0673-5

10   9   8   7   6   5   4   3   2   1

*This book is dedicated to my grandfather,
my Zayde, Morris Brustein,
who filled me with his love as an infant,
whom I lost when I was thirteen months old,
who is always with me, and who has
lived in my heart my whole life,
guiding me in my highest good—and
who plays word games with me every night.
I love you, Zayde.*

—MARGARET PAUL

# Contents

## PART III

### *Putting Love into Action*

# Acknowledgments

I am eternally grateful for my clients around the world who have had the courage to do their deep healing work and thereby contribute to the healing of our planet. I feel privileged that you have allowed me to guide you in your healing process. You inspire me!

The examples in this book are often composites of a number of my clients, and all names have been changed. If you recognize yourself, it's not necessarily because the example is about you, but because so many of us have the same issues.

I'm very thankful for all our Certified Inner Bonding Facilitators and our Facilitators-in-Training for doing your inner work to become loving role-models for others and for your clients. I'm especially grateful to Karen Kral for creating the Inner Bonding Facilitator Training Program, to Stel Fine for her wonderful work as director of training and expansion, and to Grace Escaip for stepping in to Stel's shoes as director of training so that Stel can serve as senior director of training and focus on expansion. And I'm deeply grateful for our wonderful trainers who, along with Grace and Stel, do an incredible job: Michael

Barmak, Victor Granville, and Winnie Huff. And thank you also to Jane Gosling for all your support work.

I am grateful to our assistant, Valerie Lippincott, for your many years of devotion and loyalty to us and to Inner Bonding. We could not do what we do without you.

I'm very grateful to Lee Erickson and his daughter, Elise Erickson, for all your work and support at Evermore Success in promoting our Inner Bonding launches, podcasts, courses, and other products, for dealing with the everyday webmaster challenges, and for always being available. I'm so glad I was led to you.

Thanks go to my agent, Dan Strutzel, for always believing in me and in Inner Bonding.

My deepest gratitude goes to Erika Chopich, my Golden Girl housemate and cocreator of Inner Bonding, for your unfailing wisdom when I need it the most. As I've often said to you, you are a miracle.

And finally I am grateful, moment by moment, for my higher guidance. You are my guiding light, and you never fail me.

# PART I

## *Living Disconnected from Love*

This section explores the fears we have about opening up to our higher power and how we got these fears. We take a close look at our need for control and our fear of being controlled, which blocks our direct experience of Divine love.

The material in this section, as well as in the rest of the book, has come from my personal experience with the love, truth, wisdom, comfort, and strength of my higher guidance. It is *my* truth, not *the* truth. Whatever does not feel true to you, toss aside and, using the Inner Bonding® process you will learn in part II, discover your own truth.

# 1

## Feeling So Alone and Lonely

Angie, a new client, shows up a little late for our appointment on Zoom. A very attractive woman in her early fifties, she is obviously agitated. I welcome her and ask her what led her to seek my help. She immediately bursts into tears and then apologizes for crying. I reassure her that her tears are fine.

Angie fills me in on her childhood, which, in one way or another, is similar to those of most of my clients. Some of them tell me about abuse—physical, sexual, emotional. Some tell me about being in foster homes with no sense of belonging. Some tell me that their parents treated them lovingly, but that their parents treated themselves and each other badly, so there was no role model for taking loving care of themselves.

Angie tells me about extreme neglect. She tells me how alone and lonely she feels, even though she is married and has children. She tells me of her struggles with addictions such as Facebook, sugar, and shopping. She says they are the only ways she knows to handle the unbearable feelings of aloneness, loneliness, and emptiness.

"My husband is a kind man," she says, "but we are not connected with each other. I'm on medication for depression, but it's not helping much. I've had years of therapy, and I still can't figure out what's wrong. Why do I still feel so lonely and empty?"

I take Angie through a brief Inner Bonding process, and she quickly discovers how deeply she has been abandoning her inner child—the aspect of our soul that exist within our body and often communicates through feelings. Through feelings of aloneness and emptiness, as well as anxiety and depression, her inner child had been telling her, "You don't pay any attention to me. You don't listen to me. I don't exist for you. You're always judging me, telling me I'm not good enough."

Like practically all my clients, Angie was treating herself the ways her parents had treated her and treated themselves. We tend to absorb the false beliefs and self-abandoning behaviors of our parents, other caregivers, siblings, peers, teachers, and other authorities. These beliefs and self-abandoning behaviors become lodged in our lower left brain—the lower left amygdala—along with instinctual fight, flight, or freeze reactions to fear and trauma.

In Inner Bonding, we call this part of ourselves the *wounded self* or *wounded ego*. We created our wounded self as a means of survival, but this is the part of us that needs healing.

Since a major aspect of the Inner Bonding process is to connect with a higher, wiser aspect of ourselves—the aspect of our soul that exists all around us—I ask Angie to tell me about her connection and relationship with her higher self, spirit, or her concept of God.

(To the reader: if you are uncomfortable with the word *God*, please substitute whatever term you prefer, such as *higher power, the Divine, higher self, spirit, universal intelligence, the All, Goddess, great mystery, Divine love, Nature,* and so on.)

Angie looks puzzled.

"I . . . I don't know. I can't say I believe in God or have a relationship with God. I guess I believe there is something there, but I don't know how to have a connection with it."

She takes a deep breath.

"If there is a God, then he feels like just another hurt. Someone else who is supposed to love me and care about me and doesn't. Like even to God, I'm not special enough to be loved and cared about."

Because Angie has projected her image of her unloving, neglectful parents onto her concept of God, she feels alone in the universe.

I have found that even my clients who believe in God or a higher power do not experience the love that *is* God. They don't have a two-way communication with the love, comfort, wisdom, guidance, peace, and joy that is available to all of us.

Angie bursts out in despair. "Just look at my life! There's no love or joy. I can't get off my medication, and I'm still depressed. I hate my job, and I gained six pounds this month. I've tried everything, and nothing helps."

I feel the depth of her despair. It's clear to me that Angie has no idea how to love herself. She obviously had no role modeling from her parents, who also had abandoned themselves. Without a connection with her higher self, she has no way to access the information about what is true and loving to her.

Most of us grew up with no role modeling for being a loving adult. We don't understand what it means to love ourselves—to take responsibility for our feelings of pain and joy. Since there are so few role models in our society, we need to access this vital information from a higher source of love and truth in order to be the loving adult that our inner child needs us to be. But if, like Angie, you don't know how to do this, you might be feeling the way she feels: anxious, depressed, shamed, alone, lonely, empty, and angry. These are some of the painful feelings we experience when we are abandoning ourselves.

I ask Angie to imagine an older, wiser aspect of herself, her higher self. I ask her to imagine that she is in a beautiful place in nature with her higher self. I ask her to also imagine that her inner child, around two years old, is there, and that she can see her inner child—her beautiful soul self—through the eyes of her loving and compassionate higher self.

The answer comes slowly: "She's so sweet, a really good kind person . . . loving, sensitive, curious . . . she loves nature . . . she loves to dance . . . playful . . . adorable . . . loves animals."

"Is there anything wrong with her?" I ask.

"No!"

"Is there anything about her that doesn't deserve your love?"

"No!"

For the first time in the session, Angie is smiling. I can see the relief in her face.

"Do you want to learn to love your inner child?" I ask Angie.

"Yes!"

"Then you need to learn and practice Inner Bonding, which is a very powerful pathway to learning to love yourself and connect with your higher source of guidance. Right now, ask your higher self what your inner little girl needs from you in this moment to begin to feel your love."

"She needs me to hold her."

I ask Angie to pick up a pillow and hold her inner child the way she would hold a child she loves. She holds the pillow next to her heart and rocks her inner child. I ask her to buy a doll or stuffed animal that represents her inner child.

For Angie, holding her inner child is just the beginning of learning to love herself and taking responsibility for her feelings, but it is a start. I ask her how she is feeling.

"I feel some peace inside. And I don't feel alone and lonely right now! Wow!"

This is the astonishing power of Inner Bonding. And it gets better with time and practice.

Andrew, well-educated, well-dressed, fifty-two, is telling me why he is seeking my help. Unlike Angie, his life is very full and rewarding. "I have everything I ever thought would make me happy and secure. I am highly successful, in work that I love. I have a wonderful wife and beautiful children. Yet I awake each morning with anxiety, and I often feel an emptiness inside. And I'm so lonely. I just can't figure out what the problem is."

These stories certainly differ in their details. My clients' life situations can be very different, but the suffering they feel is similar, regardless of race, gender, age, religion, or sexual orientation. Some are married, others are single, widowed, or divorced. Some are happily married, and others are not. Some have children; others are childless. Some are wealthy; others are not. Some like their jobs, and some hate their jobs. As children, some felt loved by their parents, while others felt smothered or abandoned. Some were beaten or sexually abused, while others were neglected. Some are alcoholics or drug addicts (although most are not). Some came from a rigid religious upbringing, some from a supportive religious upbringing, while others came from atheist households. Some believe in a higher power, while others don't.

Despite the diversity of their backgrounds and the differences in their present circumstances, most of the people I work with have five things in common:

1. They suffer from anxiety, depression, guilt, shame, anger, aloneness, loneliness, or emptiness.
2. They do not know how to love themselves or take personal responsibility for their own feelings and needs.
3. Because they don't know how to love themselves or fill themselves up with love to share, they do not know how to love and be loved by others without becoming needy, jealous, controlling, judgmental, or submissive. Often, they are losing themselves, giving themselves up.
4. They have tried many avenues, from therapy to prayer, from medication to meditation and plant medicine, but nothing has brought them inner peace and joy. Their efforts give them temporary relief but no true healing. They often say to me, "I've been seeking healing for twenty years, and Inner Bonding is the first thing that's working for me."

5. They do not have a direct personal experience of or consistent connection with a wise, powerful, loving, comforting, and compassionate source of higher guidance, and they don't know how to have this connection.

Regardless of whether their outer lives seem to be working well, on the inner level these people are adrift. They have no tether to hang on to, no strong hand to hold to keep them from feeling alone within and overwhelmed by the challenges of life. They have no one to guide them, no one to trust. They feel hurt, powerless, or insecure, and they often feel worthless and unlovable, no matter how much they've achieved. They are left feeling alone and lonely, like an abandoned child with no warm, loving source of strength and wisdom to turn to.

Many people have lost their way because they don't know how to connect with their source of love and wisdom. They don't trust that we each have a personal source of higher guidance that unconditionally loves us and is always here for us. They don't trust that this guidance is always available to lead us toward our highest good. As a result, they also fail to trust and connect with themselves, their own inner wisdom, the part of us that *is* a spark of the Divine. They don't know that they are truly lovable and that their spiritual guidance loves them exactly as they are. They may have the false belief that the love from their Divine source is conditional upon their being a certain "right" way—that they have to perform to be worthy of love.

When I ask my clients about whether they have any kind of spiritual connection, I get many different answers. Some believe in God or a higher power. Some do not. Of those who do believe, some resist the idea of having any connection to a spiritual source of love. They have been taught that God is judgmental and controlling. They think if they open themselves to their higher power, they will have to give up their freedom and autonomy and hand over their decision-making power. The last thing they want is some outside force telling them what to do and how to be. The last thing they want is to feel controlled.

Others believe God or a higher power exists but is not there for them personally. They think they are not lovable or worthy or important enough to be loved by their concept of God. They have not opened themselves to a spiritual connection because they think their higher guidance has already seen their flaws and the door to love and guidance is closed to them.

They are mistaken. God shuts the door on *no one*. The energy of love that is God is unconditional, constantly available, and directed personally at every single individual on earth. It is there for you, whether you believe in it or not, and whether you think you deserve it or not. It is as omnipresent as the air around you. But the people who come to me cannot accept this because they do not know the beauty of their true soul self; nor do they know how to have a firsthand and ongoing experience of the love and wisdom that is always here for all of us.

I have also met people who have opened themselves to a higher source of guidance with their whole hearts, but still do not know how to personally experience their spiritual source of love, wisdom, and guidance. Never having had such an experience, they cannot know their true worth or learn how to take loving actions toward themselves. Many of them do not even know that they have the *right* to take loving care of themselves; they think their job is to take care of everyone else. They may be exhausted from trying so hard to be loving to others, wondering when it will be their turn to feel loved. Even those who are deeply religious and have a profound love of God do not necessarily feel loved by the love that is God.

Without this deep, daily personal connection and dialogue with their higher guidance, these individuals do not know how to utilize the love, wisdom, and power of this guidance to recognize their true worth, discover their gifts and passions, take loving care of themselves, and share love with others. They do not know how to create ongoing loving relationships. They do not know how to learn the lessons of their aloneness and loneliness and discover what brings them deep, abiding joy, fulfillment, and inner peace.

If you recognize yourself in this description, and if you desire to discover how to create and maintain a daily, ongoing, and personal connection with your higher guidance, this book was written for you. Read on.

## You Never Have to Give Yourself Up to Be Loved

Like many others in our society, I reached adulthood with no sense of being loved by a higher power. I was raised by atheist parents and an orthodox Jewish grandmother who believed in a controlling and judgmental God. I rejected both my grandmother's punishing God and my parents' denial of one, but I was left with only questions, a bottomless sense of aloneness, and a thirst for understanding and healing. After forty-five years of searching for answers to my questions and relief from my suffering, I was led to discover, with Dr. Erika Chopich and the help of our higher guidance, the astonishingly powerful, transformational Inner Bonding process for connecting with my higher guidance in a deep, personal, and profound way. It moved me and my clients out of feeling like victims of our past and our pain and into personal empowerment. My purpose in writing this book is to show you how to use the life-changing Inner Bonding process yourself, or to enhance your current Inner Bonding practice.

Each day, as I've lived the practice of Inner Bonding, I've received answers to the many questions I've asked of my spiritual guidance and continue to ask. As we go along, I will share with you some of the answers I've received. So let's start with questions and false beliefs I had before I started to practice Inner Bonding.

Many of us have been taught that love is something we have to earn and that to do so, we have to give ourselves up and be what a partner, parent, or friend wants us to be. We might also project that belief onto our concept of God, thinking the Divine wants us to act in certain ways and that Divine love depends upon how we act. We may also have been told that we have to put aside what we want, give up our freedom of choice, and allow our higher power to choose for us.

I can tell you from my firsthand experience that none of this is true.

These false beliefs are sometimes perpetuated by parents or religions that want to control you. But your higher guidance does not want control over you, nor does it want you to be anything other than exactly who you are. Your wounded ego, which was created by false beliefs as part of your survival strategy, wants to control everything on the grounds that this is what will make you safe. It also believes that your higher guidance wants to control you.

As I've already mentioned, we each have two "selves": our true soul self and our false self, often called the *ego*. Your true soul self is the part of you that is a spark of the Divine—the divinity within you. This is your intrinsic way of being: your soul gifts and talents, your particular form of intelligence, your ability to love, your playfulness, joy, passion, aliveness, curiosity, intuition, and natural wisdom. It is your essence, the light within, the unwounded aspect of your soul. According to my friend, neuroscientist Dr. Jill Bolte Taylor, our ego lives in the lower left brain, while our true soul essence, our inner child, lives in the lower right brain.

Your false self is the wounded part of you, the part that learned self-abandoning, controlling behaviors to protect you from the deep pain that you might have experienced growing up: rejection, abandonment, emotional smothering, domination, neglect, shaming, and perhaps physical or sexual abuse. It is called "false" because it is not your true self. It is the facade you created to help you survive a lack of love when you were young. That facade hides a frightened, lonely, heartbroken inner child. Your wounded self has learned many ways to have control over getting love, avoiding pain, and feeling safe.

Your wounded self is your inner critic, as well as your resistance, compliance, anger, blame, and withdrawal. Your wounded self learned to numb your feelings with addictions, to disconnect from your body, stay focused in your mind, and not feel. This wounded self might believe you have to give yourself up to be loved. It may have learned to judge and criticize you to get you to do things "right," coming from the false belief that being "perfect" will enable you to get love from others and avoid rejection. Your wounded self believes you need others' approval to be OK.

If you did not get the love you needed as a child—when "love" came and went with your parents' moods, busyness, or the level of alcohol in their bloodstream—you did not feel safe. Because safety is essential for survival, you created your wounded self to get love, avoid pain, and feel safe. This wounded self can be many different ages, depending on when you absorbed a false belief or adopted an addictive or controlling behavior.

After a while, you may have completely lost touch with your true soul self and came to believe that your false ego is who you really are. Although it was created as a stopgap measure to ensure safety in childhood, it may have taken over your entire identity.

Your wounded self believes that opening to your higher self and allowing it, rather than your wounded self, to guide you means giving up your ability to control others and outcomes, which comes from the false belief that you *can* control others and outcomes.

Your false self not only fears losing control over others, but may also fear being controlled by others and by your higher guidance. When you do not trust that your higher power is always directing you toward your highest good and that your Divine source loves you and is here for you personally, the last thing you want to do is open up to your higher power. To your wounded self, surrendering to your higher guidance may mean giving up your autonomy and being controlled by an outside force. If your parents were controlling, it may feel like putting yourself back into that child position, being told what you "should" and "shouldn't" do and being shamed when you do not live up to expectations. In this case, your wounded self will naturally resist opening to your higher guidance with all its might.

Ironically, the "protection" of your wounded self causes you to feel even more pain. No matter how hard it tries to get love, you remain feeling overwhelmingly alone and lonely. On you alone falls the burden of keeping everything under control. You are probably exhausted from working so hard. You even have to do double duty: making sure everything works while making sure you do not get hurt in the process.

Once you start trying to control external things and events, life feels *anything* but free. It feels more like a burden than the sacred privilege it is.

The wounded self puts you in a terrible dilemma. If you do not invite your higher source to guide you, you must live with unbearable aloneness. But if you *do* open up to your higher guidance, your wounded self believes that you risk being controlled by an outside force. Or it believes you risk discovering that a higher power is too busy for you or that you are not worthy of Divine love. Even worse, the wounded self fears discovering that there is *nothing there*—no higher power, no spiritual source of love, wisdom, and comfort—and that you really are alone in the universe.

Our childhood experiences often lead us to make a number of erroneous conclusions about God that may make it difficult for us to open to and trust our higher guidance. These false beliefs prevent direct communion with our source of love and truth; they also trigger many of the dysfunctional choices we make in our adult lives. I have encountered eight major false beliefs about God, some of which you may harbor within your wounded self. If so, they may underlie your difficulty in having a direct and consistent experience of Divine love and wisdom:

1. God doesn't exist.
2. God exists, but not for me.
3. God is a controlling, judgmental man whose love is conditional. In order to be loved by God, I have to change who I am, give up my freedom, and be who God wants me to be.
4. I will never be good enough to please God.
5. God uses me to help others, but does not come just for me.
6. God has favorite people and showers them with blessings.
7. God made me come here to this planet.
8. If I sacrifice myself for others, I don't have to take care of myself. God will do it for me. God owes me for all the good I do.

Sometimes people try to open up to their Divine source only to find their way blocked by fear and unconscious false beliefs. You may repeat over and over, "I let go and let God," "Thy will be done, through me," or "Make me an instrument of thy peace." But in your heart, you cannot let go of control. You cannot leap empty-handed into the beckoning void. It is too terrifying. Who will keep you from falling if you let go of your control and there is nothing there to guide you?

What if you knew *for certain* that you would never have to give up any part of your true soul self in order to open up to your higher guidance? That all you have to give up are the mistaken beliefs and controlling ways of your false, wounded self? What if you knew *for certain* that spirit exists, loves you unconditionally, is here for you personally, and is directing you only toward the liberation of your true soul self and your highest good?

It would be a huge relief. Yet the only way you can truly know this is to have a direct personal experience of your higher guidance: firsthand contact with the immense force of love that cradles the universe. The good news is this experience is not difficult to have. I will show you how you can have it every day of your life.

## The Source of All Love and Truth

Let me clarify what I mean when I use the word *God*. What is "God"?

As I've said, God is love. God is the source of compassion and truth, peace and serenity, freedom and joy, creativity and beauty, healing and transformation. God is Spirit, consciousness, wisdom, and power. God is the learning, evolving, and loving force that creates and sustains all of life.

*God is not "out there" somewhere.* God is always right here, within you and around you, available to you the moment you open your heart and invite love in. When you do so, you *feel* within your heart and body the spirit of love, light, compassion, wisdom, peace, and joy that is God. You *hear* and *see* the wisdom and truth of God through an open mind. These are gifts from God that you must open to and invite within; you cannot generate them on your own. You can know and experience the love that is God only when you are truly open to learning about loving yourself and others, which is an important aspect of the Inner Bonding process.

Love is an energy, the energy that is God. When your heart is open to love, you become filled with this energy and can share it with others. When parents bring the love that is God to their children, the children feel safe and lovable; they know they are not alone. They know they are loved by God because their parents are bringing Divine love to them. They know that love exists within them because they experience it, so they know themselves to be a part of God.

If the love and wisdom and comfort that is God is available to each of us, why don't more of us experience it? Why are so many of us suffering? How did we lose our trust and faith in God? Why do we turn to food, sex, TV, overworking, drugs, alcohol—almost anything—rather than filling our emptiness with the love and grace that is God?

The immense suffering many people feel today is the result of numerous generations of spiritual abuse. Let me explain: *A direct, personal experience of the love and truth that is God is our birthright.* Therefore, anything that disconnects you from experiencing this love and truth can be called spiritual abuse. You may think that *abuse* is a harsh word to use in this instance—especially in cases where the abuse is not intentional—but as we look at its effect on children, I think you will find the use of this term is warranted.

From birth, many of us are treated in ways that disconnect us from a direct experience of the love and truth that is God. If you were taken away from your mother after you were born and put into a hospital nursery or left alone to cry, you likely became terrified. You were little and helpless, unable to take care of your own needs. You instinctively knew that if someone did not come to take care of you, you would die. Children often unconsciously translate being left alone by their parents as being abandoned by God. While most parents dearly love their children and have no intention to abuse them in any way, they may not realize how frightening it is for babies to be left alone, feeling helpless. This is how spiritual abuse, however unintentional, may begin.

Other modern child care practices continue this abuse. I was raised in the days when parents were taught that babies should be allowed to cry. "It will spoil them if you pick them up," said experts such as Dr. Spock. "Besides, it's good for their lungs." So my mother, wanting to be a good mother, gritted her teeth and allowed me to cry, denying the instincts that told her to pick me up. Not trusting herself (because she had also suffered spiritual abuse), she trusted the so-called experts instead. As a result, I inherited a substantial legacy of spiritual abuse. I have had to spend years—and a great deal of money—recovering from the fear, helplessness, and shame that I experienced at being left alone when I needed to be held or fed.

Many of us felt so abandoned in infancy and childhood that later in life, even if we do believe in God or a higher power, we don't believe that God will be there for *us*. We have problems feeling spirit's love and acceptance and opening to spiritual guidance. How can we rely on Divine love, comfort, and wisdom when our parents were not there in the way we needed? Even loving, well-intentioned parents may not know how to be there for their children in the way their children need. We may have ended up feeling alone even while knowing that our parents dearly loved us. My clients often say to me, "I know my parents really loved me, but I did not feel loved. They just didn't see me or understand what I needed." Or, "My parents were loving to me, so why did I often feel so alone?"

For many adults, being left alone is still terrifying; it may feel as if our very survival is at stake. The buried memory of infant aloneness and helplessness—when we would have died if someone did not come to care for us—is deeply etched into our psyches. My clients describe it as feeling as if they are lost in outer space with the tether to their spaceship cut, consigned to drifting in the infinite blackness until death claims them.

The intensity of these feelings can be so overwhelming that they trigger a host of dysfunctional behaviors: drinking, drug use, compulsive eating, compulsive shopping, gambling, sexual addiction. We turn to these things in unconscious desperation to distract ourselves or ease the pain.

This does not imply that leaving a child alone for a few minutes is abusive. Nor does it imply that children left in loving daycare will suffer spiritual abuse. Each child responds differently to being left alone. Besides, the intention to be loving to a child goes a long way to soften the effects of less than perfect parenting.

Having suffered from spiritual abuse does not mean that our parents were abusers. Spiritual abuse is more often the consequence of our society's child-rearing practices than of our parents' intents. Many of us suffered from unintentional spiritual abuse. It is important not to blame our parents for our difficulties. Most of our parents did the best they could, as we do with our children. Nevertheless, it is important to understand how our false beliefs and resulting disconnection from spiritual guidance may have come about.

## All Abuse Is Spiritual Abuse

Spiritual abuse is more than just not holding children when they need it. It is also holding or touching them with an intent other than to love them, such as:

- To get love *from* them
- To control them
- To physically abuse them
- To sexually abuse them

In fact, all abuse is ultimately spiritual abuse, because it undermines your sense of self and your relationship with the love that is God. Giving children anything other than love and compassion is spiritual abuse, because all unloving behavior toward children creates an ongoing problem in their relationship with their parents, which may then be projected on to their concept of God. Any behavior that teaches children that they must be different (smarter, more polite, more obedient) in order be loved by their parents or by God is spiritual abuse. Any behavior by an adult that disconnects a child from their Divine essence is spiritual abuse. Any behavior that undermines a child's belief in a higher power as an infinite source of love, compassion, and wisdom that is *always available* to that child is spiritual abuse.

Parents are supposed to be instruments of love, bringing the love that is God to their children. Unless you felt safe in the arms of your parents, you may not know that you can safely rest in the love that is God. Unless you felt unconditionally loved as a child, you may not be able to experience being unconditionally loved by your higher power—at least not until you heal from your spiritual abuse.

When parents are needy and use their children to get something from them—love, security, attention, energy, a sense of power—children learn that they are unworthy of receiving love, that they are just objects to be used by others. They may come to believe that their worth lies either in giving to others and sacrificing themselves or in accomplishments that will get attention and approval. If children only receive attention or approval when they are "good" or accomplish something, *they come to believe their worth lies in what they do rather than in who they are.* And when they feel unworthy of receiving love for who they are from their parents—their personal demigods—they feel unworthy of receiving love from their higher power.

Many clients have told me that they hated being held by their mother or father. It felt as if the very life was being sucked out of them. Many were shamed for crying when they didn't want to be held or touched, derided with words like, "What's the matter with you? You're such a cold person." Often they have carried the mistaken belief that there was something wrong with them for not wanting to be held. As they heal, they are relieved to recognize that they had good reasons for detesting their mother's or father's touch. It was a touch that *took* love, not gave it.

Parents are supposed to make sure their children are safe and healthy by setting loving boundaries, such as preventing a child from running into the street or burning a hand on a hot stove. Parents are also supposed to help their children learn to trust themselves. They do this by showing their own trust in their children's ability to know what they want and don't want, as well as what does and doesn't feel good (when safety and health are not an issue, of course).

When parents control their children through verbal abuse (shaming, judging, criticizing, discounting, threatening) or physical abuse (hitting, beating, any violence to the body) instead of setting loving boundaries and trusting the child, children learn to feel inadequate and to distrust themselves. *When children feel inadequate, they feel unworthy of love. When they learn to distrust themselves, they learn to distrust others and the love and wisdom that is God.* Trying to control a child through verbal or physical abuse is spiritual abuse.

Sexual abuse is also spiritual abuse. When parents or other adults abuse children sexually, they teach children that they are objects to be used. Sexual abuse violates not only the body but the soul, instilling shame, fear, and powerlessness and robbing children of any feeling that they are worthy of love. When adults, who are supposed to make sure children are safe, betray them by hurting and using them, children may decide that God either doesn't exist or has betrayed them.

I have heard about a few advanced souls who come into this life remembering that the spark of God exists within them, but the rest of us had no way of knowing we were worthy of being loved if our parents did not bring the love that is God through to us. If, as we grew up, we had been able to remember that we have the light of Divine love within, we would not have traded our true soul selves for the bulletproof vests and steel helmets of the false self.

But we were taught that the adults around us knew better than we did about who we are. We thought that if we were lovable and worthy, we would receive love from our caregivers. We believed that if we were good enough, they would not use us, shame us, or leave us alone with the deadly lost-in-outer-space feeling. We had no way of knowing that our parents were also wounded, that they may not have known how to love themselves any better than they knew how to love us.

As a result of our spiritual abuse, we are left without a direct experience of the love that is God, feeling desperately alone.

Fortunately, there is a way to completely heal from whatever level of spiritual abuse we experienced. Below is a very brief summary of the Six Steps of Inner Bonding. In part II, you will learn how to utilize them to heal from spiritual abuse and discover peace, joy, and personal connection with the love, truth, wisdom, and power that is God.

## Inner Bonding, Step One

Choose to move from mind focus into body focus, becoming aware of your feelings. Become willing to feel your painful feelings, rather than avoiding them with addictions. Take responsibility for the ways in which you may be causing your own pain with self-abandonment, and accept responsibility for creating your own peace and joy.

## Step Two

In the Inner Bonding process, there are only two intentions to choose from:

- The intent to get love, avoid pain, and try to feel safe with various forms of controlling and avoidant behavior.
- The intent to learn about loving yourself and others.

In step two, you consciously choose the intent to learn to love yourself and others. Making this choice opens your heart, allows Divine love in, and moves you into your loving adult self.

## Step Three

Choose to welcome, embrace, and dialogue with your feelings— your inner child. Explore how you are treating yourself and what your wounded self is telling you that is causing painful feelings. Then dialogue with your wounded self, exploring your false beliefs and the resulting behaviors. Also explore your gifts and what brings joy to your inner child.

## Step Four

Dialogue with your spiritual guidance, discovering the truth about any false beliefs and the loving action toward your inner child.

## Step Five

Take the loving action learned in Step Four: putting love into action.

## Step Six

Evaluate the effectiveness of your loving action.

These steps are a powerful road map to healing the false beliefs that may be keeping you limited and creating your ongoing disconnection with your spiritual guidance.

A belief in God or a higher power is not necessary for this process to work. I have successfully taught Inner Bonding to men and women who do not believe in anything spiritual. Instead, they learn how to call on the highest part of themselves (often known as the higher self, or older, wiser inner self) for spiritual guidance.

As you move through parts II and III of this book, these steps will become clear and usable to you. They are a powerful doorway to manifesting your dreams.

# 2

# Life without a Spiritual Connection

Spiritual abuse wreaks havoc within each of us and within our society. Being disconnected from a higher source of love and guidance leads us to operate from an earthly perspective rather than a spiritual one. This causes untold individual and planetary pain. We are operating from an earthly perspective when greed, power, and control over others, events, and outcomes are our primary motivations. We operate from an earthly perspective when protecting ourselves against what we fear—aloneness, loneliness, helplessness, rejection, being controlled by others—is more important than learning and loving. Whenever you operate from your false, wounded self, you operate from an earthly perspective.

Most of our major institutions—government, business, food production, the drug industry, education, some religious organizations, many families—operate primarily on the earthly level. As you can see by reading the headlines, greed and the desire to gain power over others (as opposed to the personal power of the loving adult), drive much of what happens in our society. Social problems like crime, violence, racism, sexism, misogyny, homophobia, substance abuse, child and spousal abuse, homelessness, food insecurity, poverty, animal abuse, environmental destruction, and war are all motivated by the intention of the wounded self to gain power and control over others. At the root of all these actions is insecurity born of fear. In fact, fear is both the primary cause *and* consequence of spiritual abuse.

The earthly level is the material level, the level of the day-to-day struggle for safety and survival. But external safety is an illusion. We can never be totally safe on the earthly level, because our bodies can be harmed or killed through disease, injury, or accident, and we can never know for sure when this will happen. Our souls, however, are eternal. The spiritual level is about creating *internal* peace and safety through loving, evolving, and expressing our soul.

The earthly perspective views situations and events within the context of this lifetime only, while the spiritual perspective views everything through an infinite continuum of eternal consciousness. We all have many challenges on the earthly level, but if we see adversity only on this level, we can never experience it as an opportunity and a privilege—in fact, a sacred privilege. Difficult events challenge us to evolve our souls, to become more loving and compassionate to ourselves and others.

In the face of these challenges, we are always being guided toward our highest good. If you see painful events such as failures, illness, loss of loved ones, or loss of money purely on the earthly level, you will see life primarily as suffering, a burden to be endured or perhaps ended in a lonely, painful death or suicide. But when you see difficult experiences as opportunities to evolve in love and compassion toward yourself and others, you will do what you came here to do: learn to love, express, and evolve your soul toward oneness with the love that is God.

You operate from a spiritual perspective when evolving and loving are your primary motivating factors and highest priorities. When you make the spiritual level far more important than the earthly level, you experience life on this planet as a sacred privilege.

## When Love Isn't Love and When Power Isn't Power

What we call "love" on the earthly level is not love at all. "Love" on the earthly level is about getting something for ourselves—approval, security, attention, understanding, sex, affection. Love on the spiritual level is about *giving* to ourselves and others—caring, compassion, understanding, attention, affection. Love on the earthly level is about attempting to fill our emptiness with things, activities, substances, and people. Love on the spiritual level is about filling ourselves internally through connecting with our own soul essence and higher guidance, receiving the energy of love and compassion from spirit and sharing it with others.

Power on the earthly level is about controlling people, events, and outcomes; power on the spiritual level is about personal empowerment within. It includes the power to receive love and wisdom from spirit, realize our creative potential, and manifest our dreams. Spiritual power is the power to remain loving and compassionate *even in the face of fear.*

Religion can operate from an earthly perspective or a spiritual perspective. Many people confuse religion and spirituality. A religion is a particular set of beliefs involved with a group experience, while spirituality is an individual, personal experience of your higher power. Unfortunately, not all churches and temples operate from the spiritual perspective, and much of organized religion has nothing to do with love. When the religion's intent is to control rather than to love, the wounded self is in charge. Religions led by people who operate from the wounded self, disconnected from their source of love and wisdom, become cults or cult-like.

Whether or not your own religious practice operates from an earthly or spiritual perspective depends upon whether you are operating, in any given moment, from your false, wounded self or your true soul self. Since your wounded self is driven by fear and the need to control, when it is in charge, religion becomes just another way for you to control things. Only when you are connected with your soul within and with your higher self can religion and spirituality come together. Then religious groups can truly become instruments of love and compassion.

## False Beliefs about God

Spiritual abuse, which disconnects us from our spiritual guidance and causes us to live from an earthly perspective, leads us to the false beliefs about God listed in chapter 1.

Let's explore each of these beliefs further (except for the last false belief about controlling God, which we'll focus on in the next chapter).

### 1. GOD DOESN'T EXIST.

When parents or caregivers give children disapproval or conditional approval and call it love, children may conclude that God doesn't exist. Few children have an inherently strong and unshakable spiritual connection, as Anna did in one of my favorite books, *Mr. God, This is Anna*, by Fynn. In this true story, Anna runs away from her abusive home at the age of four and finds a loving family to take care of her. She knows that her parents abused her not because she was bad or unlovable, but because they were wounded and unable to love. God, she knew, was "in my middle." Anna was a rare evolved child. Nothing could sway her from her connection with God. But most children are not able to do what Anna did. In the face of spiritual abuse, they may have no reason to believe that God exists, especially in homes where there is no religious or spiritual training.

Even if children are taught about God, they are often told that God is all-powerful. "But if God is all-powerful, why does God let bad things happen to me?" an abused child may ask. Even adults may ask, "Why does God allow all the bad things on the planet—the Holocaust, starvation, violence, wars, climate change?"

The concept of an all-powerful God can be misleading. In fact, the creative force of the universe gave all souls free will. Hence you decide your own purpose in life, your deepest desires, your way of being. You decide whether you are going to be loving or unloving, responsible for your own feelings and behavior or putting the blame on others. You decide if you are going to be open to learning about and lovingly managing your pain or avoid it with your anesthetics—your addictions. You decide if your deepest motivation is to love yourself and others or to maintain "safety" by protecting yourself against loneliness, rejection, and failure.

When your deepest desire is to be safe rather than loving, you close your heart to avoid pain. When you do, you cannot feel the love that is God, because love can only enter through an open heart. Free will means that our higher power has no power over your choices. *Even the love and wisdom that is God cannot control your intent—your deepest desire in any given moment—because we all have free will.*

When parents protect against feeling their pain and take their woundedness out on their children, there is no doorway through which the love that is God can enter the parents' hearts. *God is the all-powerful energy of love that you can open to and invite into your heart, but the love that is God cannot enter your heart unbidden.* Once you shift your intent and ask your higher power to help heal your wounds, teaching you to be loving to yourself and others, the spirit of love, compassion, and wisdom that is God will always be here for you. But it is you who must decide.

When our hearts are closed to ourselves, we are also closed to the suffering of others and can cause them untold pain. Because we each have free will, your higher power cannot force an abusive parent—or a tyrant or dictator—to open his or her heart. And no force outside of yourself, not even an all-powerful one, can open your heart to love when your intention is to control.

## 2. GOD EXISTS, BUT NOT FOR ME.

When parents consistently bring Divine love through to their children, the children learn that a higher power is there for them. When parents and other adults are trustworthy, children experience their concept of God as trustworthy. But when children are taught in church or temple that God exists, yet they have no experience, through their parents or other caregivers, of Divine love, truth, and wisdom, they may come to believe that God exists, but not for them. This is not unusual. Children are likely to believe that if they are not good enough to be loved by their parents or other adults around them, they are not good enough to be loved by God. *Many children project their parents' or other caregivers' feelings and behavior onto their concept of God.*

Most abused children pray to God to stop their parents from abusing them. They are too little to understand that people have free will. They do not understand that the love and guidance that is God sustains them during the abuse, but that God cannot make their abusers loving instead of unloving. They may conclude that they have been abandoned by God.

I often see adults face their false belief that God has abandoned them. "I hate God!" they shout. "God doesn't love me! God doesn't know I exist! God doesn't help me. God doesn't hear or answer my prayers. I've prayed and prayed, but God is deaf to me. God loves everyone else, but not me!" Often in facing this belief, they can come to terms with a truth they have not wanted to face: the love that is God hasn't abandoned them. It is they who have abandoned this love by closing their hearts to avoid pain.

### 3. GOD IS A CONTROLLING, JUDGMENTAL MAN WHOSE LOVE IS CONDITIONAL. TO BE GUIDED, LOVED, AND COMFORTED BY GOD, I HAVE TO CHANGE WHO I AM, GIVE UP MY FREEDOM, AND BE WHO GOD WANTS ME TO ME.

When our parents' approval and attention was conditional upon our acting the "right" way, we had to give ourselves up to be "loved" by them. Thus we learned to confuse *approval* with *love*. Since most children project their parents' feelings and behavior onto their concept of God, we may have formed the false belief that we have to be a certain way to be loved by our higher power. Children who are raised by stern, judgmental, and punishing parents tend to see God in the same way.

In addition, many children are told that God is a judgmental old man who will punish them if they are bad. Instead of a profoundly loving and creative energy, God is a force to be reckoned with, a Supreme Being whom we must please—or else. This, of course, is just a way that parents control their children and religious institutions control their followers.

The Bible talks about "fearing God," but the word "fear" has been poorly translated. A more literal translation of the original text is "awe." You are told to be in awe of God, not to fear God. Throughout the New Testament, you are told to "fear not," because God is always there; God is spirit, God is love. But parents or religious leaders who want to control their children often threaten them by saying "God will punish you," which leads to the child's false belief that God is judgmental and loves them conditionally. This is not love but approval.

Everything changes in your perception of God when you know that God is the spirit of love, comfort, and compassion, as well as truth, wisdom, peace, and joy. Love is unconditional acceptance, understanding, and caring. Everything that is conditional—shaming, judgmental, critical, withholding, or punishing—is not love and is therefore not God.

Once you directly experience God, you know that the love that is God is always here for you exactly as you are. The only way you can know that any belief is false is to directly experience the truth, which comes from God and *is* God. Later on in this book, I will show you how to experience this for yourself.

## 4. I WILL NEVER BE GOOD ENOUGH TO PLEASE GOD.

Many people grew up with parents who were never pleased with them, no matter how well they did. If they got a B in school, it should have been an A. If they received an A, it should have been an A+. Their flaws were constantly pointed out. Attention was always on what they didn't do rather than on what they did do. It's no wonder so many of us grew up feeling inadequate.

If you projected your parents' negative feelings onto your concept of God, you may believe there is nothing you can ever do that will please God. You may believe that God is a person who sees you as inherently flawed, "born into sin," and there is nothing you can do to change this. You might believe that no matter how hard you try, in the end you will be punished for your sins: God will never forgive you for being human. But if you are "created in the image of God," meaning that *you have the same love within you that is God*, it is not possible to be inherently flawed. That would mean you were created imperfect, and the creative force that is God doesn't do substandard work. Nor is the unconditional love that is God unforgiving. Unconditional love is forgiving.

## 5. GOD USES ME TO HELP OTHERS, BUT DOES NOT COME TO ME JUST FOR ME.

When we believe in God but feel unlovable and unworthy, we may believe that we can be instruments of the love that is God for others but not for ourselves. Sometimes children are taught that they are nothing, that their only worth is in helping others. Their goal becomes giving love to others so others will give love to them. This belief system fosters the giving-to-get behavior of codependent relationships. This is rampant in the helping professions. Over and over, I encounter therapists and healers who tell me that they feel totally connected when helping and loving others but not when attempting to love themselves. They can access profound truth and compassion for others but not for themselves.

## 6. GOD HAS FAVORITE PEOPLE AND SHOWERS THEM WITH BLESSINGS.

If you grew up deprived of love and you see others who were given love as children, you may conclude that God has chosen people who deserve to be blessed while ignoring others who do not. Like many of the other false beliefs about God, this conclusion comes from seeing God as an unloving, judgmental, vengeful person rather than as the spirit of unconditional love. People have favorite people; the love and spirit that is God doesn't. People think some people are more deserving than others; the unconditional love and spirit that is God doesn't. But when you believe God is a judgmental person, you may project your beliefs and experiences of people onto your concept of God.

All this changes when you experience God as unconditional love—love that is *always* here and that has *no* conditions. It is helpful to think of God as a law—the law of unconditional love— the same way you think of gravity as a law. Gravity exists for you whether you believe in it or not. It does not exist only for those who deserve it. The unconditional love that is God works the same way.

When you open your heart and invite the compassion, strength, and comfort that is God into your heart, you will know that love and guidance are always here to help sustain you, no matter who you are, what you've done, or what challenges you face on the earthly level. When you open your heart, you know that the bad things that happen to you, such as the loss of a loved one, are not a punishment. They do not mean that you are not loved by God. They just mean that bad things happen on the earthly level.

Each of us has a different journey. We cannot know why some souls learn their soul lessons through hardship while others may learn them through plenty. What you do or do not have on the earthly level has nothing to do with what you do or do not have on the spiritual level. The spirit that is God blesses every one of us. The love that is God supports your soul's journey, whatever you are facing and learning in this life. You cannot know what another's soul lessons are, or why others are able-bodied or disabled, wealthy or poor, beautiful or plain. Just know that whatever the situation, there is much for each of us to learn about our soul's growth in relationship to ourselves and others.

### 7. GOD MADE ME COME HERE TO THIS PLANET.

I often hear people say, "I didn't ask to be born," or "I didn't ask to be in this family with these parents." When you believe that God is demanding, controlling, and judgmental, you may believe that God made you come here and put you into an unloving or abusive family either as punishment (because you are inherently bad) or because God doesn't love you. This false belief relieves you of the responsibility of choosing to heal in order to evolve your soul. Your soul evolves toward lovingness through the many challenges you face on this planet, which do not exist in the spiritual realm. All forms of adversity are challenges to your soul to move beyond your current limitations into more loving behavior.

I know from my own experience that it is possible to remember life in the spiritual realm. These memories are within each of us. The more we heal, the more access we have to them. When you remember that you came here to evolve in your ability to love yourself and others and manifest the gifts you were given, you will no longer say, "I didn't ask to be here." When you know why you came here, you understand that each challenge is an opportunity to learn and evolve. You understand that being alive is a sacred opportunity, a sacred privilege.

## Life: Sentence or Privilege?

Let's take a look at where we are. We have seen that rampant spiritual abuse disconnects a child from the love and guidance that is God. We have also seen how this disconnection causes a person to draw many false conclusions about God and to oper-ate from an earthly instead of a spiritual perspective.

Making life choices based on this perspective creates many of our painful feelings and much of our unhealthy behavior, which in turn create bigger societal problems. No wonder some people say life feels more like a jail sentence than a privilege.

When you put all these factors together, you see that the consequences of spiritual abuse are indeed numerous and far-reaching. They include:

- Fear of death
- Lack of purpose
- Fear, anxiety, and depression
- Illness
- Core shame
- Harming ourselves and others
- Lack of personal responsibility: feeling victimized and powerless; blaming and controlling
- Dysfunctional relationships and shattered families
- Experiencing life as a burden instead of a sacred privilege

Let's look at each of these and see what's really behind them.

## Fear of Death

When you have suffered spiritual abuse and are disconnected from the love and truth that is God, you do not know that your soul is immortal. You think that death is the end of everything: utter blackness. This can be very frightening. When you believe that this life is all there is, you want to hang on to it at all costs.

People who want to stay on life support or have their bodies frozen in the hopes of being revived at a later date do not know that death is leaving the temporary house of the body and going to their real home, which is the spiritual realm. They have forgotten about the incredible love, peace, and joy that awaits them. If you could remember even a moment of your life in the spiritual realm, your fear of death would vanish. People who have had out-of-body or near-death experiences rarely fear death afterward.

The fear of death leads to the fear of really living life. When you fear death, you fear accidents, illness, victimization, old age—anything that could take away your life in this body. Fear of death often results in not living life to the fullest.

The fear of death may also stem from a false belief about hell. Hell, according to information I have received from my higher guidance, is not a place. It's a state of mind. When you do not experience the unconditional love that is God—which means that you are loved *no matter what you've done*—you may fear that you will be punished in hell for your bad deeds. You might be punishing and judging yourself and others, which creates hell on earth. Hell is living in fear and judgment, being disconnected from God, in life or in death. But God cannot judge or punish; people do.

If your religion has very different ideas about hell, you may find this concept unacceptable. For now, I suggest you simply consider the possibility that hell is not a place where God sends you for punishment. Later, when you have learned how to do Inner Bonding, you can ask your spiritual guidance about hell—and any other questions you may have about how God works. I am sharing with you the information I have received from my spiritual guidance, but I am not an authority on the universe. You will need to find your own answers, which you will learn how to do later in this book.

## Lack of Purpose

When we do not know that our purpose here on earth is to experience, express, and evolve our souls toward loving ourselves and others, and toward oneness with ourselves, others, and the love that is God, we may feel lost or aimless. We set goals that we believe will bring us peace and joy, such as making a lot of money, finding the right job, becoming famous, losing weight, getting a bigger house or nicer car, or finding the right relationship. Unfortunately, many people who achieve all these goals, and more, still feel alone, empty, and frightened. Until they move on to a spiritual path and devote themselves toward healing the false beliefs that block love and joy, they will continue to fill their emptiness with addictions to external things. Then they wonder why they wake up each morning anxious or depressed.

When you practice Inner Bonding, you will discover the most rewarding path for expressing love and your intrinsic gifts. Your soul's purpose lies within your true soul self, but you cannot discover it until you reconnect with your essence, the spark of the Divine within you.

## Fear, Anxiety, and Depression

The billions of dollars spent on antianxiety and antidepressant medications in this country attest to the prevalence of the consequences of spiritual abuse. When you have no faith that you are loved and supported by your higher power, you feel desperately alone. This feeling causes many people to live with knots in their stomach, numbed out on substances, or dependent on prescription or recreational drugs to take away their anxiety and depression.

We cannot live in fear and faith at the same time. When we move into faith that our higher power is guiding and supporting us, our fear and desperate aloneness disappear. To maintain faith and your personal connection with your higher guidance, you need to let go of your false beliefs and embracing the truth about yourself and God. When you do, anxiety, depression, loneliness, and emptiness will become strangers to you.

## Illness

Illness can be a consequence of spiritual abuse, because living with the frequent stress of fear, anxiety, and depression erodes the immune system. Of course, not all illness results from stress caused by spiritual abuse. We have many other factors to contend with, such as processed, devitalized, and insecticide-laden food, contaminated air and water, and hereditary conditions. But the stress of spiritual abuse on top of all this results in an unhealthy society. Spiritual abuse costs us billions of dollars in health-care costs.

## Core Shame

Core shame is the false belief that you are fundamentally inadequate, bad, wrong, defective, unimportant, and unlovable. I have never met a person who didn't have some degree of core shame. It is often the result of not getting the love we needed as children and not having done our healing inner work. We operate from core shame when we do not know the beauty and wonder of our soul—the spark of the Divine that is within us. We operate from core shame when we do not experience our essence and the Divine as one and the same: "One God . . . who is above all, and through all, and *in you all*" (Ephesians 4:6; my italics).

When we operate from core shame, we spend much of our lives trying to hide who we think we are: our false, wounded self. We cannot be authentic, honest, and straightforward for fear of being found out. We live from fear instead of love. As long as we operate from core shame, we can never feel whole or peaceful or have sustained intimate relationships. The fear of rejection and aloneness that comes from core shame causes us to act out in ways that harm ourselves and others.

## Harming Ourselves and Others

We take care of what we value. If you value your children and possessions, you take good care of them; otherwise you do not. The same is true of yourself. When you value your body and soul, you take good care of yourself physically, emotionally, and spiritually. When you do not know that your essence is beautiful, lovable, and worthy, you may not be motivated to take care of yourself.

When you operate from core shame, you may abuse yourself either in the ways you were abused as a child or in the ways you saw your parents abuse themselves. You may eat badly, not sleep enough, overwork, or abuse harmful substances. You may be self-critical, judging yourself in the ways you were judged or in the ways your parents judged themselves. You may sacrifice your own needs while taking care of others' needs. You may let others use and abuse you, not setting appropriate boundaries against disrespectful and hurtful behavior. You may even think about killing yourself. Adolescents often mutilate themselves because of the depth of their core shame and loneliness. They would rather feel the physical pain of cutting themselves than the depth of their emotional pain. Spiritual abuse can lead to self-abuse and suicide as well as harm to others.

When you do not know that your essence is love and that we are all one, you can harm yourself by harming others. When you do not believe that your core soul self is a spark of Divine love, you may not cherish the soul of others. When you feel unworthy, you may see others as unworthy. When you do not feel a sense of oneness with all living beings, you may shame, use, threaten, hit, lie to, steal from, maim, rape, or kill others. Spiritual abuse, which disconnects us from our Divine source, is the great destroyer on the earthly level. It is partly responsible for the crime, racism, violence, and planetary destruction of our time.

You may harm others when you do not know that your life will continue in the spiritual realm and that you will ultimately have to feel the pain you have inflicted. People who have had near-death experiences have said that when we leave our bodies at the time of death, we have a life review. We are asked, "How well did you love?" We reexperience all the choices we made, as well as their consequences. When we have caused suffering to others, we will feel what they felt. No one sits in judgment of us. We are not sent to any hell for our choices. But we will feel within our souls what others felt at our anger, blaming, shaming, violence, and lies. You will feel all the feelings other people had as a result of every act of kindness or unkindness on your part. You will be the only judge of whether or not you have fulfilled your soul's mission to love and evolve.

Again, if you are not comfortable accepting what I am saying here, make a note of it so you can investigate the truth later on by asking your own spiritual guidance. My spiritual guidance has confirmed that we do indeed have a life review when we die.

Many people believe that core shame is very hard to heal. Actually, it is not. *But it is impossible to heal core shame without a connection with your higher guidance.* Traditional psychotherapy that excludes spirit does not help. I have had clients who came to me after years and years of therapy, but who had not healed their core shame. Through practicing Inner Bonding and understanding that core shame is your *oldest protection,* you will learn how to heal it. We'll talk more about this later.

## Lack of Personal Responsibility

When, as a result of spiritual abuse, you feel alone in the universe and cannot connect with your spiritual guidance, you may not only feel unlovable, you may also feel powerless over these feelings. This compounds the problem.

Both these feelings—aloneness (feeling unlovable and alone in the universe) and loneliness (having no one to share love with)—are very painful. Aloneness is the black, hollow, empty feeling you have in the pit of your stomach or in your chest when you are alone *inside*. When you are disconnected from your soul self, you feel like a child drifting alone in a vast and indifferent universe. Loneliness, on the other hand, is the aching or burning feeling in your heart or solar plexus when you have no one with whom to share love. You can feel lonely when you are by yourself, but you can also feel lonely when you are with others whose hearts are closed.

If you are disconnected from your soul self and your higher guidance, you will feel both alone and lonely. Your heart will be closed, so you cannot bring Divine love through to yourself. You will feel empty and alone inside and consequently will have no love to share with others. This despair often leads people to act out addictively.

When your heart is open, you will not feel alone, because you will feel Divine love within. Nevertheless, you may still feel lonely. The important thing to remember is that when you are connected with your spiritual guidance, *you are not alone in your loneliness*. You do not feel alone when you experience the presence of Divine love in your life. When you move into deeper levels of healing and connection with your spiritual guidance, you can feel your oneness with others even when their hearts are closed. This does not mean that you will not feel sorrow at not being able to share love with someone, but it does mean that you will be able to handle the loneliness in a way that is loving to yourself and them. We'll look at this more deeply in the chapters on relationships.

We often feel helplessness or powerlessness as intense agitation or frustration. Because these feelings are so unpleasant, we naturally want to have control over *not* feeling them. We may use addictions to block these feelings. We may also defend against them—especially powerlessness—by trying to control others with anger, criticism, or coldness. Unfortunately, because controlling behavior is a major cause of relationship failure, our efforts may backfire. We may end up feeling more powerless and isolated than ever.

When we operate from an earthly perspective, we tend to see others as responsible for our feelings and behavior. One of my clients, Jennifer, frequently blows up at her husband, convinced that he doesn't care about her. Because she was abused in childhood, she has deep abandonment wounds that lead her to feel unlovable and victimized. Not loving herself or being able to truly love her husband, she projects these feelings onto him; she becomes convinced he doesn't care about her, when in fact he loves her deeply. Whenever she suffers the consequences of not taking good care of herself—that is, of abandoning herself—she blames him for the resulting feelings. "You don't care about me!" she screams at him. "What about me? What about what I need? If you loved me, you would spend more time with me!" She feels like a victim of his behavior. If this goes on long enough, she may drive him away, thus confirming to herself that he never really did care about her. Sometimes she even places the blame for her feelings on her children.

Unfortunately, this is a common scenario in families. Jennifer's unloving behavior toward herself and others perpetuates her core shame, which she will hand down to her children. Because her intention is to control rather than to love herself and others, she cannot experience love within herself, and her own unloving behavior causes core shame in her children. Spiritual abuse breeds spiritual abuse—and all the negative consequences that follow.

## Dysfunctional Relationships, Shattered Families

Our core shame, coming as it does from spiritual abuse, cannot help but create dysfunctional, codependent relationships. In such relationships, we hand over the job of defining our worth and lovability to someone else. We try to control how they define us, and we feel angry and rejected when they do not make us feel worthy and lovable. Because we don't take personal responsibility for our own feelings and behavior, we end up feeling like victims and blaming others for our pain. The consequences are misery, anxiety, depression, and often illness.

A friend of mine, Lester, is a very talented healer. He is highly intuitive and very connected with the healing energy and information that comes through him from his higher guidance. Like many people on a spiritual path, Lester has learned to attune to higher energies, but he has never brought that love inside to take care of his inner child. His connection to spirit has been his addiction, his way of *avoiding* dealing with his feelings. Because he has never done his own inner work and healed his wounded self, he doesn't take responsibility for himself and his own feelings. Instead, he makes women responsible for his sense of worth and lovability. He is a pushover for beautiful women, and each time he gets into a relationship, he gives himself up by taking responsibility for the woman's feelings while ignoring his own. When Lester does not receive the love he wants, he feels trapped and resentful. He blames the woman for not loving him, never realizing that he is the one who is not loving himself. Lester is not only going through his third messy divorce, but at age fifty, he has also recently been diagnosed with throat cancer. No matter how much he has prayed, how well he has eaten, how many supplements he has taken, and how many people he has healed, the added stress to his immune system—caused by not healing from his spiritual abuse—may be the factor that is costing him his life.

Every day, couples come to see me who are suffering from the consequences of the spiritual abuse they experienced as children. They respond to their deep fears of rejection and abandonment by controlling instead of loving. They constantly attribute their problems to their partners. Their love is ground down to nothing as their wounded selves pound each other with anger, blame, and withdrawal. Without inner healing, such couples have no chance for a loving and passionate relationship. Families are shattered when the two partners leave each other to find happiness elsewhere, instead of looking within. They err in seeking a "better" partner when they should be seeking to *become* a better partner.

This is especially sad because when both partners are willing to do their inner healing work, very often they can repair their relationship, no matter how damaged.

When you add up all the consequences of spiritual abuse, it is no surprise that for some people, life feels like a burden instead of a sacred privilege. Having to control everything—getting love, avoiding pain, feeling safe—is an exhausting job. Believing that you have to do this yourself (because spiritual guidance doesn't exist or has abandoned you) makes life a misery.

## Living with a Spiritual Perspective

People who have a deep experience of God as love, either because they were appropriately loved as children or because they are healing from spiritual abuse, operate at least some of the time from a spiritual perspective.

They know that we are all spiritual beings, that our souls are eternal, and that our present choices affect our souls. They do not fear death because they know the soul transcends the body. They know that life on earth is a transitory learning, evolving, and discovery experience and that our true home is the spiritual realm.

Those who live from a spiritual perspective see life on this planet as a gift. They have a sense of purpose. They know that they are here to express their unique gifts and evolve their souls toward love, compassion, truth, and joy, and to heal their blocks to loving and being one with all of life and with spirit.

They know that the love that is God is not a static entity, but a living force that evolves as we evolve. They see adversities as opportunities to learn more about love.

Such individuals recognize that all of us have the spark of the Divine within, that we are all one, regardless of race, religion, culture, gender, or sexual orientation. They know that each of us is a unique and important part of a giant puzzle whose whole is the love that is God, and that to harm one harms all, including themselves.

Those with a spiritual perspective see their bodies as temples for their souls. They accept the sacred privilege of caring for their bodies by eating well, exercising, getting enough sleep, lovingly managing stress, and doing whatever else it takes to be physically healthy. They see our planet as a gift and accept the sacred privilege of keeping it healthy. They also have faith that their spiritual guidance is leading their souls toward their highest good. They do not live in constant fear and do not attempt to control everything. They try only to express and evolve their souls, leaving the outcome to spirit.

Such individuals take personal responsibility for their own pain and joy. They do not blame their higher power or others for their misery, knowing that their feelings are often a result of their own thoughts, beliefs, and actions. They embrace the sacred privilege of emotional and spiritual growth and move continuously toward more lovingness and joy.

Spiritually oriented people set appropriate and loving boundaries against being disrespected, used, and abused by others. They resolve conflicts by caring about both their own and the other's highest good.

They create balance in their lives, giving themselves time to be alone, pray and meditate, work, play, and express their creativity, passion, laughter, and love. They find work and activities that joyously express their unique gifts. They operate primarily in the moment, with love, rather than obsessing about the past and projecting it onto the present and future.

It would take an enlightened being to operate from the spiritual perspective all the time, and I have never met an enlightened being. But we can all move toward this ideal.

## Love in the Face of Fear

It is easy to be loving when we have no problems, when we feel safe and secure. It is very hard to be loving when we are frightened. Yet it is our challenge—and our sacred privilege—to evolve the fabric of love and compassion as we learn to be loving when confronted with the hardships of being on earth. Life on this very difficult planet gives us an opportunity that we do not have in the spiritual realm: *to love in the face of fear*. In the spiritual realm, we do not have to contend with the earthly challenges that create fear, such as loneliness, pain, hunger, disease, financial loss, rejection, loss of love, and physical death. We have each courageously agreed to leave the safety of our true home, the spiritual realm, and come here to learn the things we can only learn in a body. We came here knowing full well that we would forget our original agreement with ourselves to evolve in lovingness and would have to discover it anew. We may feel lost until we remember that we came here to evolve in our ability to love.

Parents can regard caring for their children as a burden or a sacred privilege. Those who see taking care of their children as a sacred privilege happily learn from the hard times, while those who see it as a burden feel resentful and depleted.

So it is with our life here on this planet. How you see it determines your experience. We can face the hard times with the courage and determination to learn as much as we can about love, or we can run from fear and hardship by hiding behind addictions. In *The Lion King*, the shaman Rafiki, trying to convince Simba to take his rightful place as the lion king, hits him on the head and says, "You can either run from it or learn from it."

Moving out of fear into love is a *process*, not an event. There are many paths to wholeness, and we each need to find the process that works best for us.

Ask yourself this: "Am I suffering enough to do something different? Am I suffering enough to learn how to experience the love and guidance that is God and take responsibility for myself? Do I want to learn to be loving and connect with my higher source of love and wisdom, or would I rather get someone or something outside of myself to fix my pain for me?"

This book teaches the powerful process of Inner Bonding for moving out of the earthly and into the spiritual perspective, out of fear and into love. (Those of you who have used Inner Bonding before will find the process expanded here.) Inner Bonding heals our false beliefs and teaches us how to live in truth. It shows us how to take loving care of ourselves and share our love with others. It enables us to develop our connection with our soul self—our inner child—and connect deeply with our spiritual guidance.

# 3

# Traveling the Wide Road: The Intent to Control

When loving and being guided by our higher power isn't our highest priority, what is? If we are not willing to open to our spiritual guidance, what then? What do we do when we do *not* choose spirit as our guide?

Jesus said that we have only two paths to choose from: "Enter ye in at the strait gate: for wide is the gate, and broad is the way, that leadeth to destruction, and many there be which go in thereat; Because strait is the gate, and narrow is the way, which leadeth unto life, and few there be that find it." (Matthew 7:13–14). We can choose the wide and easy way, or we can choose the narrow way, also known as the "strait gate," or, as Robert Frost and M. Scott Peck call it, "the road less traveled."

There are many other names for these two paths: earthly or spiritual, dark or light, fear or faith, low road or high road. These two roads are the choices we make to control or to love, to avoid or to learn, to close or to open, to get or to give. When we choose the wide road, we are motivated by a desire to *get* love rather than *give* it. Ironically, the wide rode is the road to loneliness, because our intent to get rather than give love disconnects us from ourselves and others.

There is not a right or a wrong path in regard to whether we are loved by God, because love is unconditional. But we will *experience* Divine love only when we choose the narrow path, the road less traveled. That's because the narrow path leads us to our spiritual guidance, which teaches us that we are inherently lovable. The wounded, wide-road-walking mind would have us believe otherwise.

Likewise, our worth as human beings is not determined by the path we choose. Our true soul self is inherently worthy. However, whether we *experience* ourselves as worthy is determined by the path we choose.

Walking the wide road leads to further difficulties. If you are operating from your wounded self and do not know your own worth, you let yourself be defined by others. Your highest priority becomes getting love and validation. If other people like you or love you, you feel worthy and lovable. If not, you feel unlovable. This is like having a baby and instead of loving it yourself, trying to give it to others to love. This innocent child has already been rejected by you, so fear of rejection will rule the child's life.

When we are desperate for approval, it's not enough to *try* to get it. We *must* get it. We must have *control* over getting it. It is a life-or-death matter to us. That's why the wide road is the road of control.

Earlier I asked, "When loving and becoming one with our higher power is not our highest priority, what is?" The answer is *control*. Control is what remains without higher guidance. We become addicted to controlling everything—maybe even our higher power—to get love and feel safe. Since no one likes to be controlled, we inevitably end up feeling alone.

Scott is a fifty-one-year-old screenwriter who came to see me after his girlfriend broke up with him. Although Scott said he wanted my help in learning to love himself, unconsciously he wanted me to tell him he was worthy and lovable. He started each session telling me in detail how well he was doing and how much progress he was making. Then he would wait for my response. After listening to him do this for a few sessions, I addressed the issue.

"Scott, when you are reporting this to me," I asked him, "what are you wanting the most?"

He thought about this a moment. "I want you to know what I've been doing."

"Anything else?"

"I thought you would like it."

"Like hearing about it or like what you have done?"

"Both, I guess."

"You want me to approve of what you've done?" I asked.

"Sure."

"And what does my approval give you?"

"It lets me know I'm OK. That I'm doing the right thing."

"So the only way you know you are OK is if I—or others—approve of you?"

"I guess so. I never thought about it like this before. Actually, I guess I spend a lot of energy trying to avoid rejection. But doesn't everyone? Nobody likes rejection. It feels awful, like just about the worst thing that could happen. I just don't know how to handle it. I go right back to being the little kid I was with my dad. You know, always feeling there's something wrong with me."

"Have you been doing your inner work?" I asked, purposely keeping my question vague.

"Yes, I do it every day. But nothing seems to be happening. I don't *feel* anything in my heart. I can't seem to feel the love in my heart."

"I'd like to hear what you're doing."

"I pray to God for help."

"What do you say to God?" I asked.

"I say, 'God, help me feel better. Give me your love so I don't feel so alone and lonely.'"

"Scott, it sounds like you're trying to get God to fix you, to heal your aloneness for you, rather than inviting God into your heart so that you can heal yourself," I told him. "You need to open to the love that is God so *you* can give it to yourself."

Stunned, Scott just stared at me. He had been on a spiritual path for some time but had never realized that he was still trying to get his concept of God to do it *for* him rather than *with* him. He wanted to get love rather than become a loving person. Scott had always played the role of caretaker in his relationships, giving to others to get love from them; he kept trying to control getting love. Even though Scott believed in God, he had never invited the love that is God into his heart. He had never decided to define and love *himself.* He always tried to get others, and God, to do it for him.

"This is amazing!" Scott exclaimed. "I never saw this before!"

"Are you willing to invite the love that is God into your heart so you can see who you really are and give love to yourself?"

"Yes."

And he did. In that moment, Scott shifted his deepest desire from *getting love from God* to *giving love to himself.* A surprised look came over his face, and he smiled at me.

I could see that Scott had made a new decision about what was most important to him. All his life, getting love and approval had been his deepest desire. But in that moment, he had changed his mind—which we can *always* do, because we have free will. Scott had decided that it was more important to give love than to get it.

## Why Do We Think We Can Control Love?

Some of us were brought up by parents whose "love" was conditional. We had to earn it by our acting the way they wanted us to. In the process, we learned many ways to control getting "love"—which, in reality, was approval. We probably projected our parents' feelings and behavior onto our concept of God. We believed we could win God's love by being "good" and doing things "right." This got us into even deeper confusion, since "good" and "right" are usually defined by parents, teachers, and other authorities rather than by our own spiritual guidance. In reality, *good* is whatever is truly loving to ourselves and others.

Children are often taught to try to win love from others and God. We train them in the art of control by controlling them and rewarding their attempts to control us (by giving them candy or kisses or approval when they do what we want). Parents try many ways to control their kids: anger, threats, sarcasm, punishment, criticism, judgments, withdrawal, violence, treats, money, shame, and smothering. Kids, in turn, may try to get parental approval or attention by being nice, by caretaking (giving themselves up and doing what parents want them to do), overachieving, becoming invisible, becoming ill, acting out, or having temper tantrums. Whenever we role-model controlling behavior by trying to control our children or reward their manipulative behavior with our attention, we teach them the soul-deadening art of control.

Some of our most famous children's songs teach kids that they can control the outcome of things by being "good," like the one that tells them Santa knows when they've been good or bad. This song not only teaches the art of control by telling kids how to make Santa do what they want, it practices control by telling children they will only get gifts if they are good. By implying that Santa Claus sees and judges all, the song suggests an aim to keep children in line.

Some people see God the same way they saw Santa Claus. They believe they can manipulate God into loving them by being good or doing things right. Until they learn that the love that is God is a free gift and cannot be bought or bargained for, they will try endless ways to get it. They will say their prayers, try to be perfect, follow all the rules, rigidly keep the Ten Commandments, be polite, always be right (or righteous). Being good may mean suppressing their sexuality or sexual identity. Being the "right way" may mean dieting or starving oneself to look right. It may even include beating up people who are smaller and weaker. When parents beat their children for being "bad," they teach that it's OK to hit someone smaller when it's "for their own good."

For children, being good may include denying their own feelings and taking responsibility for others' feelings. Children are routinely told that focusing on themselves is selfish. When people with this kind of training grow up, they may continue the pattern by following the rules of a church, being a community do-gooder, or sacrificing themselves, not because they are moved from their hearts to do so, but in the hope of earning approval from others and God.

All this training in control leads to the avoidance of personal responsibility for our needs, feelings, and behavior. Ultimately, it leads to deep feelings of aloneness and loneliness.

Just as you attempt to control outcomes with others, you may attempt to control the outcome with your concept of God. You might pray, go to church or temple, tithe, or do volunteer work to attempt to make God love and protect you. Have you noticed that even some religious dogma is based on an attempt to control God? For example, some Christians believe that only if you confess Jesus Christ as your personal Lord and Savior will you go to heaven. This gives them a sense of control over God: I only have to believe the "right" thing, and I am safe.

Each religion has its rules for ensuring God's grace: don't work on Saturday; give away a percentage of your earnings; don't divorce; sacrifice yourself for others. Unfortunately, none of these rules has anything to do with love and compassion. Worse, they teach you to deny your own inner truth and follow someone else's teachings so as to experience Divine love. In fact, they teach that *only* by giving yourself up will you experience Divine love. While this may give you a sense of safety, it does not help you become a more loving and compassionate person.

The doctrines and dogma of religion have nothing to do with being guided toward love, which is what spirituality is all about. Opening or "surrendering" to your higher guidance does not mean ignoring your own needs or your own truth. It means that releasing the will of your false ego self and inviting in the will of love, compassion, and wisdom. You cannot surrender and attempt to control the outcome of things at the same time. Letting go of outcomes is not a matter of avoiding decisions or neglecting to move toward your goals. It means that you come from the faith that spirit supports your highest good at all times and that you cannot always know what is best for your soul's growth.

I have often been asked, "How can ending up homeless or hungry be in our highest good?" Issues such as homelessness and hunger have nothing to do with God: they are caused by people motivated by greed and control. Even so, can you consider that the homeless person might have soul lessons to learn through the homelessness? Or that he or she is giving others an opportunity to learn soul lessons through offering their help? On the earthly level it makes no sense, but on the spiritual level it can make sense. Sometimes a very evolved soul will agree to a life of illness or poverty in order to give others the opportunity of evolving through helping.

## A Homeless Man's Soul Lesson

A good example of one homeless man's soul lesson is an experience Dr. Erika Chopich had with a homeless man. As Erika relates it:

> I was in a grocery store behind a gentleman who was trying to buy a sandwich and a carton of milk. He was $1.57 short, so I quietly leaned over to the checker and said, "Please just put the whole purchase on my bill." The gentleman, who was clearly homeless, was touched by my offer. He thanked me; I smiled at him and wished him well. I turned back to the checker and asked, "Is this one of your regulars?"
>
> "Nah, he's just some homeless guy," he replied.

As I exited the store, the man was waiting for me. He said, "Ma'am, I have $4 here that I want to give to you to at least pay my part, and I appreciate what you did very much," (which of course I didn't take.) We struck up a conversation, and I learned that he had spent twenty-six years in the Army. I immediately recognized the ring on his finger. He had been an Army Ranger.

He was a high-functioning homeless person: neatly dressed, very clean, and everything he owned was in order. He told me he had lost his job during Covid. When he could no longer pay the rent, he had to live in his car, but someone stole it.

The man said, "Wait a minute. I have something for you." I watched him carefully reach into his backpack and pull out a brand-new bar of dark chocolate, which he quickly opened, and he broke off a piece for me and a piece for him. Chocolate to someone living in the streets is worth gold, yet he wanted to share it with me. We clinked our pieces of chocolate together like glasses of fine wine and enjoyed the moment of connection. He reached again into his backpack and pulled out an unopened bag of Milano cookies. He said, "I'll bet you've never tasted this," as he offered me a cookie. "Remember, only eat dark chocolate, because that's the healthiest." I was struck that he knew that and wanted me to know it as well.

As we chatted, he asked me what I did for a living. Rather than intimidate him by telling him I was a PhD psychologist, I told him I was a chaplain (which I am). He quickly smiled and said,

"Then we work for the same boss!"

"How is that?" I asked.

"I used to fight for the country," he said, "and now I fight for the people here. You have no idea how dangerous it is when the sun goes down for the women and children here. It is my mission and my training to protect them and to look after them. God gave me a strong body and the training to do what needs to be done out here, so that is my mission. Now, instead of fighting for my country, I fight for the people who need protection." He said, with a twinkle in his eye, "I may not look like much, but I can still take them down with one punch and always will if they threaten any kind women and children who live in the streets."

I struggled to keep the tears out of my eyes and kept my smile as I held eye contact. This gentleman, who had lost everything, managed to have the internal resources to give his life purpose and meaning. He was an extraordinary man, and I will always remember him. I promised to look out for him when I go back to the store, and I will. This man gives a great deal and should not be overlooked.

When we are devoted to the rules and dogma of religion, the wounded self often operates from judgment instead of compassion. We may judge the homeless person as somehow bad, wrong, or undeserving. When compassion has a higher value than control, we do not judge things in terms of right and wrong. Instead, we look at our own and others' behavior and try to understand the values and preferences behind this behavior. We try to understand the very good reasons we all have for feeling, believing, and behaving the way we do. We try to *learn and understand* rather than *judge*.

# Penance, Suffering, and Self-Abuse

Unfortunately, control rather than compassion has become the most prevalent way of life. Through the ages, certain techniques for attempting to control God have become common, such as:

- Penance, suffering, and self-abuse
- Prayer with intent to control
- Giving to get approval
- Self-sacrifice
- Shame
- Victimhood and blaming

If you believe that God wants you to suffer to prove your love and devotion, you can feel safely in control of God's love by suffering. When I was in Mexico as an adolescent, I often saw people inching toward church on bleeding knees. I was appalled to see this self-abuse and could not understand it. Later I read about priests and nuns who ritually flagellated themselves to prove their love of God. While some forms of self-chastisement may be a means of entering into an altered state in order to connect with God and attain clarity of mind, often these rituals are really just attempts to control God. Doing hours and hours of prayer or chanting when you are hungry and tired may bring clarity and connection—or it may be an attempt to win God's love through suffering.

Likewise, doing penance when you have done something you believe was wrong may also be a way to control God. Often confession and penance are ways to get back into God's grace so that you can go ahead and do what you want again, such as getting drunk, hitting your spouse, having an affair, or cheating someone. If you were truly sorry for your behavior, you would make amends and get the help you need so that you will never do that again.

When your heart is truly open and you receive a direct experience of God, you know that the last thing Divine love wants is suffering. The spirit that is God wants to express itself through us as love, compassion, joy, peace, creativity, and beauty. Self-inflicted suffering usually comes from fear, not love.

## The Power of Prayer

More and more people are recognizing the power of prayer. Many ask, "How do I pray? What is the best way to pray?" The "how" of prayer is not nearly as important as the "why." Intent matters most.

We either pray from an open heart—the true soul self—or a closed heart—our wounded self. Think of your prayers for a moment. Who prays? Your soul self or or the false self that wants to get some blessing or remedy from God? In the latter case, your prayers are simply an attempt to control God. These are demanding, begging, and bargaining prayers, which you may be doing merely because you think you should. Since the wounded self always has an outcome in mind and wants control over it, these prayers have an expected outcome attached to them. You pray in the hope of getting God to fix things for you. These prayers will go unanswered because they do not come from a desire to learn about love.

Prayer coming from love is another matter. Here the intent is to invite Divine love into your heart, surrender your individual will, and become an instrument of higher will. You are not asking God to fix things for you. You are asking for help in becoming one with Divine love so you can bring love, compassion, kindness, and truth through to yourself and others. Instead of trying to get, you are offering to give. Prayers that come from love include a period of contemplation, of listening to your higher guidance, so you can hear its instruction to you. Our higher power is always speaking to us, but most of us never take the time to listen.

I have discovered that prayer is far more powerful when I thank the love that is God for what I have and for what I know is on the way than when I try to get spirit to give me something. One of my past challenges was to trust my inner knowing about what is true for me. It seemed easier to trust my knowing about what I know is true for others.

Many years ago, my dear friend Erika was very ill. For a while we thought she was dying. As she lay in bed, her higher guidance told her of her life's purpose: to start a service organization called Hope America, whose primary purpose would be to help the homeless. Erika was shown pictures of her and other chaplains trained in Inner Bonding traveling the country in motor homes, helping people living on the streets who needed help.

This vision was the beginning of Erika's healing. She began establishing the nonprofit organization, having no idea how she was going to get the first motor home. I had a deep sense of knowing that when Erika was well enough to go on the road, the motor home would be there for her. I told her, "Don't worry; it will be there," and thanked spirit for the motor home that I knew was on the way. Sure enough, it showed up, the gift of a generous person.

When it came to trusting my knowing for myself, however, it was not as easy. What if I was wrong? What if my inner knowing told me something, but it never happened? I hadn't worried about this with Erika, because I knew spirit would show up for her, but what about me? I realized that I believed in the power of my prayer for others, but not for myself. I finally decided to start trusting my knowing for myself and to pray in gratitude for what I had and what I knew was coming. This has made an enormous difference in my ability to surrender to my guidance and manifest my dreams. By trusting my deep sense of knowing, I am trusting the love that is God. Today I continue to pray and express my gratitude for the help I continually receive.

Our prayers of gratitude raise our frequency, and our prayers for help in loving ourselves and others will always be answered. So will our prayers for help in facing the darkness in the way of our being pure instruments of love. Whenever you invite the love that is God into your heart, you will be presented with the lessons you need to continue on your spiritual path. Spirit always supports your highest good—not necessarily in the material sense, but in the spiritual sense. You may not get into the school you want or get the job, house, or relationship you want, but you will always get the knowledge you need to evolve toward love.

Similarly, your loving prayers for others' highest good will also be answered, but you need to accept that you do not know what is in their highest good. If you pray for someone to heal from an illness, but it is time for them to leave this planet, you may believe that your prayers have not been answered.

When I was writing some of this chapter, I was in an airport in Springfield, Missouri. My flight had been delayed, which meant I would probably miss my connecting flight from St. Louis to Los Angeles, where I lived at that time. It was fairly important for me, on an earthly level, to arrive in Los Angeles early, so I was certainly hoping to make my connecting flight. But I also knew that I had no control over the outcome and that whatever the outcome, I could learn something. So, while I hoped to make my flight, I was simply praying for my highest good, which I cannot always know. I prayed the first part of the Serenity Prayer:

> God grant me the serenity to accept the things
>     I cannot change,
> The courage to change the things I can,
> And the wisdom to know the difference.

By praying these words, I was asking for spirit's help in making inner peace more important than arriving on time. By thanking my guidance for the opportunities to learn and evolve, I managed to stay lighthearted instead of feeling put out by the vagaries of air travel.

The more you pray from gratitude, love, and faith, the more powerful your prayers are. We are in fear when we do not have the faith that we are being spiritually guided. We are in fear when we are operating from our wounded self, feeling separate from our higher power. We are in faith when we invite higher will into our hearts.

## Giving to Get and Self-Sacrifice

Self-sacrifice comes from the false belief mentioned in the previous chapter: "If I sacrifice myself for others, I don't have to take care of myself. God will do it for me. God owes me for all the good I do."

Giving for the pure joy of giving is a wonderful expression of your true soul self. Often, however, many of us *give to get,* which is just another way to control. Sometimes it takes the form of praise, affection, or sympathy, which we offer others as a way to win their approval. The same can be true of giving time to charities. It all depends on intent. People often find it hard to connect with you when you are giving to get. Instead, they feel your pull on them to give you what you are not giving to yourself, and they may withdraw. If you often feel lonely with people, this may be part of the reason.

Many religious doctrines teach that being a good person means self-sacrificing and if you do not sacrifice yourself for others, you are selfish. This is backwards. What's truly selfish is trying to control others into sacrificing themselves for you.

Many of the people I work with ask me, "If I do what I want and someone else is upset by it, aren't I being selfish?" I tell them the story of my grandmother who, being an orthodox Jew, believed we shouldn't do anything on Saturdays. She lived with us and took it upon herself to make sure I was a "good girl." When she caught me breaking her rules by doing my homework on a Saturday, she shamed me mercilessly, shaking her head while making a tsk-tsk sound. "How can you do this to me?" she would say. "You are so selfish." I quickly learned that whenever I did what I wanted, even with no intent to harm anyone else, I was considered selfish if someone was upset by it. Only after I grew up and started healing did I realize that my grandmother was being selfish by expecting me to fall in line with her beliefs.

Our society's definition of selfishness, which parallels my grandmother's, often makes it difficult for people to take responsibility for themselves. Instead, they are praised for sacrificing themselves and taking responsibility for others. The result is a nation of people embroiled in dysfunctional, codependent relationships and loneliness.

Since the love that is God is a free gift, it cannot be won by self-sacrifice. It is far healthier to stop trying to control others and your concept of God by sacrificing yourself for them, and instead taking responsibility for making yourself peaceful and joyous. Then you will naturally give because it makes you happy to do so, not out of fear, obligation, or guilt.

## Shame

It can be difficult to see how shame is a form of control. Let's start by reviewing how core shame—the false belief that you are essentially bad—begins. When we were neglected, shamed, or abused as infants and young children, we had only two choices. We could see the truth: our parents were wounded and did not know how to love us, and we were helpless to do anything about it. Or we could believe the abuse was our fault—that we were defective, inadequate, unworthy, and unlovable.

Because admitting we were helpless might have filled us with despair, most of us chose to avoid the truth. Instead of blaming our parents, we blamed ourselves. We developed core shame ("It's my fault they don't love me. I'm worthless") as a defense against that despair. After all, if we believe that it is our fault we are not loved, then the power to change this situation is in our hands: we can try to be good. In this way we can control getting love from others—or so we think.

Operating out of shame—believing that you are inherently bad and inadequate—may be your way of trying to get others to do things for you. If you really believe you are inadequate, you obviously cannot take care of yourself. Someone else has to do it for you. This is how core shame absolves you of personal responsibility.

As long as you hang on to your false belief in your unworthiness, you can think you can fool others into loving you by hiding your shame and trying to do things right. You may become addicted to shame because it protects you from the truth that you really have no control over others or over the love that is God. You can't *make* people love you, and Divine love is always here for you, whether you know this or not.

Although we can influence whether others like or approve of us, we have no actual control over them. Yet if we operate from the false belief that our best feelings come from others loving us, we will continue to try to control their responses to us. Until we know that our best feelings come from giving ourselves the love we need and sharing it, we will continue to try to get what we need from others, driven by the pain of core shame.

Until you give up your illusions of control, you will never understand what you do have control over: your own choices and intent. Personal power is knowing what we do have control over and taking action, but it will elude us until we accept that we are helpless in regard to others. We cannot move into personal power until we accept our powerlessness over everything but ourselves.

Giving up control becomes easier when you open to the love that is God and discover that it is irrelevant to try to make God love you. *There is nothing you can do to earn unconditional love and nothing you can do to stop it, other than shutting it out of your heart.* You can abandon love, but the love that is God will never abandon you. Divine love for you is as ubiquitous as the air you breathe. When you know you are loved no matter what, control becomes superfluous.

Despite what some religions say, knowing the love that is God and feeling shame are mutually exclusive. When you know Divine love, you also know that it exists within you. At that point, you move beyond shame and beyond the need to manipulate.

Shame may also serve as a defense against being confronted with things about yourself that you do not want to look at. I once had an employee who used her shame to control people in this way. If ever I was the slightest bit unhappy with something she did, she felt terrible about herself and started crying. This made it difficult to let her know when something needed to be done differently.

You might use shame in the same way with your concept of God. It is one way of avoiding your higher guidance's lessons and instructions: "God won't talk to me. I am nothing. I am not good enough." By clinging to your shame, you protect yourself from learning the Divine will for you, and you escape having to act upon it. Your shame may be your wounded self's way of avoiding personal responsibility as well as emotional and spiritual growth.

For years I attempted to help people heal their core shame, yet over and over I found they could not get free of feeling inadequate. Affirmations didn't help. Therapy didn't help. Nothing seemed to help. One day when a client was expressing her feelings of shame, I got the sense that shame was not the root feeling. Then I heard my spiritual guidance telling me that her shame was a protection against far more painful feelings: helplessness, loneliness, grief, and heartbreak. I was told that this woman's shame was so hard to heal because it was an addiction. An addiction is anything we use to protect ourselves from what we deeply fear, and this woman feared her deeper painful feelings.

Shame is simple to heal, but it is not necessarily easy. Your shame will vanish when:

1. You have the courage to compassionately feel your heartache when someone's heart is closed toward you rather than attempting to control the heartache by deciding it is your fault.

2. You have the courage to feel and accept your helplessness over whether someone opens or closes his or her heart to you.

3. You are willing to take responsibility for compassionately managing your painful feelings and gratefully accepting this opportunity to evolve your soul.

## Victimhood and Blaming

Emotional victimhood means choosing not to recognize that as adults, we have choices. When we are acting as victims, we deny that we have free will to choose our path and that our feelings are a result of the path we chose rather than of others' choices. The moment we think our wounded pain is caused by something outside ourselves, we choose to be victims. Although the pain of life can be caused by external people and events, we remain responsible for lovingly managing these feelings.

In her wonderful book *Anatomy of the Spirit*, Caroline Myss states: "Managing the power of choice, with all its creative and spiritual implications, is *the essence of the human experience*. . . . Choice is the process of creation itself."

In her profound book, *The Choice: Embrace the Possible,* psychologist Dr. Edith Eva Eger, who is at this writing one of the few living survivors of Auschwitz, brings us on her journey from being victimized and traumatized by the Nazis to surviving and thriving, and helping others to move out of victimhood and into personal power. She says:

> Most of us want a dictator—albeit a benevolent one—so we can pass the buck, so we can say, "You made me do that. It's not my fault." But we can't spend our lives hanging out under someone else's umbrella and then complain that we're getting wet. A good definition of being a victim is when you keep the focus outside yourself, when you look outside yourself for someone to blame for your present circumstances, or to determine your purpose, fate, or worth.

The seeds of victimhood are planted when we try to control God and others. Then, ironically, we end up with the very feelings that our tactics were designed to prevent: aloneness and loneliness. When we try to control God, we feel alone because we cannot connect with our higher guidance, and we feel lonely because others back off from us when they sense that we are trying to control them. We then blame God and others for our painful feelings. We may also believe that if only we feel miserable enough, God and others will see our misery and bail us out by giving us the love we want.

Emotional victimhood and blaming someone in the past or present always go hand in hand. If you believe you are a victim, then it is the fault of someone else that you feel so badly. When you blame someone, you make them responsible for what is going on inside you. Until you accept the truth that *your* wounded feelings come from *your* choices and that *you* are responsible for your thoughts, beliefs, and actions, which create these feelings, you will be stuck.

It is especially difficult to take personal responsibility for our own feelings and behavior when someone is behaving in a way that feels hurtful: attacking, blaming, lying, shaming, and the like. We want to think that our feelings of anger, hurt, or guilt are caused by the other person's behavior (or from God or fate bringing that person into our life). How often have we said or thought, "You make me so mad!" or "You hurt my feelings"?

But if you pay close attention to your feelings, you will discover that it is not others' behavior that creates your distress, but your own thoughts and behavior in response. For example, let's say my friend Mary is angry with me because I haven't called her in a long time. The truth is, I don't feel a real connection with her, and I haven't been motivated to call. One day Mary calls and says, "You don't know how to be a friend. I have to do all the reaching out. If I didn't call, we would never talk. I don't think you even care about me."

I've learned that how I respond to Mary and how I end up feeling are the direct result of whether I come from fear or love. If I come from my fearful, wounded self, then I too will use blame and shame to regain control. I may attack back: "How dare you blame me for the problems in our friendship! Whenever I do call you, it takes you forever to return my call. You're just projecting your own lack of caring onto me." I may pacify: "Mary, please don't be angry with me. You're right; I haven't been a very good friend lately. It's not that I don't care about you." Or I may become defensive: "Look, Mary, I've been overwhelmed. Things are really difficult for me right now. If you were really a good friend, you would find out what is going on in my life before getting angry at me."

Once we end the conversation, I may feel like a victim of Mary's blame, or I may berate myself for not calling her more often. I will either blame her or myself, or both. I may also blame God for bringing into my life people who treat me badly.

Regardless of whom I blame, I end up feeling bad, and I believe that how I feel is a result of Mary's anger at me, that I am a victim of her choices. If I just say I don't feel a connection with Mary and I'm not motivated to call her while she is angry at me and in her wounded self, the conflict will escalate. So first I ask if she is open to learning with me. I tell her that I have some very good reasons for not calling her and ask whether she is interested in learning and exploring this with me. If she opens, I will tell her about not feeling connected with her, and we can explore why. If she doesn't open, then there is no point in saying this to her, because she will just continue to blame me for it.

What if instead of coming from fear, I come from love? Then I have the choice to open my heart to my spiritual guidance, asking for help in responding to Mary in a loving way. I have the choice to surrender to a higher will and allow my response to come *through* me from my guidance instead of from my wounded self. In this case, I might say, "Mary, I understand that you're feeling hurt and uncared for by me, and I'm open to hearing your pain. Can we talk about it without the blame? I do have some very good reasons for not calling you. If you'd like to explore this with me, perhaps we could resolve this in a caring way. If you just want to blame me, then I'd rather talk about it when you're not angry."

By setting a boundary against being blamed and not taking responsibility for Mary's feelings while letting her know that I am open to resolving the issue, I respond in a way that is loving to both of us. If Mary refuses to stop blaming me and is unwilling to open up and explore her desire to blame, then I can disengage from the conversation: "Mary, I'm unwilling to continue a conversation when I am being blamed. Please call me when you are open to resolving this with me."

Continuing the conversation when I am being shamed and blamed is not good for me—or Mary. Even though she may feel furious that I will not allow her to blame me, this is still the most loving action I can take for both of us. I may feel sad that Mary will not open up to me. I may feel a pang of heartache about it. But I will not feel angry, hurt, or victimized. By taking responsibility for myself through staying connected with my own feelings and spiritual guidance, I am able to take loving action for myself as well as supporting Mary's highest good by refusing to accept her unloving behavior. This leaves me feeling empowered instead of victimized.

As adults, we are no longer helpless over how we feel. Whenever I allow others to treat me disrespectfully, I feel victimized. Whenever I do not set good boundaries against being treated badly or respond with anger or blame to another's anger or blame, I feel awful. It is easy to think that this is because of how I have been treated instead of how I am treating myself and others. But the moment I set loving boundaries against disrespectful behavior while refusing to treat the other person with disrespect, I feel powerful, lovable, and worthy.

None of us like to think of ourselves as victims. Therefore it comes as a shock to realize how often we allow ourselves to be victims. We are victims any time we give another person the power to define our worth. We are victims any time we make our addictions to approval, sex, substances, things, or activities responsible for our feeling happy and lovable. We are victims any time we blame another or God for our feelings of fear, anger, hurt, or disappointment. When we define ourselves *externally*, we hand away our power to others and feel controlled by their choices. When we define ourselves *internally*, through our connection with our higher guidance, we move into personal power and responsibility.

When there is no loving adult to set appropriate boundaries against being controlled, the wounded self often protects itself by going into resistance. Resistance is a form of control—over not being controlled. This is such a big subject that we'll need to spend some time with it. So the next chapter deals with resistance.

# 4

# Resistance and Procrastination: Keeping Your Life Stuck

Raymond was raised by a mother who tried to control his every thought and action. There were rules for everything, from the right way to speak to her to the right way to wipe his bottom. The moment he didn't do things her way, she withdrew, becoming a block of ice. Because Raymond's father was not around much, his mother was all he had. He needed her to survive. So Raymond capitulated, giving himself up to get what he thought was her love. He did everything her way. He allowed her to take over his life until almost nothing of the real Raymond was left.

But a tiny part of him refused to give in. It found little ways to resist, to keep him safe from being completely consumed. One of these was dawdling. Not only would Raymond dawdle, but when he finally did what his mother wanted, he did it badly, always making some mistake that drove her crazy.

Now, as an adult, Raymond resists and procrastinates, even over things he wants to do, such as connecting with his higher guidance or taking loving action. The moment he knows what the loving action is, he procrastinates. He puts off acting on what is loving to himself. He just doesn't get around to it. When he does act on it, he makes mistakes. Because Raymond doesn't understand why this happens, he can't change his behavior. He is stuck.

Whenever his higher guidance speaks to him, Raymond's wounded self hears his mother's voice and automatically resists. His mother's need to dominate him, which came from her own unhealed spiritual abuse, left him with a terror of being consumed by anything or anyone, including his concept of God.

The old power struggle between little Raymond and his mother is now being reenacted inside the adult Raymond. The part of him that wants to stay safe from control struggles with the part that wants to open to loving himself. Until Raymond becomes aware of this inner battle, his resistance will keep winning.

People who resist learned early on that this was the only way to maintain a bit of integrity in the face of invasive, controlling parents or caregivers. This may have been true when they were children, but it's not true now. In fact, when you are driven to resist, you are not free to make your own choices. You are not even free to do the things you want to do. Paradoxically, *you are actually being controlled by your resistance.* What used to safeguard a bit of your integrity now cheats you out of your freedom and sabotages your ability to grow.

The problem goes even further. Like Raymond, people who had to resist controlling parents often transfer this resistance to their relationship with their higher power. They find it impossible to open to their higher guidance for fear of being controlled. They believe on the deepest level that they would have to give up themselves to receive Divine love. They do not understand that real love is unconditional rather than controlling.

I discovered this pattern while working with clients who seemed to be stuck in their healing process. It occurs when your fear of being controlled is so great that resistance becomes your identity, your essential way of interacting with the world. Just as a fish cannot see the water it swims in, you may not even be aware of your resistance. You cannot see it, but on some level, you believe you must have it to be safe.

Resistance often explains why people get stuck in their recovery, why their healing seems to go just so far and no further. It is a key reason why people have not been able to open to their guidance and experience Divine love firsthand. We'll spend this chapter looking in depth at resistance and seeing how it plays out in different people and different situations. As you read, see if anything rings a bell for you. In my experience, the simple act of recognizing your resistance and choosing not to continue it is like taking an express train to emotional and spiritual well-being.

## Six Forms of Resistance

There are six main symptoms of resistance. Most people who are caught up in resistance will identify with at least three of them.

1. **Being stuck.** No matter how much therapy you have or how many workshops you attend, nothing is working. You are stuck in your unhappiness, and you often feel alone and misunderstood.

2. **Controlling parents.** One or both of your parents were controlling—invasive, overprotective, abusive, shaming, or critical.

3. **Wanting to change but not taking meaningful action.** You intend to take care of yourself in new ways, such as improving your health, cleaning your house, or getting your work done on time. You decide on some new actions, but somehow you never seem to carry them out for more than a few days or weeks. No matter how many resolutions you make to follow through, you never do.

4. **Denying your real motivation.** You say you want to change—to become loving, successful, happy, spiritually connected, and so on—yet it never happens. You are in denial about the

fact that you have a goal that is more important to you: not to be controlled by anyone or anything, *not even by what you actually want.*

5. **Resenting the goal.** Although you say you want to be loving, successful, responsible, and so on, you resent the very thing you claim to want. You may even judge it as an unworthy goal: "People who jog are too obsessed with their appearance. Why are looks such a big deal in our culture?"

6. **Getting satisfaction out of others' frustration with you.** When people react negatively to your behavior or your lack of action, you feel gratified, like a rebellious adolescent who is winning the power struggle with his or her parents. You might even feel a gloating satisfaction when your therapist is unable to help you get unstuck. You might feel this same satisfaction with regard to your higher power.

## Control over Not Being Controlled

Why is not being controlled so important? How did resistance become so much more important than love? Resistance is a consequence of spiritual abuse. If your connection with your spiritual guidance was cut off in childhood, you do not have a consistent source of love and safety. As a result, you must protect yourself from your wounded self. You may do so by resisting all forms of control.

This is especially true if your parents were invasive and consuming in their attempts to control you. You might have felt overwhelmingly helpless and alone. These are almost intolerable feelings, especially for a child. In fact, the deeper purpose of all addictions is to avoid these feelings. So you came up with little (or big) ways to resist your parents, assert your power, and hang on to some tiny part of yourself. Over time, this resistance came to be the only thing that made your wounded self feel safe. You became addicted to it. Resisting became part of your identity.

## Resistance to Others

Let's look at resistance to others first. Resistance to being controlled by other people falls into two categories: overt and covert. Overt resistance includes all the ways we openly try to stop others from controlling us: explaining to them why they should not be treating us the way they are, defending our position, blaming them, and getting angry at their invasiveness. Covert resistance includes surreptitious ways to thwart others' efforts to control us: withdrawing our attention or fading out, digging in our heels and being stubborn, giving them the silent treatment, procrastinating, forgetting, making mistakes, doing the opposite of what is being requested of us, getting tired, falling asleep, lying—and denying that we are doing any of this.

Let me tell you about my first clear experience with what I now recognize as resistance.

Elisa had been working with Inner Bonding for a few years and had done much healing around her past abuse issues, especially with her mother. Her work and relationships were going well. From the outside, Elisa seemed to have everything, but much of the time she felt anxious, empty, and sad. When she was with others, she frequently got angry at them about minor things. She found this especially disturbing because it was exactly the way her mother had treated her.

Elisa clearly heard her inner voice asking for what she wanted—such as less stress and more sleep—but she didn't respect these wishes or take responsibility for her feelings. She also heard the voice of her spiritual guidance, yet she rarely asked it for advice and even more rarely acted on what she heard. Elisa knew that her inner child existed and needed her compassion, yet she persisted in hating her. When she looked at her life, she was mystified at her inability to love herself and take loving action on her own behalf.

Elisa attended one of my five-day Inner Bonding intensives to try to break through her stuckness. On the fourth day, she was working one-on-one with me and feeling frustrated with her lack of progress.

"I hate my inner child," Elisa told me. "I think she is bad. I don't want to love her. I can't love her. I know I should. I know I'm supposed to. I know no one else can do this for me, but I don't want to."

As I listened to these words, something in Elisa's voice and manner suddenly struck me: she looked and sounded like a rebellious adolescent gloating over the fact that her parents could not make her do what they wanted. "Ha, ha, you can't make me" was the feeling I picked up. I later came to recognize this gloating satisfaction as one of the six symptoms of resistance.

"Elisa," I asked, "Do you feel resistant?"

"Yes!" she shouted. "That's exactly what I feel."

I knew that Elisa was brought up by an extremely controlling mother. "Elisa, what do you think your mother wanted from you the most?" I asked.

"She wanted me to love her," she promptly replied.

"So you did everything she wanted you to do. You gave in to her control, except in this. She could not make you love her. Is that right? She could not control you in this area?"

"That's right! I remember being seven and deciding that I would never love her. I knew that no matter what she did to me, she could not make me love her. And it was not just her she wanted me to love. She wanted me to love my sister and be loving in general. She wanted me to be a sweet, loving girl."

"So this is where you took your stand against being controlled? This is where you said 'No, you can't make me?'"

"Yes!" Elisa's hands tightened into fists. "She could make me do everything else, but she couldn't make me be loving."

"So in order for you to be loving now to your inner child, you would have to give in to your mother's demands? You would have to let her think she has won?"

"Oh my God! That's what has me stuck! I can't be loving because my mother will think she has control over me, and I can't stand that thought."

"So you would rather be miserable than let your mother think she won?" I asked softly.

Elisa was silent for nearly a minute. Then she looked directly at me and said, "That is exactly what I've been doing, but I didn't realize it. And you know what? I don't want to do that anymore."

"What if your mother thinks she has finally gotten control over you?"

"That makes me feel kind of sick inside, but it would be better than being irritated and angry so much. Yes . . . I think I can live with her thinking she has control over me."

"Maybe you've been in a power struggle with your mother all this time without even realizing it—one that you seem ready to let go of. Do you think that through resisting control by your mother, your life has been controlled by the power struggle?"

"Yes," Elisa said. "I see that now. It's like I've been controlled by my own resistance!" Excitement had flooded her cheeks with color. "This makes so much sense. I feel like a door is opening in me!"

I saw the shift in Elisa as she sat before me, and I knew that this insight would profoundly change her ability to love herself and others. But Elisa would have to address another part of her resistance before she could fully heal.

"Elisa," I continued in a gentle voice, "Being a loving person means loving yourself: loving your inner child, the part you keep saying you hate. But I don't think it's your inner child you hate. I think your wounded self thinks you are bad. The part you call 'bad' is just like your mother—angry, irritated, controlling. Really loving yourself means dropping any judgments you have about yourself and healing the false beliefs of your wounded self. You have been very resistant to showing up as a loving adult for both your wounded self and your inner child and doing the healing work you need to do."

"I get it. Because my mother tried to make me love her, I resisted, and that meant resisting loving any part of myself that was like her, and also resisting loving my inner child. The thing is," Elisa continued, shaking her head, "I do love my mother, even though she is still controlling sometimes. And I really am just like her sometimes. So I guess I can learn to love that part of me if I don't have to resist her control anymore." She let out a deep breath. "Whew . . . I feel so relieved!"

Elisa's face broke into a radiant smile I'd never seen on her before. She was shining, bubbling over with joy. When I saw her the next morning, she was still exuberant, laughing, hugging other people in the workshop, overflowing with joy. Her soul was beginning to taste freedom after all those years of bondage to the power struggle inside her. Resisting control, instead of loving, had been Elisa's savior, her God, albeit a false one. Now she was free to choose the path of love, the love that truly *is* God. Watching her from across the room as I sipped my tea, I realized that Elisa looked as if she had just been let out of prison.

The next time I noticed the resistance of the wounded self was at another five-day intensive a few weeks later. I was working with Annette, whom I had just met. Annette had not used Inner Bonding before, but she had sought out many other forms of healing for her misery. Like Elisa, she was stuck.

As Annette sat with me on the second day of the intensive, she kept collapsing into the helpless, miserable tears of a victim. As I looked at her, something did not feel right to me. Here was a very attractive, obviously bright and talented woman in her forties, with an aura of power and a loving and generous heart, yet she was unhappy. She felt victimized. Something was definitely wrong.

I suddenly realized that Annette was resisting something. Remembering my experience with Elisa, I asked, "Annette, was one of your parents controlling with you?"

"Yes, my mother was very controlling. Everything had to be her way."

"Did you give in to her?"

"Yes. I was a good girl."

"What do you think your mother wanted from you the most?"

Without hesitation Annette answered, "To be happy. She used to point her finger at me and say, 'Be happy. Just be happy.' I think she felt if I wasn't happy, she wasn't a good mother."

"Were you happy?"

"No, I never was."

"So you gave in to your mother's control in everything else, but this is where you took your stand. This is where you tried to maintain some sense of self, some sense of integrity. In this one way your mother could not control you. She could not make you be happy."

"That's right! Wow! I just remembered throwing stones in the creek one day when I was about ten and vowing to myself that there was nothing she could do to make me be happy!"

"So all these years you have been in a power struggle with your mother, refusing to be happy, believing on some deep level that you were maintaining your integrity and sense of self by resisting happiness?"

"Yes. I really have . . . That's pretty ironic!" Annette said, giving me a wry grin. "I'm the one who's suffering from not being happy, not her!"

In that moment, I saw the dark cloud under which Annette had lived her life start to lift. I sat there stunned at the seemingly instant transformation. Annette's tears dried up, and her wry grin was replaced by a beatific smile that slowly spread across her face, a smile that I would see often during the remaining three days of the intensive. After many years of resistance, Annette was finally free to be happy.

## The Authoritarian Self

On the flight home after the intensive, I thought hard about what had happened with Annette, and earlier with Elisa. Their healing seemed so quick, so magical, like opening a jail door and freeing the soul. Had I stumbled onto something wonderful that could help people who were stuck? Was it really that simple? Did people only have to *recognize* the resistance that had been running their lives to be free of it?

In the weeks and months that followed, I started seeing resistance everywhere, every time someone was stuck in their healing process. Although some people who recognized the power of their resistance were freed from it, others had a harder time choosing true freedom over the illusion of freedom from control.

Neil, a young man in his midtwenties, was an example of this difficulty. His mother, who tried to completely run his life, had always wanted him to be thin, while his highly critical and financially successful father wanted him to make a lot of money. When Neil came to see me, he was immobilized in his life. As you might guess, he was seriously overweight, emotionally shut down, and unwilling to find meaningful work, even though he was a brilliant young man. Resisting his parents had become far more important to him than getting unstuck and taking good care of himself.

Unfortunately, recognizing how resistance was controlling his life did not even begin to free Neil from it. Instead he made the conscious choice to continue to resist. In Neil's case, resisting his parents was truly more important to him than loving himself. Being right about how awful his parents were, and punishing them for it, was more important than being happy.

Looked at in these terms, doesn't Neil sound more like an angry seven-year-old than a grown man? That's exactly what's going on behind the scenes. When your wounded self is in charge of your life—as Neil's was—you may eat doughnuts for dinner, get to work an hour late, and skip your exercise routine. The next day, however, you may do just the opposite. You may force yourself to get up an hour early, have a green salad with no dressing for lunch, and jog four miles instead of two.

You enact this Dr. Jekyll/Mr. Hyde behavior because at any given moment, your wounded self is being either permissive or authoritarian, just as your parents were. Both kinds of behavior are based on false beliefs, and both are unloving.

This is how addiction to resistance makes us resist even ourselves. All of us absorb the wounded, controlling voices of our parents and others, telling us what we "should" do, what we "must" do, what we "have" to do. Whenever your wounded self tries to exert power over you with the same rigid rules, internal criticism, and unilateral decisions that you absorbed from one or both of your parents or others and that ignore your feelings, you are trying to have control over yourself. This sets off an internal power struggle between the authoritarian part of your wounded self and the permissive, resistant, indulgent part, which resists being controlled with all its might.

Let's say your authoritarian part lays down the law:

"From now on, I'm cutting out sugar."

"I will write down everything I eat."

"No more drinking. It's ruining my marriage, and it's time to stop."

"Tomorrow morning, I will start my new exercise program."

"I'm putting myself on a budget right now. No more extras."

"I will get up early tomorrow and clean up the clutter."

What usually happens when you do this? Your good intentions are short-lived, aren't they? They don't result in long-lasting change. That's because they become sabotaged by your resistant, permissive wounded self, which experiences any attempt at control—even self-control—as threatening to your freedom and integrity. It will fight tooth and nail to resist it. This makes sense, because when you are caught in resistance, resistance has become your identity. Any assault on your identity feels like an attack. So your resistant, permissive part responds to the authoritarian part with fury: "You can't tell me what to do! I can eat whatever I want."

"One drink won't hurt."

"I'm the boss of me. I don't have to do what you say. I don't like exercise."

"Leave me alone. I'm really tired. I need to sleep in."

The result of this inner power struggle is a standoff. Neither side wins, and you become immobilized. The voices of the authoritarian part and the resistant, permissive part are equally loud and convincing. Behind each of them is a compelling set of false beliefs. For example, your authoritarian part may believe: "I have power. I can control what and how I eat, drink, smoke, and spend money. I can control my health, my weight, and my addictions. I can do this by myself, without help."

In the meantime, your permissive, resistant, indulgent part believes: "I am nurturing myself and rewarding myself when I eat whatever I want, drink whenever I want, sleep in, watch TV instead of exercise, and buy whatever I want. The only way I can be my own person is to resist what is demanded of me, even if I am resisting myself."

Paradoxically, the goal of both parts is to keep you safe. But it's a goal you can never reach without giving up the very strategy you think is protecting you.

## The Fear of Giving Up Resistance

Giving up lifelong resistance can be very frightening. I saw this clearly in a client named Brittany. She and I had worked together for a number of months, and she had done a lot of growing, but now she was stuck. Her friendships and love relationships were not going well, and her employer was constantly yelling at her (as had most of her previous employers). Her connection with her guidance was sporadic.

Brittany seemed to fade out whenever difficult feelings came up. Sometimes she would even fall asleep during her work with me. This, combined with the fact that she had a controlling father, suggested to me that she might be stuck in resistance.

"Brittany," I asked her one morning, "what do you think your father wanted from you the most?"

"He wanted me to listen to him."

"So you gave in with everything else, but he couldn't get you to listen?"

She broke into a sheepish yet self-satisfied smile. "Yeah. It drove him crazy. He would end up yelling at me, 'Why don't you ever listen?'"

"So this was where you drew the line? He could not force you to listen. He could force you to do a lot of other things, but not to listen."

Laughing, Brittany said, "Yeah, that's right!"

"What does your employer say when she is yelling at you?"

Brittany's eyes widened. "I can't believe it! She says the same thing! She is always saying to me, 'Brittany, why can't you just *listen*?' It drives her crazy." Again came the gloating, self-satisfied laugh.

"What about in our sessions?" I asked. "Do you think I am trying to control you when I bring up difficult issues?"

"I guess so," she conceded, shifting in her chair. "It feels like you are invading me somehow."

"So you just fade out?"

"Yeah, but that doesn't make sense. I'm here to get help."

"Maybe resisting what you perceive as control or invasion feels safer. Maybe it's more important to feel safe than to get help."

"But it's ruining everything—my work, my relationships. Nothing is going right."

"That's true. But your first priority seems to be keeping yourself safe by resisting control. Until you decide it's more important to be loving to yourself and others—which means being willing to listen and learn, even if it feels like you are being controlled—you will keep fading out."

"But that's crazy!"

"Not to your wounded self. To your wounded self, it makes perfect sense to resist, to hold the line against being totally consumed."

"Margaret, I feel like going to sleep right now."

"I guess your wounded self doesn't like being unmasked."

"I know I've got to deal with this for my life to get better, but I sure can feel the part of me that would rather fade out, no matter what the cost."

Brittany shifted her gaze and stared out the window. After a few moments, she said in a small voice, "The idea of giving up this resistance feels so scary. It feels like I'm going to die." Tears filled her eyes. She looked terrified.

The desperate intensity of Brittany's reaction made perfect sense to me, and I have since seen it in many people who are confronting the need to drop their resistance. I think there are three reasons for it.

First, if you have used resistance all your life to try keep yourself safe, giving it up must feel at first like opening the door to a lynch mob. Unless you have learned how to set loving boundaries against being controlled by others, it is just too scary to give up your resistance. In addition, you may have spent so much time resisting that you have no idea who you are other than a person who resists. You may even fear that underneath all the resistance you are empty, dark, full of holes, that you have no true self, no soul essence. If so, losing your identity as someone who resists, even if it's a false identity, may feel life-threatening. Finally, because resistance was the primary way you protected yourself from the pain of feeling powerless, it came to be an addiction. And giving up an addiction that is keeping your pain at bay feels like dying (or so your wounded self believes).

Brittany faced a hard decision. She could give up her resistance and start to listen to other people, thus accepting the fact that she might feel at first as if others were controlling her. Or she could continue to create a facade of safety based on her resistance, thereby accepting the fact that she would continue to suffer problems in her work and her relationships. She had to decide which was more important to her: resisting control or being loving.

Of course, what Brittany wanted was to continue to resist while enjoying the results of being loving. If she persisted in her denial, lying to herself that this is possible, she would stay stuck. Fortunately, once she started to see the dire consequences, she decided that learning to love herself was worth facing her fears.

## Revealing the Hidden Agenda

Being stuck in your life, work, or relationships is a painful way to live. Yet time after time new clients tell me, "I decided to work with you because I am stuck. I am repeating the same patterns over and over again, both at work and in my relationships. I can't seem to find my way out of this rut I'm in. There must be more to life than this." Although they think they truly want to get unstuck from their problems, they actually have a hidden agenda.

See if this fits for you: Consciously, you want to be unstuck and free from your pain, but unconsciously something else is far more important to you. Getting unstuck means that you need to change your mind about your deepest desire and motivation. You have to move off the wide road onto the narrow road—the spiritual path, the path of love, starting with learning to love yourself.

You may say that you desire to be loving and open to learning. You may say you are on a spiritual path, eager to evolve and connect with your higher power. However, the fact that you are stuck indicates that you have a more prevailing intent: *to have control over not being controlled.* As long as safety from being controlled is more important to you than love, you will stay stuck.

As you can imagine, resistance can wreak havoc with intimate relationships.

Suzanna came to see me because she was unhappy in her marriage. She had been married to Jason for thirty-one years and was confused about why she was so unhappy, since she knew that she still loved him. Not only was she depressed and lonely, she was sick much of the time and couldn't seem to discover the reason.

As we talked, it became apparent that Jason was very stuck in his neediness and resistance. As a child, he had an invasive mother and an absent father. He had withdrawn early in life to protect himself from being engulfed by his mother's invasiveness. While Jason professed great love for Suzanna, his actions were not caring. He was either pressing her to meet his needs, being as invasive as his mother had been, or he resisted giving her what she wanted, especially caring, empathy, and intimacy—just as he had resisted giving in to his mother. Although Suzanna saw that she sometimes *was* controlling, she also saw that Jason perceived her as controlling even when she wasn't.

Over time, Suzanna worked hard on letting go of her controlling behavior, hoping that Jason would be able to drop his resistance, but things got even worse. As soon as she disengaged herself from her struggle to control him, Jason felt abandoned. His alarm bells went off, and he started pulling on Suzanna for time, sex, and attention. Then, as soon as she started coming toward him again, he retreated emotionally. She couldn't even offer a suggestion to Jason without his shutting down and resisting. Suzanna finally realized that Jason saw her as his mother, no matter what she did.

Jason was trapped between a rock and a hard place, between fear of engulfment and fear of rejection. He was stuck and didn't want to do the inner work necessary to get unstuck. In the end—and much to Jason's dismay—Suzanna made the difficult decision to leave the marriage. She realized that she was far less lonely when she was alone than when she was with Jason.

Everyone who is unhealed has both of Jason's fears in varying degrees. People who have a terror of engulfment have an even deeper terror of rejection. As children, they suffered from unbearable rejection when they did not capitulate to their parents' demands. Because they were not taught that their very essence is love, they let others define their essence. In doing so, they became dependent on someone else's definition of who they were and thus put themselves at risk for even greater rejection. *Fear of rejection is a direct result of not having defined our own worth or knowing our own light and lovability.*

When you are intimate with someone, fear of rejection can make you think you have to give yourself up, do everything they want, and take responsibility for their feelings. Naturally, this triggers the fear of engulfment. In the heat of this fear, you withdraw and shut down, as Jason did, cutting off the very connection you seek. The person on the other end gets confused. First, they see you desperately wanting to connect with them and pulling on them to get it. But if they open up to connecting with you, you pull away.

Sonya and Ian had a relationship similar to Suzanne and Jason's, but with a much better outcome. They came to one of my intensives, during which Ian recognized his own addiction to resistance. He even remembered making the decision early on to not do what his mother wanted him to do, no matter what. Ian would act as if he was complying, but each time he found some way to sabotage his performance.

When Ian interacted with Sonya, whom he loved very much, his wounded self was in charge. He would shut down to whatever she wanted from him, which resulted in a total lack of affection and connection with her. Ian also professed to want affection, yet he pulled away whenever Sonya reached out to him. When she withdrew, he called her cold. Sonya ended up feeling lonely, confused, and frustrated. She just couldn't win. When she voiced her frustration, Ian would tell her that it was her fault because she was so controlling.

At the intensive, Ian gained a clear understanding of his addiction to resistance and how it was affecting his relationship. But I did not encourage him to release it. Instead, I told him to continue to resist but *to choose resistance consciously rather than unconsciously*. This, as I will explain below, is the first step out of the resistance trap.

When Ian watched himself *choosing* to resist, he stopped operating on automatic pilot. Suddenly a new choice became available to him. He could choose to resist or choose to act a different way. For the first time ever, he was able to reach out to Sonya with love rather than holding back. There wasn't a dry eye among us as we witnessed them openly expressing their love.

Ian learned another crucial lesson that day. He discovered that when he stopped resisting control by Sonya, he became able to connect with his higher guidance. He no longer resisted its love and wisdom.

Resistant people tend to be terrified by the thought of surrendering to their guidance and being controlled by some outside force. It triggers all their old fears of engulfment. This presents a terrible dilemma: you cannot know who you really are, the love that is your very essence, without a connection with your higher source of love and truth; yet in connecting to your guidance, you fear losing yourself. Fear of rejection plays a big role in resistance to guidance: you might believe you have to let God control and consume you in order to win Divine love, and that God will reject you if you don't do it right.

If your parents didn't bring through Divine love to you, the only way to know your own light and lovability is by receiving that knowledge from your spiritual guidance. Yet you cannot connect with your guidance when you are resisting being controlled by your concept of God. And without a spiritual connection, you have no consistent source of safety and love. So you must protect yourself. Which means resisting all forms of control. Which means you can't connect with your guidance.

Is this really a vicious circle? Yes! But there is a way out!

## The Freedom to Choose Differently

You can do three things to break this cycle of resistance:

1. Notice that resistance is a choice, and notice yourself making that choice.
2. Notice the consequences of that choice.
3. Make a new choice: that becoming a loving human being is more important than not being controlled.

Once you have accomplished these tasks, you will be able to use the Six Steps of Inner Bonding to have a deep daily dialogue with your higher guidance, which is essential for moving beyond both aloneness and loneliness.

The first task is to notice—*without judging yourself*—when you choose to resist. This may sound simple, but it represents a huge shift in consciousness. When you really see that resistance to any given situation is a choice, you no longer operate on automatic pilot. You have taken the first step out of denial and into awareness. In that moment, you start seeing that you can make other choices, such as choosing love instead of control. Noticing when you choose to resist is the beginning of changing your intent.

If you resist seeing your resistance—that is, if you resist the awareness that resistance is a choice—back up a step. Start watching yourself, noticing your feelings kindly and without judgment. Notice how you feel when someone wants something from you. Do you feel uncomfortable? Do you think those feelings are being caused by the other person? See if you can tune in to the fact that your feelings arise from your own fear of being controlled, not from what the other person is saying or doing. No one can make you feel the discomfort of the fear of engulfment. They may trigger the fear, but you are the source of these feelings.

For example, if someone calls you a cheapskate and you know you are not, you may laugh or simply dismiss the remark.

But if deep inside you feel you really *are* a cheapskate, that person's remark may bring up feelings of anger or shame. Your reaction is *your* responsibility. How do you end up feeling when your fear forces you to resist? How do you feel when you make resisting control more important than loving?

Now ask yourself this: are there things that you want for yourself but resist because someone else also wants them for you? Notice what happens inside if someone urges you to do something you actually want to do, such as be on time, eat well, exercise, or let go of an addiction that's harming you. Watch yourself procrastinate, and notice how you feel when you do. Do you feel like a child who's winning a game, or an adolescent who's getting away with something? Later, once your procrastinating self has won, do you still feel like a winner? Or do you end up feeling that you are the one who lost?

If you are honest with yourself, you will discover that instead of maintaining your integrity, you have lost it. You will see that it is false to believe that resisting maintains your integrity. In fact, you maintain your integrity only when you make choices based on spiritual guidance, on what is truly loving to yourself and others.

Once you notice that your resistance is a choice, you are ready for the second task: noticing the consequences of your choice to resist. Choosing to live from fear forces you to walk the wide road, the earthly path. It closes your heart and ruins your relationships. It pushes you into addictions and makes you turn to others for attention and approval.

You may be reading this book because you are stuck. Being stuck is the consequence of choosing resistance instead of growth and spiritual connection. Look at your life. In what areas is it not working? Is your love relationship thriving, or is your resistance keeping you from having a relationship? Are you satisfied at work? Do you have a caring circle of friends? Do you take good care of your body? Are your home and work spaces peaceful or cluttered? Do you want to change but find that nothing works? Now ask yourself if resisting control is really worth all that pain. Would you consider making a new choice?

Now that you have noticed the choice you are making and have faced its consequences, the door is open to take the final step. The third and final task in breaking through resistance is to consciously decide that becoming a loving human being is more important to you than protecting yourself from being controlled, or from someone thinking they control you. In other words, you actually need to be *willing to be controlled* without putting up your wall of resistance.

This does not mean, however, that you *will* be controlled. That's the paradox of giving up your addiction to resistance: when being a loving human being is more important to you than resisting being controlled, *you never get controlled.* That's because when you choose to be loving, you can move into Inner Bonding, through which you will experience Divine love, heal your wounded self, and learn to set healthy, loving boundaries against being controlled. When you are in resistance, you only focus on what's happening externally: someone is trying to control you, and you've got to get safe by resisting. When you change your intent and choose to make loving more important, you focus on what's happening internally. You create safety for your inner child and do whatever you need to do to take care of yourself. (You will learn how to do this later in the book.) You no longer have to avoid being controlled. Instead, you learn to handle engulfment and rejection in ways that are loving to yourself.

There's a boomerang effect with resistance: the more the wounded self tries to make us feel safe, the more unsafe we feel. The more we try to protect against loss of freedom, the more unfree we feel. True safety and freedom can never come from strategies of control. In fact, the more you use this approach, the more unsafe and insecure you feel. *That's because each time you choose control instead of love, you undermine your sense of self.*

Attempting to control others not only violates them, it violates your true soul self, which is love. This violation creates a lack of safety, security, peace, joy, and freedom. When you allow yourself to be guided by the love that is God instead of your controlling and resistant wounded self, you will discover your personal power and true integrity.

# PART II

## *Living with Love*

This section describes the Six Steps of Inner Bonding for healing your false beliefs and experiencing the unconditional love, truth, wisdom, and power that is God. This process will enable you to replace your false beliefs with truth. Shame is healed as you learn to love yourself and embrace the beauty of your true soul self.

# 5

## Inner Bonding: Laying the Foundation

In the first four chapters, we saw what life without love looks and feels like. Now we are going to start to change things. You are going to experience the astonishing power of the Six Steps of Inner Bonding, which hundreds of thousands of people practice to have direct daily contact with their higher guidance, define their own worth, heal their aloneness, and fill themselves with love to share with others so that they are lonely no more.

First, I want to share with you how Inner Bonding came into my life.

### The Path of Discovery

I was born on a farm in upstate New York. I have clear memories of being outside in my playpen when I was around eight months old, communing with nature and feeling what I would now describe as a oneness with the love that is God. I remember the warmth of the sun, the freshness and openness of the air, the smell of the grass, and the exquisite beauty of the butterflies that drifted past. I remember the feelings of joy and peace and the connectedness I sensed with everything around me.

My paternal grandfather, who lived on the neighboring farm, would come and sit with me each day. I felt our deep love for each other—a depth of connection that I didn't have with my parents. I'm grateful that I experienced this profound heart connection with him.

When I was thirteen months old, we left the farm for Los Angeles. I never saw my grandfather again. Our country was at war, and fear hung over the city. I recall lying on a bed in a dingy apartment complex and looking up at the air. I could see the denseness and darkness of the energy (babies often see things that adults can't). I had lost the brightness and clarity of the air in the country. I had lost the warmth of the sun and the smell of the grass. I had lost my grandfather, as well as my sense of connection with a source of love.

Soon after coming to Los Angeles, I got very sick and almost died. At that time, I established a false belief that governed much of my behavior in my relationships: if I am not deeply connected with someone, I will die. As a result, much of my behavior became motivated by my desperate need to get this connection with others.

Looking back, I can see that the search for connectedness drove my actions from the time we left the farm. I hated being an only child. I used to beg my parents to give me a brother or sister. My deepest desire was always to connect with others, to feel our oneness instead of my loneliness, anxiety, and fear. My parents did the best they could, coming from their own deep woundedness, but I was a mystery to them. Unable to connect with themselves or a higher source of love, they could not connect with me in the deep way I needed.

My profound desire to connect with others and to heal my almost constant anxiety motivated me to begin a spiritual search in my early twenties. This search took me into many different forms of therapy: psychoanalysis (four days a week for four and a half years); Jungian, neo-Reichian, Ericksonian, humanistic-existential therapy, Transactional Analysis,

Psychosynthesis, rebirthing, Rolfing, past-life regression, and hypnosis. I joined a meditation group and worked with various healers in my attempts to connect with myself, others, and a higher source of love and wisdom.

Each experience was beneficial, but none brought me the inner peace and joy I sought. Why was the deep connection and inner peace I longed for so elusive? What was I missing?

I married and struggled for years trying to discover how to have a loving relationship. I had three children and learned a great deal, which my then husband and I wrote about in our best-selling book *Do I Have to Give Up Me to Be Loved by You?* But something was still missing. I still had no personal connection with a higher power, and my connection with my husband was sporadic. No matter how hard I tried, I couldn't keep my heart open to others during conflict. I wanted so much to be loving, but I was often angry, critical, and controlling. As a result, my ability to maintain a deep connection with others was limited.

I tried prayer and meditation, but that didn't seem to be the answer either. Sometimes when I prayed with others, I got a fleeting sense of a higher presence and was filled with hope. Then it would be gone. Try as I might, I couldn't make that connection on my own. I just didn't know how.

During those years, I also grappled with illness, going from doctor to doctor, from chiropractor to homeopath, trying to understand why I was exhausted and hurting so much of the time. I studied nutrition, ate only organic foods, took supplements, exercised. I rented an art studio and took two days off a week to pursue painting, something I had always loved. Yet I was often in a puddle of tears in my studio, feeling sick, miserable, and lonely, wondering what could be so wrong.

By 1984, I had run out of things to try. On the outside, things looked fine. I was married, had three beautiful children, a career I loved, a successful book, an art studio, and enough money to do what I wanted, and I'd had tons of therapy, but I still wasn't happy. I felt lost and anxious much of the time. Like it or not, I had to face the fact that I needed more help than I knew how to get for myself. So I prayed for a teacher to come into my life, someone to lead the way, someone I could learn with and learn from.

It has often been said that when the student is ready the teacher appears. I guess I was ready. A few months later, I met Dr. Erika Chopich, who has since become my best friend, coauthor, companion on the spiritual path, and Golden Girl housemate. Erika had half of the Inner Bonding process, and I had the other half. Along with help from our higher guidance, Erika and I developed Inner Bonding. I wrote a book by that name, and we wrote two books together, *Healing Your Aloneness* and *The Healing Your Aloneness Workbook*.

Most importantly, however, it was through Erika that I finally learned how to have a direct personal experience of my higher guidance.

## The Teacher Appears

One morning in late 1992, Erika called me in a panic. She had moved the previous year to Santa Fe, New Mexico, and was living in a beautiful house on pristine land.

"I think I'm going nuts!" she told me. "I must be hallucinating!"

"Why? What happened?"

"This is really crazy. Last night I got into bed, and there, at the foot of my bed, was an old Indian woman. I got scared, thinking she was a homeless person who had somehow got in. I asked her who she was and why she was in my house. She said, 'I am your spiritual Master Teacher.'"

"That's great!" I replied. Among the many things I'd tried in order to heal my own anxiety and unhappiness was contacting my spiritual guides, messengers of spirit who could bring me Divine love and wisdom and let me know the higher will for me. It had never worked.

"No, it's not!" Erika shouted. "I told her I didn't want a teacher. This is all too hooey-wooey for me."

I smiled, thinking of Erika's medical training and her sci-entific mind.

"Don't tell her to leave!" I said. "You aren't crazy. She's here to teach you."

"I don't want this stuff. This is too weird."

Of course her spiritual teacher came back. No protests from Erika could stop it from happening. Finally, she accepted that her teacher was here to stay and let herself learn from her. She also remembered that her spiritual teacher was with her as a child and had helped her through a very abusive and traumatic childhood.

The closest I had gotten in my own attempts to meet my spiritual guidance was when I painted. Each time I stood before a blank canvas, I saw a beautiful silver-haired woman smiling down at me and radiating light. So I painted what my "artistic imagination" saw.

One evening, after Erika had learned how to contact her spiritual teacher, we were talking on the phone. I wasn't feeling very well and was lying on my bed.

"Erika, do you think you can see my teacher?" I asked.

"I don't know," she answered, "But I'll try."

There was silence on the phone for a few minutes. Then I heard, "Oh my God. This is really weird!"

"What?"

"I'm here in my house, but I think I'm also in your house. I see your teacher working on your body. Are you lying on your bed? Wearing a pink sweatsuit?"

I was—and I was stunned.

When Erika described my teacher, I recognized her instantly. She was the radiant silver-haired woman whose image popped into my mind when I was painting.

I longed to know more. "I only see her when I paint," I pro-tested, "and she doesn't talk to me. Erika, please ask her how I can see her and hear her when I'm not painting."

There was a short silence. Then Erika said, "She says that to connect with her you must be in the same creative state that you are in when you are painting. She says . . . well, she says to try it in the bathtub."

As peculiar as this suggestion was, it proved to be life-changing. That night, as I relaxed in a tub of steaming hot water and tried to connect with my guide, it worked. As I lay there and imagined myself painting, the radiant image of my guidance suddenly filled my mind. I was thrilled. I held the image in my mind, and I realized that when that image came to me while painting, I had never thought to ask her a question. So now I asked her question after question, and I was overjoyed to receive clear answers—some in words, some in pictures, and some through feelings. I now converse with my spiritual guidance each morning when I walk, and throughout the day when I need guidance. Through her, I gradually learned to feel the Divine within and around me each moment.

Having this contact with spirit has completely changed my life. I am no longer exhausted. Writing used to be hard. Lecturing and teaching seminars used to be hard. Even my hobbies, drawing and painting, used to be hard. Now they are easy, thanks to my direct and tangible connection to my higher guidance. My relationships are thriving, and I walk through my day knowing I am a beloved child of the love that is God. The sick, miserable aloneness and loneliness I lived with for so long are gone.

Often I also receive information from other people's spiritual guidance in the form of pictures and words. This is how I do my work with my clients. I also help my clients connect with their own spiritual guidance. I have done this successfully with clients ranging from construction workers and housewives to artists, physicians, lawyers, and accountants. I will teach you how to do this too, if you desire to have higher guidance. However, it is not necessary to imagine a guide in order to have direct contact with the love that is God. There are many ways of establishing this contact, which you will learn in a later chapter.

Inner Bonding has changed my life. As you can see, I struggled for years to find inner peace and joy. I prayed to be shown how to overcome the shame, fear, and false beliefs that ran my life. I yearned to evolve my soul and become an instrument of God on this planet. I prayed for a process that would teach me how to rediscover my soul self and connect with unconditional love and truth.

My prayers were answered when Erika came into my life and our higher guidance helped us to develop the Inner Bonding process. Erika and I have been evolving Inner Bonding for the past forty years. As each year passes, she and I receive a deeper understanding and experience.

Spirit gave us Inner Bonding for a purpose. Each of us is on this planet to be an expression of Divine love. Being "God's pencil" (as Mother Teresa put it) means being the loving hands, voice, intent, and actions of God. Through our loving actions, we bring the Divine spirit of love and compassion through us, and we express the love that is God on this planet. The Six Steps of Inner Bonding will show you how to become an instrument of Divine love.

## Laying the Foundation: Definitions

Let's start by defining the terms you'll need to understand before using the Six Steps. I have referred to some of these in previous chapters, but here I present them in detail. This section will also serve as a review of the key points you need to understand for the Six Steps of Inner Bonding to work.

## Intent

Our *intent* is what governs how we think, feel, and behave. It is the most powerful and creative force we have; it is the essence of free will. Your intent is your deepest desire, your primary motive or goal, your highest priority *in any given moment*.

There are only two primary intentions:
- To learn about loving yourself and others, even in the face of fear and pain.
- To control: to protect yourself from fear and pain with addictive, controlling behavior and thereby avoid responsibility for your feelings and actions.

When your intent is to learn to love, you are willing to face your fears and feel your painful feelings in order to understand how you may be creating them and discover what you need to do differently. The deeper purpose here is to become one with yourself, others, all of life, and the love that is God. When you open to learning, you move toward this state of oneness. No fear gets in the way. When your intent is to learn to love, your deepest desire is to find your safety, peace, lovability, and worth through an *internal* connection with your higher source of love.

When your intent is to control, you protect yourself from fear and pain and avoid responsibility for your feelings. Your deepest desire is to find your safety, peace, lovability, and worth through externals, such as attention, approval, sex, money, substances, things, and activities. When you believe that others are responsible for how you feel, you try to control them in order to feel powerful, safe, and worthy.

In every moment, each one of us chooses one of these two intents. When you desire to heal from your spiritual abuse and become one with love, you choose the spiritual path, the path of the heart, the path of courage. The road less traveled. Although the choices that others make may influence you, no one but you has control over your intent—not even your higher power, since that would negate your free will. In each moment, you choose what is most important to you, and in each moment you have an opportunity to change your mind.

The *intent to learn* is not the same as the *intent to know*. The intent to *know*—to gather information—often comes from the wounded self wanting to know what to do and how to do it "right" in order to have control over getting what it wants. People can even become addicted to gathering information, believing it will give them more control. By contrast, having the intent to *learn* means that you do not have to know what to do. You only need to open to your spiritual guidance, and you will be directed.

## Soul Self and Wounded Self

We have already talked a little about the soul self—also called the true self, or essence, or inner child—as well as about the false, wounded self. It is helpful to imagine the soul self as a bright and shining child, the natural light within that is an individualized expression of Divine love. This aspect of ourselves is ageless: it always has been and it always will be; it evolves through our life experiences. Our soul self contains our unique gifts and talents, our natural wisdom and intuition, our curiosity and sense of wonder, our playfulness and spontaneity, and our ability to love. This immortal part of us was not harmed by spiritual abuse. Instead, the soul self was hidden away, and it waits to be retrieved. Because this part of us is unbroken, complete healing can occur. Your healing is complete when you have fully retrieved and deeply know this aspect of yourself, who you really are: a Divine child created in the image of the love that is God.

Your wounded self can be any age in any given moment, depending upon how old you were when you learned a particular false belief, addiction, or way to control. We can absorb our false beliefs, which fuel our addictions and ways to control, in infancy or even prebirth, through adolescence to early adulthood. The wounded self can often pretend to be an adult, like a child or adolescent who had to take care of things that should have been beyond his or her responsibility. Our wounded self is often a mirror image of one or both of our parents. Even though we may have said, "I'll never be like that," the wounded self learned to be just like our parents or caregivers. You might even notice that your voice sounds like one of your parents when your wounded self is in charge.

Your wounded self has many parts that were developed to handle abuse, especially if it was severe. You may have a mean, angry, or violent part, a withdrawn part, a lewd or obscene part, or a "nice" part who learned to be a "good" boy or girl. You may have a part that uses food, drugs, or alcohol to numb out fear and loneliness. All these parts need healing, and they can be healed only through compassion, acceptance, truth, and love. Once you understand that they were your survival strategies in childhood, you can feel grateful and compassionate toward them instead of judgmental.

The wounded self is always trying to protect against a perceived threat of rejection, engulfment, or loss that was experienced in the past and projected onto the present or future. Through its various devices, it hopes to ward off what it fears or control getting what it wants. In addition, the wounded self is in denial—protecting itself from the pain that results from *its own choices*. The wounded self sees itself as a victim of others' choices. It believes others, or even God, cause its pain.

Almost any activity can be used as a protection against pain. Meditation can be used to connect with your higher guidance and learn about loving, or it can be used to bliss out and avoid dealing with your feelings. Many people have meditated for years without improving their lives because they have used it merely to avoid pain. Likewise, reading the Bible can be a way to open your heart and move into your desire to learn, or it can be used as an anesthetic to avoid your fear. In such cases, it often becomes a tool to control others or make God reward you.

The intent to control automatically closes your heart. In that case, you cannot bring through truth and Divine love, and you cannot give and receive love with others. You are alone inside, and this drives your wounded self to try to control getting love to stop the painful feelings of emptiness. Can you see what a vicious circle this is?

The wounded self falsely believes that we, as separate egos, cut off from the love that is God, can have power over ourselves and others. But we cannot control others' behavior without violation. The ego is willing to violate the soul self and others to have this control. As wounded egos, we violate ourselves through substance and process addictions. We violate others through controlling and sometimes violent behavior.

Your wounded self is codependent: it depends upon others to define its worth. You hand the job of defining your worth over to others and continue the cycle of self-abandonment by trying to get their love, approval, and attention. The wounded self has learned to abandon your inner child—your feelings—in four primary ways:

1. Staying in your head and ignoring the feelings in your body
2. Judging yourself
3. Numbing your feelings with addictions
4. Making others responsible for your feelings

## False Beliefs

In chapter 2, we looked at the eight major false beliefs about God that are held by the wounded self. But the wounded self has *hundreds* of other false beliefs, many of which we adopted when we were very small. A false belief is a belief about ourselves, others, the world, the universe, or God that limits and disempowers us, causing us to fear. Our false beliefs are the conclusions we drew about ourselves and the world as a result of spiritual abuse. Such beliefs cause much of our pain and much of the behavior that causes us pain. For example, if you concluded from your childhood experiences that you are bad, unlovable, or unworthy, you will generally behave as if this were true. Your resulting behavior, such as anger or withdrawal, which is geared to protect you from the rejection you fear, may actually lead others to reject you—which is just what you expected. This brings you pain and reaffirms your false belief about being unlovable. In addition, controlling behavior is itself a rejection and abandonment of your soul self, and reaffirms your belief in your unworthiness.

We know a belief is false when the belief itself causes us anxiety, depression, guilt, or shame. We then protect against the pain *caused by our false beliefs and resulting self-abandoning, self-rejecting behavior* by sinking further into self-abandoning behavior.

The following chart lists of some of the false beliefs carried by the different parts of the wounded self. These are the wounded parts of us that need welcoming, embracing, and healing. As you read this list, be sure to put your judgments aside and compassionately embrace the parts you identify with.

## FALSE BELIEFS OF THE WOUNDED SELF

### The Domino Effect False of Core Beliefs

- I am a victim. I am not responsible for my own feelings and behavior. Others' or God's unlovingness to me causes my feelings and behavior.
- God is judgmental, controlling, too busy or non-existent. God doesn't love me, just as my parents /caregivers don't love me. I project my parents' feelings and behavior onto God and conclude that God has abandoned me.
- Therefore, I am alone in the universe and I cannot handle the pain of aloneness.
- I won't survive if someone I love/need disconnects from me.

As a child, unable to bear the helplessness and despair of this aloneness, I concluded:

- It is my fault I am not being loved because I am intrinsically odd, defective, damaged, bad, wrong,
- inadequate, unimportant, unlovable or unworthy (development of core shame).

Without God to define me, others are responsible for defining my worth and lovability. Therefore:

- I must and can have control over getting the love I need to feel worthy and avoiding pain to feel safe.
- I must and can control people, my feelings, God, and the outcome of things to feel safe and worthy.

- I can control by hiding my flaws through looking good or doing everything right.

## Aspects of the Wounded Self
The wounded self develops many controlling aspects that come from the victim and core shame beliefs.

### Defender
- Belief: I can explain to others how they should see things and get them to see me the way I want to be seen. I can talk them out of seeing me as bad or wrong.

### Fixer/Lecturer
- Belief: I know what is right and it is my job to point it out to others when they are wrong. My worth is in advising and fixing people and in being right.

### Blamer
- Belief: I can intimidate others with anger and blame into feeling afraid or guilty enough to give me the love, attention, affection, sex or approval I want/need.

### Critic/Judge
- Belief: By criticizing and judging myself and others, I can get myself and others to change and be the way I want.

### Complainer/ Martyr
- Belief: If I complain verbally or with silent suffering, others will feel sorry for me and give me the love, attention or sympathy I want.

### Pleaser
- Belief: If I compliment others, do nice things for them and smile a lot, they will give me the approval I need.

### Caretaker/ Rescuer
- Belief: I'm responsible for others' feelings and behavior.
- Belief: If I sacrifice myself to take care of others, they will give me the love and approval I need.
- Belief: I am selfish if I take care of myself.

### Taker
- Belief: I can control getting the love, attention, sex or approval I want by invading others' boundaries with touch, anger, invasive or needy energy, incessant talking or emotional drama.

### Bully/Predator

- Belief: If I physically control others through threats, violence or rape, I can get what I want from others and feel powerful and safe from being violated and controlled by others.

### Avoider

- Belief: I can find a way to feel good if I deny my pain, my fear and the truth about myself and others.

### Worrier/ Obsesser

- Belief: If I think long and hard enough, or if I perform certain rituals, I can control how others feel and act and the outcome of things. If I worry enough, I can stop bad things from happening.

### Clown

- Belief: If I can be funny enough, I can control getting others to give me the approval and attention I need, and I can prevent them from withdrawing, getting angry or disapproving of me.

### Perfectionist/Performer

- Belief: If I look perfect, act perfect, say the right thing, achieve and perform right, I can control how others feel about me and treat me.

### Resister

- I can stay in control and avoid being controlled by others, by God, or even by my own inner critic by numbing out, spacing out, forgetting, withholding or procrastinating.
- Belief: Resisting being controlled is essential to my integrity.

### Addict

- Belief: I can fill the emptiness, avoid pain or feel safe if I can fill up from outside or numb my feelings with food, drugs, alcohol, sex, approval, love, spending, connection with others, things or activities such as T.V.

False beliefs can have a devastating impact on our natural spirituality, as we see in the following true story told to me by a man I knew many years ago, Don Eaton, a teacher, singer, and songwriter.

A girl was born deaf at a time when nothing could be done medically to restore her hearing. Like all children, she was born with a strong connection to the love that is God and was naturally happy and loving and open. People loved her in an especially compassionate way because they saw her as handicapped. They noticed how loving she was toward everyone. Her parents took her to church and Sunday school, but she could not hear the sermon or teachings of the adults.

One day, when she was eight, a "miracle" happened. Medical advances made it possible to restore her hearing. Her parents took her to have the operation, and her hearing was restored. Everyone thought she would be happy to be able to hear—and she was, at the time. But when she became an adult, she looked back and realized what she had lost when she gained her hearing.

Being able to hear the words of other people powerfully affected the little girl. She heard whom she should play with and whom she shouldn't, who the "good" people were and who the "bad" people were—which seemed to depend upon the color of their skin, what church they belonged to, what their parents did for a living, or what neighborhood they lived in. She learned to fear people. She learned whom to love and whom not to love, and who would love her and who wouldn't. She learned about sin, hell, and being thrown out of a Garden that she thought she had been playing in all this time. She learned about a God who was harsh, strict, and judgmental—one who was completely different than the one she had known inside herself as a child.

She tried to be a good girl, so she learned all of the "right" beliefs, and over time she learned not to trust her own experience of life. Eventually, the "right" beliefs that she was taught became her reality.

Now, as an adult, she challenged that reality. She knew that everything she learned from hearing the adults was the *opposite* of what she had experienced as a deaf child. She saw that although she gained her hearing, she lost her joy, her natural loving spirit, and her God. She worked to turn that around, to become deaf to all of those "right" beliefs that robbed her of her joy and her connection with God. She now knows how powerful beliefs can be, and that what you believe is what you get. She is on the path of love that leads her back to her original experience of oneness with herself, others, and God.

## Inner Child, Soul Self

When I use the term *inner child*, I am referring to the true soul self, the beautiful light that is the light of our soul essence. (I am using the terms *inner child* and *soul self* interchangeably.) The ego wounded self does not know that this light is within, because it operates from the false belief that who you are is essentially inadequate and unworthy—that your essence is dark instead of light. Only when you are able, as a loving adult, to bring through to the inner child the love that is God will the wounded self become healed enough for your inner child to shine and be all you have come to this planet to be.

Your inner child is an infallible communicator. It lets you know through your feelings what is good or bad, right or wrong for you. The feelings that come naturally from it are joy, peace, and love. Nevertheless, the inner child also has the natural feelings of sadness and sorrow (over people's inhumanity to one another, for example), loneliness (when you have no one with whom to share love), heartbreak (over loved ones being unloving), grief (over loss), helplessness (over others' unloving choices), and outrage (over injustice), as well as fear of real and present danger.

By contrast, the feelings that are caused by the wounded self include anxiety, depression, anger, hurt, aloneness, neediness, emptiness, misery, guilt, shame, jealousy, envy, and fear (of a perceived rather than an actual threat).

When we are present in the moment, we will not feel the projected fear coming from the false beliefs of the wounded self. On the other hand, we will continue to feel the fear of real danger when it is present. This is a natural physical reaction:

the fight-or-flight response. Too many of us, however, are often in the fight-or-flight response over dangers imagined by the wounded self. This is the anxiety that troubles many people.

Anxiety and depression can also come from eating junk food, devitalized processed foods, sugar and high-fructose corn syrup, factory-farmed foods with antibiotics and pesticides, and foods with industrial seed oils such as corn, canola, sunflower, and safflower. These create an imbalance in the gut microbiome and can send toxins into the brain through the vagus nerve, creating anxiety and depression as well as sending toxins into the organs and creating illness. These nonfoods also lower your frequency and make it much harder to connect with your higher guidance.

*All* of your feelings let you know whether what you are doing and thinking is right or wrong for you. They let you know whether someone is open or closed, dangerous or safe. The tightness in your stomach in reaction to someone's threatening anger tells you something important, as is the safety you feel when someone is being truly loving. Your anxiety, anger, or depression tell you that you are not taking loving care of your inner child physically and/or emotionally, while peace and joy let you know that you are being truly loving to yourself. Trusting these feelings and discovering what they are telling you will help you take personal responsibility for your own well-being.

Because I grew up being a caretaker as my primary way to control, whenever my stomach was tight around others, I took this as a sign that something threatening was happening that I needed to fix. I would immediately attempt to pacify the other person so he or she wouldn't be angry with me. This would give me a temporary feeling of safety, but it would disappear as soon as someone else got upset with me. Now I know that my tight stomach is my inner child telling me to take care of her. Instead of trying to fix others so I can feel safe, I take action for myself. My feeling of inner safety is no longer temporary and no longer depends upon others.

## The Loving Adult

The loving adult is the emissary through which the spirit of love and compassion that is God thinks and acts. The loving adult receives love, truth, comfort, and strength from spirit and then takes loving action in the best interests of the inner child and others. The loving adult puts the love that is God into action.

Many of us do not yet have a strong, spiritually connected loving adult who knows how to truly nurture and protect us and love others without trying to control them. Many of us do not have a loving adult who knows how to set appropriate inner boundaries against harming ourselves or others, or outer boundaries against being controlled and consumed by others; nor do most people have a loving adult who knows how not to take rejection personally. This is because we may have had little or no role modeling on how to be a loving adult. If your parents (and their parents before them) were operating primarily from their wounded selves, doing the best they could coming from their fears and false beliefs, they could not provide the necessary role modeling.

Until we develop a loving adult, the wounded self is generally in charge. You, however, have the opportunity to practice the powerful healing process of Inner Bonding, which creates new neural pathways for the loving adult—the loving inner parent. If you do not have role models for loving behavior, do not despair. We can all learn to access our higher guidance as role models for loving action. In the next chapter, you'll start learning how to access this guidance.

There are generally two circumstances under which we decide to open to learning. One is when we are in a lot of pain and realize that our protections are not working to bring us the safety, peace, and joy that we want. The other is when we remember that we came here to this planet to love and evolve in our lovingness. *The memory of our soul's mission is within each of us.* Spirit attempts to remind us each day of our soul's mission in the hope that we will not have to hit bottom to shift our intent. Those who learn to hear the voice of spirit may then open to learning.

## Two Life Paths

Let's put together all of the terms we've covered so far and look at the two life paths you can choose to take and their consequences. (See chart on the next page.) The first section of the LifePaths chart, "Reactions to Fear," shows the choice, purpose, intent, and desires of the wounded self on the earthly path of fear, and of the loving adult on the spiritual path of love and courage. As you can see, the intent determines whether the heart is open or closed.

The next section of the chart shows the reactions to fear of the wounded self and the loving adult.

Sometimes it's confusing to people to see something like reading listed as an addiction. As we saw earlier when we talked about meditation, whether or not any behavior, thing, activity, or substance is an addiction depends upon your intent. You can read for pleasure and learning, or you can read to avoid your pain. You can watch TV for enjoyment or to avoid your anxiety. You can eat for nutrition and pleasure, or you can eat to numb out painful feelings. The substance or the process itself does not define the addiction; *the intent behind it does.*

When you choose the spiritual path of love and courage and open to learning about loving yourself, then your reaction to fear is to move into doing the Six Steps of Inner Bonding.

The last section on the chart shows the consequences of choosing the earthly path of fear. These consequences will always result from using addictive, controlling behavior to avoid responsibility for your painful feelings.

Putting it all together, you can see the eventual results of practicing the incredibly powerful steps of Inner Bonding.

# LIFE PATHS

| EARTHLY PATH OF FEAR<br>THE PATH OF THE WOUNDED SELF | SPIRITUAL PATH OF LOVE/COURAGE<br>THE PATH OF THE LOVING ADULT |
|---|---|
| **CHOICE: CONTROL in the face of FEAR**<br><br>**PURPOSE:** To get love and avoid pain<br><br>**INTENT:** Find happiness, safety, lovability and worth through EXTERNALS such as people, sex, things, activities, substances<br><br>**DESIRES:** To PROTECT against pain and AVOID RESPONSIBILITY for feeling it | **CHOICE: LOVE in the face of FEAR**<br><br>**PURPOSE:** To give love to self and others<br><br>**INTENT:** Find joy, peace, safety, lovability and worth INTERNALLY by connecting with God's unconditional love<br><br>**DESIRES:** To LEARN TO LOVE and TAKE RESPONSIBILITY for own pain and joy |
| **THE HEART CLOSES** | **THE HEART OPENS** |
| **REACTION TO FEAR: You turn to ADDICTIVE, CONTROLLING BEHAVIOR**<br><br>ADDICTIONS TO MANIPULATING OTHERS<br>Anger, blaming, interrogating, criticizing, bitching, judging, shaming, perfectionism, threats, violence, withdrawal, resistance, denying, caretaking (giving in order to get), people-pleasing, complaining, demanding, arrogance, defending, lying, analyzing, convincing, lecturing, pulling, explaining, dismissing, telling feelings to blame, drama, illness<br><br>ADDICTIONS TO PEOPLE<br>Attention, approval, love, connection, romance, sex<br><br>ADDICTIONS TO ACTIVITIES & THINGS<br>TV, computer/internet, busyness, gossiping, sports, exercise, sleep, work, making money, spending, gambling, shopping, worry, obsessive thinking, self-criticism, talking, telephone, reading, gathering information, meditation, religion, crime, danger, pornography, masturbation, glamour, beautifying<br><br>ADDICTIONS TO SUBSTANCES<br>Drugs, alcohol, nicotine, food, sugar, caffeine | **REACTION TO FEAR: You turn to THE SIX STEPS OF INNER BONDING®**<br><br>STEP 1   Willingness to feel pain/fear and take responsibility for your feelings and security.<br><br>STEP 2   Choose the intent to learn about love and fear; invite Spirit into heart—open heart to compassion, becoming a loving Adult.<br><br>STEP 3   Welcome and dialogue with wounded selves, exploring fears, false beliefs, memories and resulting behavior that is causing the pain. Explore gifts and what brings joy to Core Self.<br><br>STEP 4   Dialogue with spiritual Guidance, exploring truth and loving action toward Inner Child.<br><br>STEP 5   Take the loving action—put God into motion.<br><br>STEP 6   Evaluate the effectiveness of your action. |

| FEAR INCREASES | FEAR RESOLVES |
|---|---|
| **RESULTS:** <br> You feel UNSAFE and INSECURE | **RESULTS:** <br> You feel SAFE and SECURE |
| **WITHIN SELF** | **WITHIN SELF** |
| • Sad, depressed, alone inside, lonely <br> • Victimized, powerless, helpless, fearful, anxious, desperate <br> • Empty, numb, hopeless, unfulfilled, purposeless <br> • Angry, hurt, jealous, envious, insecure, untrusting <br> • Ashamed, guilty, unlovable, unworthy <br> • Trapped, stuck, going in circles | • Empowered, self-trusting, free <br> • Grace-filled and spiritually growing <br> • Authentic, integrated, service-oriented <br> • Grateful, at one with Spirit and others <br> • Joyful, peaceful, serene, aware of intrinsic worth <br> • Creative, curious, passionate, alive, playful, spontaneous |
| **IN RELATIONSHIPS** | **IN RELATIONSHIPS** |
| • Codependent: taker/caretaker system, dependent <br> • Disconnected, distant, unsupportive <br> • Conflicted, angry, blaming, locked into power struggles <br> • Violent, violating, disrespectful <br> • Nonsexual, unable to give or receive love <br> • Dishonest, suspicious, undermining | • Part of a spiritually-growing circle of love <br> • Able to resolve conflicts lovingly <br> • Interdependent, supportive, empowering each other <br> • Intimate, honest, trusting <br> • Respectful, kind, gentle <br> • Passionate <br> • Creative, playful |

## The Safe Umbrella and the Love Umbrella

Imagine that over each side of the LifePaths chart is an umbrella under which you can choose to live. Imagine that the Earthly Path of Fear is covered by the "safe umbrella," while the Spiritual Path of Love and Courage is covered by the "love umbrella."

You can choose which umbrella you want to shelter you. People who have chosen the path of love, as well as people who have chosen the path of safety, will be loving when they feel safe. Both will stand under the love umbrella when they feel safe. When they are frightened, both kinds of people will run under the safe umbrella to protect themselves against pain. The difference is that people who are devoted primarily to their own safety will huddle in fear under the safe umbrella *until other people come and make it safe for them* to risk loving again. People who are devoted to the path of love, on the other hand, want to move back under the love umbrella as soon as possible, so they *take responsibility for making it safe* for themselves to do so.

When you are devoted to safety, you operate from the false belief that your emotional safety is based on things outside yourself, so you try to have other people create safety for you. In your heart, you believe that *others* are responsible for you feeling safe. When you are devoted to love, you know that your emotional safety comes from having a loving inner adult taking care of you. You do your own inner work to create safety for yourself.

People who live under the safe umbrella open their hearts only when there is an external, dependable source of love. They depend upon others to be their source of love. Because they have no dependable internal source of love, they will close their hearts as soon as their external source of love is cut off, even if temporarily.

When you feel you have to walk on eggshells around certain people, it is often because they have decided to live under the safe umbrella and will retreat to anger, blaming, or complaining as soon as you do something they don't like. They will stay in a bad mood until you comply with what they want. Everyone around them has to make it safe for them to be nice again by doing everything "right." They take no responsibility for their own feelings or behavior. One of my clients described her childhood as "always trying not to wake the bear." The children had to tiptoe around, trying to avoid upsetting their father so he wouldn't yell at them.

People who live under the love umbrella are much more secure than the people who have chosen the safe umbrella. They develop a loving adult who connects to their spiritual guidance as their dependable source of love.

## Inner Bonding versus Traditional Methods

Traditional psychotherapy attempts to heal the wounded self by remembering the past, talking it out, releasing anger and grief, and gaining insight. But it usually ignores the spiritual aspect of healing and therefore does not help us develop a loving adult. I have worked with many clients who have given up on traditional psychotherapy because the wounded self cannot be healed without a spiritual connection: the grace of God, which is love.

What about traditional spiritual or religious practices? Can they provide full healing? While many spiritual practices do help us connect to our spiritual guidance, bringing a momentary sense of peace, they generally ignore the feelings of the inner child and the crucial healing of the false beliefs of the wounded self. Inner Bonding unites the effects of psychotherapy and spiritual practice by both healing the wounded self *and* freeing the soul self. It does so by bringing Divine love inside to the inner child and expressing it through the actions of the loving adult.

In many cases, neither psychotherapy nor traditional spiritual practice significantly improves the quality of our lives.

But the consistent practice of the Six Steps of Inner Bonding *does*. It accomplishes this by giving you a direct, moment-by-moment experience of your spiritual guidance and enabling you to experience life more frequently from a state of grace—a complete feeling of love, peace, and joy within.

Inner Bonding does not exclude any other therapeutic or spiritual practices. Rather, it provides a framework that includes them. It works no matter what your concept of God is. It works even if you do not believe in a higher power, because you can begin using Inner Bonding by accessing the highest part of yourself, your higher self, for your guidance. Eventually, if you keep practicing, you will have a firsthand experience of the love that is God.

Step One of Inner Bonding—the willingness to feel your feelings and take responsibility for them—can include any therapeutic modality that helps you gain access to your feelings. This includes all forms of bodywork and breathwork, yoga, energy work, shamanic journeying and soul retrieval, dream work, movement, and art therapy, as well as the more traditional forms of psychotherapy.

In Step Two—moving into the intent to learn—you can use any process or meditation for opening your heart to learning. Inner Bonding can be adapted to any religious or spiritual system and any other healing process.

Inner Bonding works to heal deep past and present wounds as well as to resolve minor everyday problems. It works with both children and adults (providing there is no psychosis: there must be some grounding in reality to begin the process). No matter how deep your abuse, Inner Bonding can bring you into truth and love. The Six Steps of Inner Bonding provide a clear road map to healing and loving yourself and sharing your love with others.

Here is the heart of Inner Bonding: understanding what your inner child needs to feel loved by you and then taking the action necessary to heal past and present pain and bring in joy and connection with the love that is God. It is an astonishingly powerful process for moving out of the false, limiting beliefs that lead you to violate yourself and others. By learning about your false beliefs and replacing them with a truth experienced directly from a higher source, you eliminate the causes of your fears and anxiety as well as the need for addictive and controlling behavior.

Inner Bonding creates communion with your higher power and opens you to your buried essence, your beautiful inner child, your untarnished and innocent soul. This profoundly creative spiritual process allows you to heal the wounded self and move ever deeper into actualizing your potential and becoming a truly loving and joyful human being.

# 6

# Becoming More Aware: Steps One and Two

I will now show you how to use Inner Bonding to have a direct, moment-by-moment experience of the love, compassion, truth, wisdom, and strength that is God. This chapter takes you through the first two steps of Inner Bonding. Steps Three through Six are covered in chapter 7. Although the Inner Bonding pathway is simple, it is not always easy, so I am going to spend some time explaining it to you. Once you understand it, you will probably find that, with practice, it is relatively easy to use and can often be done very quickly.

Let's say you have a run-in with someone at work. Maybe someone has said something that felt rude or disrespectful to you. You might react by feeling hurt or angry. That happens to all of us. Most people just let feelings of hurt or anger dissipate in the course of the day, believing that they are caused by the other person's unloving behavior. But if you are willing to take responsibility for your feelings and spend ten minutes (or more, if necessary) to do an Inner Bonding process, you can learn about how you might be abandoning yourself in the face of the other person's unloving behavior, which may be the real cause of your hurt and anger. Once you have done that, you will know what action you need to take (which may or may not involve the other person), and you will quickly move back into inner safety and peace.

Naturally, if you have a big upset or uncover some very deep, old feelings that hugely affect your life, you will need to spend more time with them, and maybe get some help. You will probably find that these old feelings will show up again and again when you do the Six Steps of Inner Bonding. That doesn't mean you are doing it wrong. It means that you are slowly learning about and healing the deep wounds inside you.

You can also choose to use Inner Bonding as an open-ended inner exploration without waiting for an upset in your life. As I walk you through the whole process, I will give you tips on how to do this.

## Step One

*Choose to be aware of your feelings, and be willing to feel your painful feelings. Be willing to take responsibility for the ways in which you may cause your own pain, and accept responsibility for creating your own peace and joy. Make use of somatic (body-based) therapies to have access to your feelings.*

You cannot begin a journey without the *willingness* to do so. Otherwise, you will not begin the journey of healing and evolving your soul. "Doing whatever it takes" means that you are ready and willing to feel, understand, and take full responsibility for the whole range of your feelings—from fear, anger, hurt, shame, depression, aloneness, and loneliness to safety, worth, lovability, and joy. Willingness also means that you are ready to see how you are responsible for your own feelings; you become aware that you create them with your wounded thoughts, beliefs, and actions.

Willingness is a huge step forward in emotional and spiritual growth. It means that you have decided to face your fears, your demons, the shadow side of yourself you might hide from everyone. It also means you are ready to stop hiding *from yourself*—to stop denying the pain you are causing for yourself. You are willing to see how much you want control. Until you are willing to see, *without judgment,* how much you want to control everything, and all the overt and subtle ways you try to do so, you cannot open your heart to the love and guidance that is here for you.

Finally, willingness means that you are ready to ask for help from your higher power—and from others who can bring Divine love through to you. It means admitting to yourself that you cannot find the safety you seek without spiritual guidance and that you are ready to invite spirit into your heart to nurture and guide you. It means that you have embraced the journey, the sacred privilege of learning about love.

When I tell people that they need to be willing to feel their pain, they often say to me, "What's the big deal about that? I feel my pain all the time." But there is a world of difference between feeling pain and having the *willingness* to feel it in order to learn from it. Willingness includes the capacity to move toward the pain, explore it, and own it. There is no healing merely in feeling and expressing your pain. You can cry and rage forever, but unless you are willing to take responsibility for your pain and for lovingly manage it, it stays stuck. It cannot move through or out of you.

Sometimes people respond with, "Why? Why feel my pain? What's the point?" They believe that feeling pain, especially the pain of childhood, is a waste of time. "Why cry over spilled milk?" they argue. "Why can't we just try to find our joy and skip the pain?" The answer is: *because love, joy, and pain are in the same place in the heart.* When you stuff your pain back inside, you put a lid on your joy and your ability to love. You choose to live an emotionally stunted life. You also close your ears to information about how you might be abandoning yourself and to what might be happening externally.

Pain is how your inner child lets you know that you are behaving in ways that are not in your highest good. Pain is your teacher, both physically and emotionally. For example, if you are sawing a piece of wood and you accidentally slice into your finger, the pain tells you to stop sawing. Similarly, your emotional pain tells you to stop doing what is causing the pain. Otherwise, you will go on behaving in ways that continue to cause you pain. You will also develop unhealthy, even harmful, mechanisms for avoiding your emotional pain, such as addictions of all kinds.

Ask yourself this: when you want to binge, eat sugar, drink alcohol, use drugs, smoke, blame, hit, appease someone, resist someone, run away, turn on the TV, play endless video games, glue yourself to social media, gamble, shop, masturbate with pornography, demand sex from your partner, or compulsively act out in any way, *what are you feeling?* Look back at the results listed on the Earthly Path half of the LifePaths chart in chapter 5. Are your actions driven by any of these feelings? Are you turning to your addictions to distract you from painful feelings? Can you commit to learning about what these feelings are telling you without blocking them with addictive behavior?

Before I learned how to do Inner Bonding, I was willing to feel my pain only about 10 percent of the time. Now it's more like 95 percent. I am telling you this to keep you from thinking that perfection—being willing to feel your pain 100 percent of the time —is your goal. We are all human. You simply want to strive for being *more* willing, *more* open, *more* aware than you are now. As I said, I can't stay open to loving all the time, and I don't know anyone who can, but moving toward that is the most worthy goal I know.

The idea of feeling long-suppressed emotional pain may be scary to you. The truth is, you can handle it. Your fear of those feelings is based on the beliefs about pain that you acquired in childhood, *beliefs that are false now that you are an adult.* Let's look at some of them.

# False Beliefs about Pain

When we were very small, we could not handle our pain alone. Our little bodies were too small to endure the huge energy of pain, so unless we had loving parents there to help us, we learned various ways to numb it out. As adults with grown-up bodies, we can now handle the big energy of emotional pain, but most of us don't realize this. Nor do we realize that we are no longer victims. We now have choices about whether to stay in painful situations—choices we didn't have when we were young. We can leave a painful situation, call a friend or therapist for help, and learn to bring through Divine love to manage painful feelings.

What beliefs do you have about your pain? See if any of these feel true for you.

- I can't handle my pain. It's too much for me. I'll go crazy or explode into a million pieces and die from it.
- If I open to my pain, it will be unending, a bottomless pit with no way out. Better to keep a lid on it.
- There is no point in feeling my pain.
- No one wants to hear my pain. If I open to my pain, I will end up alone.
- Feeling and showing my pain is a sign of weakness and will lead to rejection.
- Feeling my pain makes me too vulnerable to being controlled by others and by God.

To move beyond these false beliefs, you must be willing to test them, to *prove* them false. To do so, you must resist the urge to blunt your pain with addictions and other forms of controlling behavior. Until you stop numbing out in the face of your pain, you will never know that you *can* feel it without going crazy or dying, that your pain is not endless, and that it can be a source of information and strength rather than weakness.

In all the years I have been working with people, I have never had anyone die, explode, or go crazy from opening to their pain. I have never met anyone whose emotional pain was unending. Nor do people kill themselves from feeling their pain when they are willing to learn how to heal it and reach out for the appropriate help. It is not opening to pain and learning how to manage it lovingly that causes suicidal feelings; it is sitting in pain with no inner or outer help. When you open to feeling, learning about, and healing your pain and learn how to release it, there is no longer a need to avoid it.

## Breaking Old Patterns

Even when we are willing to feel our pain, it can take some practice to do so. Many of us are so used to ignoring our feelings that the moment we feel a twinge of fear, anxiety, or loneliness, we open the refrigerator, pour a drink, grab a cigarette, or turn on the TV. We may even find ourselves doing this before we *consciously* know we've had a feeling.

To break this pattern, you have to be willing to feel what is going on inside your body. This means learning to pay attention to physical sensations—tightness, fluttering, heaviness, emptiness, or burning in your stomach, chest, legs, jaw, throat, or anywhere else in your body. Remember, feelings are sensations. Old feelings and memories from childhood are often stored in the body's musculature; so are feelings from the present. Because the wounded self tends to treat you the way you were treated by your parents or the way they treated themselves, Most of your present painful feelings come from the thoughts and beliefs you learned in the past. For example, if you believe, "I have to do everything right or I will be rejected," you will probably feel anxious or panicky. Some of the anxiety in your body may be old, coming from past rejections, but most of it is current, coming from the pressure you put on yourself and your *expectation* of rejection.

Whatever the origin of your pain, you are responsible for feeling it, learning from it, and healing it. If you need help to feel your feelings, you can use various therapies. You might try dream work, yoga, meditation, or massage. You may have spent so many years numbing out and ignoring your body that it will take you time and practice to get back in touch with your feelings. If they overwhelm you, you can seek out trauma work, such as EFT (the emotional freedom technique), TRE (trauma release exercises), EMDR (eye movement desensitization and reprocessing), or SE (somatic experiencing). These therapies release patterns that are stored in the energy system of the body.

Some people have such deep pain from childhood abuse that they will not be able to endure opening to it until they have a solid, loving, spiritually connected adult in place, which you can learn to do through Inner Bonding. It is not advisable to attempt to open to the pain of severe abuse on your own. If you suspect that you may have deep buried pain or if you have not succeeded in feeling your pain despite a genuine willingness to do so, it is imperative that you receive therapeutic help while practicing the Six Steps of Inner Bonding.

Brian came to see me because he was severely depressed and addicted to masturbating with pornography and acting out sexually with prostitutes, despite the many therapies and processes he had used to deal with these problems.

The first thing I noticed was that Brian was seriously out of touch with his feelings. When he tried to talk to his inner child, nothing happened. It was as if there was no inner child in there. I assured him that he did indeed have an inner child—his soul—but there was some good reason his inner child did not want to talk to him right now. Instead we concentrated on helping Brian develop his loving adult.

Throughout each day, Brian practiced talking with his spiritual guidance, learning what it meant to take care of his inner child. As Brian strengthened his spiritual connection and his ability to take loving action on his own behalf, he began to sense that his inner child was filled with pain. Eventually, when Brian's inner child felt safe that a loving adult was there to handle the pain, he let Brian know about the severe physical and sexual abuse that had occurred before the age of six at the hands of his father.

Brian had dissociated during the abuse, leaving his body in order to endure the pain, both emotional and physical. As a teenager, he learned to use sex to numb out the old pain he carried. He could not stop his sexually compulsive behavior until he knew what this behavior was protecting him from, and he could not open to the old pain until he developed a loving adult. Once he did so, Brian was able to feel the depth of his pain and heal it. Once his inner child felt seen, heard, understood, and loved, Brian no longer felt alone and depressed, nor did he need to act out sexually.

No matter what therapy you use to become aware of your feelings, remember this: it will not work unless you are truly willing to *learn* from your feelings, not *avoid* them. I cannot emphasize this enough. Willingness means being ready to learn about what your feelings are telling you about how you may be treating yourself from your wounded self. Willingness means you are ready to learn about past abuse that might be repressed. It means you are ready to learn how to lovingly manage the pain of life rather than avoiding it with addictions.

This can be a tall order. Don't be dismayed if you don't succeed immediately. Letting go of controlling behavior and breaking the habit of numbing out with addictions takes time, but when you are willing to take responsibility for your feelings, you can learn to move inward and attend to the signals that your inner child sends you in the form of feelings. This is the beginning of the path of healing your loneliness, because when you learn to deeply connect with yourself, you will eventually be able to connect with others.

Of course, you do not have to be in pain before listening to your feelings. You can practice Step One by regularly tuning in to your body to see how you are feeling. *Remembering to do this is the challenge.* You can set the alarm on your watch or phone to go off every fifteen minutes to remind you; you can put notes on your mirror, your refrigerator, and the dashboard of your car. Remembering to tune in is a major challenge, because most of us have practiced tuning *out* for most of our lives.

As you practice turning your focus inward and becoming aware of your inner experience, you will become more acutely aware of what is going on around you as well. Your feelings can tell you whether you are safe or not, whether someone is being loving or unloving with you, and whether someone is lying or telling the truth. The more disconnected you are from your feelings, the more disconnected you are from your experience in the world.

With time and practice, you can learn to stay in Step One all the time by being present in your body and aware of your feelings. I call this "having your inner baby monitor on," because loving parents use baby monitors to know when to attend to their babies. Being present in the body lets us know when we need to attend to our feelings. This means becoming more and more aware of what you are feeling in the present moment.

The Six Steps of Inner Bonding can be done at any time, not just when you are in pain. The more you practice, the better you will become at it, and the more loved your inner child will feel. Consequently, the less you will act out addictively, and the safer and more peaceful you will feel.

If you are still not willing to feel your pain, you can pray for willingness, and your guidance will help you. If you are not willing to feel your pain and are unwilling to pray for willingness, you are not ready to heal. Your higher power cannot help you until you ask for help. But please remember that the love that is God is always here for you, whether or not you are ready. Divine love is unconditional, but you will not *feel* that love until you are willing to invite it into your heart. And without willing-ness, you cannot move to the next step on your healing journey: opening to learning about love.

Here again, is Step One:

*Choose to be aware of your feelings, and be willing to feel your painful feelings. Be willing to take responsibility for the ways in which you may cause your own pain, and accept responsibility for creating your own peace and joy. Make use of somatic (body-based) therapies to have access to your feelings.*

## Step Two

*Choose the intent to learn to love yourself and others. Making this choice opens your heart, allows Divine love in, and moves you into your loving adult. Use any meditation or spiritual practice or any-thing else that helps you open your heart to love and learning. Invite the love, compassion, truth, strength, wisdom, and courage of higher guidance into your heart.*

Once you can feel your wounded feelings, you can choose to learn what you may be thinking or doing to cause them. Knowing this will enable you to make new, more loving choices. Choosing to love yourself releases your individual will and allows Divine love into your heart so that you can operate as a loving adult. You cannot learn unless you are a curious, loving adult, and you cannot be a loving adult unless you allow your higher power to guide you. Surrendering your individual will, letting go of control over the outcome of things, and inviting the presence of Divine love into your heart are the results of mov-ing into a true intent to learn with your higher guidance.

Many people are uncomfortable with the word *surrender*, so let's talk about what surrender is and what it isn't. It is not an act of acquiescence, but an invitation to spirit to use your being as vessel of love, compassion, and truth. Surrender does not mean giving up the things that are important to you. It does not mean that you have no personal goals and are just waiting to see what spirit does with you. Nor does it mean relinquishing your free will or giving up your present life for a more ascetic one.

In moments of surrender, you are willing to hand the reins of your life to your higher source of love and truth rather than to the wounded self. As a result, you can *embrace* your wounded self rather than *being* your wounded self. Surrender means opening your body, mind, heart, and soul to your spiritual guidance. It means letting go of attachment to controlling your feelings, others, and outcomes and opening to an exciting journey of discovery.

Learning to love sounds simple, but it is not always easy. The wounded self hates to give up control and will do everything it can to convince you that listening to your guidance is a bad idea. The wounded self wants you to believe that it knows how to keep you safe, and it will continue to attempt to undermine and sabotage your Inner Bonding process. It wants to convince you that you will end up alone or be taken advantage of if you listen to your higher guidance, or that there *is* no higher guidance. Therefore, in order to open to your higher guidance, your desire to learn to love must be stronger than your desire to protect yourself against pain. You need to decide that loving yourself and others is more important to you than anything else. Your wounded self does not understand that the more you develop your powerful, loving adult, the *less* you will be controlled, hurt, or manipulated.

Even when we say we want to be loving, keeping our heart open is always a challenge. When we feel angry and hurt, we want to blame someone rather than learning about how we might be abandoning ourselves in the face of challenges. When we feel victimized, we are usually unwilling to open to spirit because we do not believe that we are causing our own pain. As long as you focus on blaming your past, others, or your concept of God, you have no power to do anything about your pain. As we saw in Step One, although your childhood experiences may have caused you much pain and created your false beliefs and resulting behavior, the beliefs and behavior are now *yours*. They are the principal cause of your current pain.

Even if your pain is being caused by others' unloving behavior or by painful events, it's still up to you to learn to lovingly manage the pain in the face of these adversities. Openness to learning means taking loving responsibility for all your feelings—both the ones you cause and the ones caused by others and by life.

## Bridges to Learning

When you are stuck in the anger, blame, or numbness of your wounded self, you need to find a bridge that will take you into a state of openness. Bridges are things you can do to open your heart. Of the many bridges you can use, prayer is probably the most powerful. Prayer can take many forms, such as dialogue, meditation, recitation, or song. The choice is up to you. I have found that repeating a simple prayer of gratitude throughout the day helps me stay open to learning. I use some version of the following:

*Dear God, sweet Spirit of Divine love, I will to will thy will. I deeply desire to be an instrument of your love and compassion. Thank you for helping me heal all blocks to being this pure instrument. Thank you for helping me support my own and others' highest good. Thank you for the challenges in my life that provide me the opportunities to learn and evolve my soul toward love.*

Generosity is another bridge. Many of us focus on how we can get what we want or avoid getting hurt. But one of the quickest ways of moving out of a closed heart and into openness is to ask your guidance: "What can I *give* to myself and others?" The moment you sincerely ask this question, with no attachment to its outcome, your heart will open and Divine love will rush in. The love that is God is abundant, unconditional, and always there for you when you ask for help.

Everything changes when you decide to go through life thinking about how and what you can give. For example, if you are going to a party where you don't know anyone, you can create anxiety for yourself by worrying: "How can I get people to like me? How can I avoid being alone?" However, if you walk in thinking, "What can I give? I can give people my smile, my interest, my listening, my acceptance, and my sense of humor," you will feel great. The moment you decide to give, your heart opens, and spirit fills you with love and peace.

Many of us fear that nothing will happen if we open. The wounded self does not believe that the love that is God is here for us; it believes that if we let go of trying to get what we want, we will end up feeling very alone. Our fears of being rejected, feeling alone, being controlled by God, or even dying from being alone and helpless (the old infant feelings) may be so strong that we are unwilling to open our hearts. Until you are willing to take a leap of faith and open your heart through your intent to learn, you will not know that you are never alone.

Sometimes you are too stuck in your woundedness and can't pray from the heart, or you may not believe in prayer. When this is the case, try other bridges. These include:

- Listening to music
- Taking a walk
- Being in nature
- Talking with a friend
- Reading spiritual or inspirational literature
- Journaling
- Drawing or other artwork, like sculpture or collage
- Dancing
- Attending Twelve Step or other support group meetings
- Playing with a child or a pet
- Being held by a loving person
- Letting yourself cry
- Releasing your anger with the Inner Bonding Anger Process (follows)

Remember, though, that these bridges will only open your heart when your intent is to learn to love. If your intent is still to protect against pain and fear, no bridge will work.

## The Inner Bonding Anger Process

Releasing anger can help you open your heart, but it will work only when you intend to learn about what's causing your angry feelings. If you just want to use your anger to blame, control, and justify your position, you will stay stuck. The following three-part anger process moves you out of victim mode into open-heartedness.

1. Imagine that the person you are angry at is sitting in front of you. Let your inner child yell at him or her, saying in detail everything you wish you could say. You can put a pillow in front of you and pound on it while you release your anger. Unleash your anger, pain, and resentment until you have nothing more to say. (You don't tell the person directly, because this kind of cathartic, no-holds-barred "anger dump" would be abusive to them.)

2. Now ask yourself who this person reminds you of in your past—your mother or father, a grandparent, a sibling? (It may be the same person as in step one. That is, you may be mad at your father now, and he may be acting just as he did when you were little.) Now let your inner child yell at the person from the past as thoroughly and energetically as in part one.

3. Finally, come back into the present and let your inner child do the same thing with *you*—with your wounded self— expressing its anger, pain, and resentment for your part in the situation or for treating yourself the way the people in parts one and two treated you. Let your inner child rage at you for abandoning yourself. This brings the problem home to personal responsibility, opening the door to exploring your own behavior.

Anger at another person is generally a projection of your inner child's anger at you for not taking loving care of yourself. Recognizing your anger at others as a projection can move you into an intent to learn.

## Good Reasons for Your Feelings

There is another essential aspect of the intent to learn: you must believe that there are *good, compelling reasons* for your present feelings and behavior. These reasons may be the false beliefs of your wounded self or the promptings and desires of your soul self. Understanding that you have good reasons for your feelings and behavior is the opposite of being judgmental. It is being compassionate. Your inner child will not open to you if you are shaming and judgmental of him or her. And if your inner child doesn't open to you, you will not be able to learn what is causing your pain.

There *are* times when we have to make judgments about things, but there is a big difference between judgment intended to discern your highest good and judgment intended to condemn. If you approach an actual child and ask, "What are you feeling?" in a condemning tone, the child will not feel safe in giving you an honest answer. If you ask that question in a compassionate tone, the child is more likely to tell you. The same is true of your inner child. *Compassion is the natural result of understanding that you and others have good reasons for your feelings and behavior: your false beliefs and resulting fears.* You cannot be judgmental and compassionate at the same time. Accepting that you and others always have good reasons for your feelings and behavior will move you out of judgment into the open heart of compassion.

## Subtleties of the Intent to Learn

A true intent to learn is not driven by the wounded self. It is not focused on an outcome, such as getting rid of the pain or changing yourself so you can find a partner. Your wounded self may like to think that you are open when you strive for answers, but often this is just an information addiction based on the false belief that finding the "right" answer will give you more control.

A true intent to learn is an invitation to spirit to enter your being and enlighten you. You must be willing to be in a process of adventure and discovery rather than striving for a certain result. *The only outcome we are looking for in a true intent to learn is to become a more loving human being.* We are not trying to get rid of pain, win love, or get a new job. There is nothing wrong with having these goals, but they are different from opening your heart to evolving in love. When we open to learning about loving ourselves, we are just trying to do what we came here to do. If you have any other goal, you will not truly intend to learn. Sometimes people decide to learn to be a loving human being so they can find a partner. When they don't find one, they are angry because they didn't get the result they expected. But a true intention to learn means learning to be loving, period!

Often in my work, people think they are in an intent to learn when in fact they want answers. Their wounded self believes that I have the answer for them and when they find out what it is, their pain will stop. As long as they are focused on ending their pain and believe the answers are outside themselves, they are not truly open to learning.

At other times, individuals think they are in an intent to learn when actually they are trying to control how I see them. Because they have not defined themselves as worthy and lovable, they depend on me to do so. If they think I like them, they feel worthy, and if they think I don't like them, they feel inadequate. They may interpret my offering them information about their wounded self as judgment and go into resistance, closing down instead of learning about their self-abandonment. The wounded self always hears information about itself as an *attack*, while the loving adult hears it as a *gift*.

Until these people are willing to define their own worth, they will have a hard time being open to learning. Often when I help them connect with their spiritual guidance and see their inner child through the eyes of that guidance rather than through the eyes of their wounded self, they suddenly find that they can hear the information I am offering with curiosity and interest. It is a profound experience to see how quickly a person can move from defensiveness into curiosity when they connect with Divine love and truth.

Some people just want my approval or sympathy. They are unwilling to give themselves these things because they don't see and value themselves; they believe that another person's approval or sympathy will make them happy or heal them. I'm a very empathic person, and it's natural for me to give approval and care to others, including my clients. I can easily see their beautiful soul essence, but because they don't see and value themselves, it's hard for them to take in my caring. Instead, they want me to give them approval for who they are in their wounded self, but if I were to do that, I would enable them in being dependent with me. If I don't, they are angry and feel I do not care about them (which always indicates that they are in their wounded self). But when these individuals open to learning and allow me to help them connect to their own spiritual source of love, approval, and compassion, they begin to heal.

## The Practice of Learning

Moving into and maintaining an intent to learn is among life's greatest challenges. Had we been brought up in loving families with parents who were spiritually connected, we would naturally be in this state. But since many of us had parents who were operating from their wounded selves, trying to control in order to feel safe, that is what we learned. It takes time and practice to remember that we have the option of choosing the intent to learn when painful feelings come up. For thousands of years, people have responded to such feelings with various defenses. These patterns are not easily broken. But unless we break them and become role models for our children and their children, we will continue to suffer the negative consequences of our controlling behavior.

Each time you remember to open to learning, especially when you are distressed, that choice becomes easier to make the next time. The results of being open to learning are so satisfying that the more you do it, the more you want to do it. As your self-worth and inner peace increase, you will find it easier to move directly into the intent to learn whenever you experience internal or external conflict.

Becoming a loving adult is a skill that takes practice. Here many people run into a problem: until you either hit bottom or remember your soul's mission to love and evolve, your wounded self will resist the process at all costs, because it does not want to lose its illusion of power. It is the age-old battle between love and fear, between God and the devil. Your wounded self is like a little demon sitting on your left shoulder, whispering in your ear, telling you that you will be hurt unless you continue to act out in addictive and controlling ways. It is often very hard to hear the quiet voice of the little angel—your soul self—sitting on your right shoulder, urging you to open to learning. You may find yourself grabbing a candy bar or yelling at someone before you even recognize that you are in pain. Your pain becomes a trigger for your wounded self to instantly initiate your protective, controlling behavior. As we saw in Step One, it takes time and effort to break this immediate response and move into learning. Sometimes the only way to break this dysfunctional pattern is with help.

I have many clients who, for the first three to twelve months of their work with me, are able to practice being a loving adult only in their sessions with me, with a lot of help. Sometimes the only way they can open is when I'm creating the safe space for them. But eventually they develop enough of a loving adult to do Inner Bonding on their own.

To remind you, here are Steps One and Two of Inner Bonding:

**Step One**. *Choose to be aware of your feelings, and be willing to feel your painful feelings. Be willing to take responsibility for the ways in which you may cause your own pain, and accept responsibility for creating your own peace and joy. Make use of somatic (body-based) therapies to access your feelings.*

**Step Two**. *Choose the intent to learn to love yourself and others. Making this choice opens your heart, allows Divine love in, and moves you into your loving adult. Use any meditation or spiritual practice or anything else that helps you open your heart to love and learning. Invite the love, compassion, truth, strength, and wisdom of spirit into your heart.*

The steps of Inner Bonding build upon each other. You will not be able to move into the intent to learn—Step Two—until you choose to be aware of your painful feelings and take responsibility for them: Step One. And you cannot move into Steps Three and Four, the important dialogue processes, until you are open to learning about loving yourself and others.

# 7

# Inquiry, Discovery, and Loving Action: Steps Three to Six

The next four steps in the Inner Bonding process bring you into dialogue with your inner child, your wounded self, and your higher guidance. You are then asked to act on what you have learned in these dialogues by taking effective loving action on behalf of your inner child and others.

## Step Three
*Choose to welcome and learn with the inner child—your soul self—and with your ego wounded self. Embrace and dialogue with your inner child and your wounded self to discover how you are treating yourself and what you are telling yourself that is causing your wounded feelings. Explore with your wounded self the underlying false beliefs causing your self-abandoning behavior. Explore what might be happening with a person or situation causing your painful existential feelings of life. Also explore your gifts and what brings joy to your inner child.*

In Step Three, we open our arms to our inner child and wounded self. Although one goal of Inner Bonding is to integrate all parts of ourselves, in order to heal, we first need to separate the various aspects of ourselves. Eventually the energy from our wounded self merges with our inner child and our loving adult, creating an inner family that flows between our higher self, our loving adult, and our inner child. Some of the immense energy that once went into protecting and avoiding is free to go into playing and creating (activities of the inner child), and some will go into taking loving actions (the role of the loving adult). The more you operate from this flowing state of connection between your inner child, your loving adult, and your higher guidance, becoming a vessel of Divine love, taking loving care of yourself and sharing your love with others, the less alone and lonely you will feel, and the more integrated you become.

When you talk with your inner child, you are asking about what you are telling yourself, how you are treating yourself, what you are doing or not doing, as your wounded self, that is causing your wounded feelings. Remember, no feelings are ever wrong or bad. You have all of them for good reasons. By using Step Three's dialogue process gently and with great compassion, you will be able to discover what your feelings are telling you about how you are treating yourself.

When you dialogue with your inner child, you can ask questions like:

- What am I telling you, or how I am treating you, or what am I doing or not doing that's causing you some pain?
- Are you angry with me? I'd like to hear what it's about.
- Am I letting you down in some way?
- How do you feel about how I am taking care of you?
- What do you need from me right now?
- Are you happy or unhappy with the work we do? With our relationships?
- What are some of the things you've always wanted to do, but have never done? Have I kept you from doing them?

Sometimes it's hard to know exactly what you are feeling, especially if you have spent much of your life avoiding your feelings. If you can't identify a feeling, that's OK. Perhaps you just know if you are feeling good or bad, or full or empty, or you might be feeling nothing. All of this is information.

Here are some of the ways your inner child might feel when your wounded self is in charge:

- Fearful
- Terrified
- Anxious
- Insecure
- Panicked
- Trapped
- Helpless
- Angry
- Jealous
- Murderous
- Alone
- Empty
- Numb
- Depressed
- Guilty
- Ashamed
- Unworthy
- Unlovable
- Inadequate
- Unimportant
- Damaged
- Hurt
- Needy
- Excluded
- Abandoned

You may discover deeper existential feelings, such as:

- Loneliness
- Grief
- Heartache or heartbreak
- Helpless over another person or a situation
- Sorrow

If this is the case, bring compassion and understanding to these feelings so you can learn from them. Eventually, they can move through you and be released into spirit. You don't want them to get stuck in your body.

Often you are trying to avoid these feelings with self-abandoning behavior, because your wounded self believes you can't manage them (and you couldn't as a child.) The more you develop your spiritually connected, loving adult, the easier you will find it to feel your feelings, learn from them, and release them.

The next part of Step Three is to compassionately dialogue with your wounded self to discover the false beliefs and resulting behaviors that might be causing these feelings, as well as your memories of where and when you absorbed these false beliefs and self-abandoning behaviors. You can ask your wounded self and inner child about the events in childhood from which your false beliefs arose. Tears and anger may come up as you do this.

For some people, using a doll or stuffed animal as a surrogate inner child is very helpful; you can hold this surrogate child and comfort yourself when painful feelings come up. You can dialogue with various aspects of your wounded self, as well as with yourself at various ages, from a young child to an adolescent.

Look at this as an exploration into the layers of yourself. Welcome rather than judging or condemning anything that comes up. Here are some of the aspects of your wounded self that you might invite to dialogue with you:

- Victim
- Defender
- Fixer/lecturer
- Blamer
- Critic/judge
- Martyr/complainer
- Pleaser
- Caretaker/rescuer
- Taker
- Predator/bully
- Avoider
- Resister
- Obsessor/worrier
- Clown
- Perfectionist/performer
- Addict

When exploring your false beliefs, ask your wounded self, what are you trying to control, avoid, or protect against when you abandon your inner child with:

- Self-judgments
- Ignoring our feelings
- Numbing with addictions
- Making another person responsible for your feelings of worth and safety

Once you understand what you are trying to control, avoid, or protect against, you can ask other questions, such as:

- Why do you believe that judging yourself is the way to get yourself to do things right and be perfect?
- Why do you believe that if you are perfect, you can control how others feel about you?
- What are you afraid will happen if we feel our deeper existential feelings rather than avoiding them, or if we feel our wounded feelings?
- Why do you feel you have to be nice to everyone?
- What would happen if someone didn't approve of you?
- What are you afraid will happen if we take care of ourselves instead of everyone else?

Sometimes the pain you explore will turn out to be about the past, and you will find yourself delving into old memories and the false beliefs that resulted from them. At other times, the pain will be from the present, a result of your own unloving choices. The present illuminates the past, and the past illuminates the present. Healing your pain means healing the false beliefs from the past that create your current unloving behavior. Step Three is primarily about uncovering these false beliefs.

Another vital part of Step Three is to embrace, dialogue with, and learn about what brings your inner child joy. As your inner child learns to trust you, he or she will let you in on what is fun for you, as well as your true calling. Here are some questions you might ask.

- What brings me joy? What's fun for me?
- What is my calling? What is my true work?
- Where does my passion lie? What are my gifts and talents?
- How can I express my creativity?
- What will fulfill my soul?

## Hints for Successful Dialoguing

An important aspect of dialoguing is to be aware of who is asking the questions: is it your loving adult or your wounded self? Are you really in a compassionate intent to learn, or are you asking the questions from your fear and woundedness? Do you want to learn about how you may be causing your pain (your loving adult) or are you just trying to get rid of it (your wounded self)? You will not receive helpful or accurate answers when your wounded self asks the questions. This is why it is *imperative* to do Steps One and Two before starting to dialogue.

When you begin, it is best to dialogue with your inner child out loud or in writing, so that you don't get lost in your wounded self. A written or recorded account of your dialogue can also be helpful later, when you look back at your early process. After a year or so of regular spoken or written dialoguing, many people find that they can dialogue silently.

Were you surprised just now when I said, "a year?" I have been doing Inner Bonding for almost four decades, and the wonderful thing about this process is that it is not just a quick fix. It is a way of life. It is a way of creating and maintaining a daily connection to your innermost self and the sacred. As you grow and your life goes on, more and more challenges will come your way. You can use the Six Steps of Inner Bonding for dealing with all of them, the big ones and the small ones. Some of these challenges will bring up old pain from childhood events. You can use the Inner Bonding process to address those feelings too. Inner Bonding is a tool that you can use again and again to connect to your higher guidance and the wisdom of your inner soul self.

## Listening to the Answers

When you are ready for your inner child to answer your questions, be sure you are present in your body with your feelings.

The answers will come from deep within you rather than from your head.

If you can remember to use Step Three whenever you feel hurt or lonely or angry, you won't have to act out addictively. Instead, you will be able to find out what you really want by dialoguing with your inner child. You might ask, "What is it you are *really* seeking or feeling hungry for?" The wounded self grabs for a short-term fix—new clothes, sugar, sex, Scotch, weed, cocaine. But embracing and listening to your inner child can show you what your soul self *really* wants and needs.

Of course, the answer is always love. Your inner child wants to experience Divine love coming to him or her through your loving adult. It is only when you learn to bring through the love that is God to yourself that your hunger, emptiness, and aloneness will be filled. You will feel both alone and lonely until you heal your separation from the love that is God. Using Step Three, you can discover the false beliefs and resulting fears that are in the way of receiving Divine love.

Often people tell me that they have been dialoguing with their inner child, but they don't seem to be getting anywhere. When I ask them to show me exactly what they have been doing, I invariably discover is that they have not taken the time to first open to learning by inviting love and compassion into their heart. They *think* they are open because they are asking their inner child questions, but the tone of their questions is curt, bored, condemning, or embarrassed. I gently remind them to go back and do Steps One and Two, so they are in a true intent to learn.

If your inner child still refuses to talk to you, that's OK for now. Go ahead and skip to Step Four. Eventually, when you have developed a solid, loving adult, your inner child will open to you.

## Step Four

*Dialogue with your spiritual guidance to discover the truth and the loving action toward your inner child.*

Once you understand which of your false beliefs and actions are causing your pain, you are ready to learn the truth about those beliefs and discover what new, loving action you need to take on your own behalf. This information will come to you through a dialogue with your spiritual guidance.

## Accessing the Spiritual Realm

All matter vibrates at a specific frequency. This has been confirmed by science. The spiritual realm exists at a higher frequency, a higher vibration, than the earthly realm. One way to understand the concept of frequency is to imagine a room filled with people who are sharing love and joy with one another. This room has a feeling of lightness—a high frequency—whereas a room filled with angry, tense people has a feeling of heaviness—a low frequency.

To access the higher frequency of the spiritual realm, you must raise your own frequency. You can do this in a number of ways. First, though, you must truly have the intent to learn with your guidance about loving yourself and others. When you have a true, pure intent to learn, your frequency automatically raises. None of the actions I suggest below will raise your frequency without this intent. However, once you have it, the following actions can help to further raise your frequency.

**Keep your body clear**. Your body is an energy system. If it is clogged with drugs, alcohol, nicotine, sugar, high-fructose corn syrup, industrial seed oils (such as canola, soy, sunflower, safflower, corn), heavy foods, lots of food, genetically modified (GMO) foods, foods contaminated with pesticides, preservatives, artificial sweeteners, or any of the thousands of chemicals that are added to processed foods, your frequency is lowered. It's much more challenging to connect with your guidance when the frequency of your body is low as a result of its hard work in managing these nonfoods and a lack of nutrients.

**Move into your imagination.** Your imagination is a gift from spirit. When you move into your imagination, you raise your frequency and tap into the source of your creativity and inspiration. (As you might recall, at first I was only able to see my spiritual guidance when I was painting. As soon as I stood in front of a blank canvas, I moved into my imagination.) Our willingness to move into and trust our imagination is essential to connecting with our spiritual guidance When you first begin to utilize your imagination, you might feel as if you are just making things up. However, as you take the risk of trusting what you think you are "making up," you will discover that it really is coming *through* you from your guidance rather than *from* you.

**Pray.** Sincere prayers of gratitude and asking spirit for help in healing all blocks to loving can raise your frequency.

**Chant.** Repetitive prayers (such as the rosary), chants, and mantras can open you to higher frequencies, as can singing in general.

**Dance.** Rapid repetitive movement, such as Native American drumming dances, may open you to higher frequencies.

**Spend time in nature.** The frequency of a city is far lower than the frequency of nature. Being among trees and flowers, near a river, creek, or lake, at the ocean, in the desert, or on a mountain can raise your frequency.

**Listen to classical or spiritual music,** such as Bach, Vivaldi, Handel, and some of Mozart's work, as well as Kitaro, Taizé, and Gregorian and Indian chants. Throughout the ages music has been used to raise frequency.

**Do creative, artistic activities,** such as painting, drawing mandalas, or working with clay. Moving into your creative imagination raises the frequency.

**Use incense or do smudging.** Incense has been used for centuries to raise the frequency and invite spiritual connection. Smudging is using the smoke from dried plants such as sage, pine, cedar, and lavender to clear the energies in a room and raise the frequency. This practice has been used for thousands of years by indigenous peoples throughout the world.

## Connecting with Your Guidance

Dialoguing with your spiritual guidance means different things to different people. Our spirituality is as individual as we are. Some people find they can dialogue directly with God as a person, an energy, or simply light. Others dialogue with a personal teacher (also called a Master Teacher); an Ascended Master; a religious figure like a saint, a guide, or a guardian angel; a beloved deceased relative, friend, or pet; a power animal; or with an image of an older, wiser part of themselves. Even young children can contact their guidance by imagining a coach or a fairy godmother.

If you would like to create a personal guide or mentor to dialogue with, try the following exercise. Put on some beautiful music and have someone read the following visualization to you very slowly, or tape it and play it back for yourself.

Close your eyes and imagine that you are sitting somewhere in nature, in a place that is very beautiful for you—the mountains, the desert, a forest, a brook or waterfall, a lake, a meadow, the ocean. Imagine that you can hear the sounds around you, smell the smells, feel the temperature of the air on your skin. Use your imagination to see, hear, and feel your surroundings. Imagine yourself feeling content and peaceful, surrounded by love.

Sometimes it is hard to imagine the energy of love, so pretend that it is the color violet. Imagine that what you need to feel filled and to flourish is the color violet. Imagine that throughout your life you have been seeking to get bits of violet from others and from accomplishments. Now imagine that the space around you is filled with violet, and all you have to do to be filled with it within is to open to learning about loving yourself.

Allow the light, the love, the violet to fill your whole body, within and without, surrounding you in a cocoon of violet, a cocoon of love. Imagine yourself resting, relaxing into this love. Breathe it in, and breathe it out in a circle of light. Imagine that circle of light connecting with Divine light, Divine love, the source of all light, the source of all love. Breathe it in, and breathe it out. Each breath in and each breath out allows you to go to a deeper place of spiritual peace and relaxation. Deeper and deeper . . . surrendering the control as you relax and rest into spirit.

In this place of beauty and relaxation, you have the opportunity to create the perfect guidance for you. Imagine that you become aware of a light or presence next to you and around you. This is your spiritual guidance, which desires to appear in whatever form is most acceptable to you. Your guidance is the most powerful, loving, and wise being that you can imagine. It can be a man, a woman, or an androgynous being. It can be any race that you have an affinity for—Caucasian, American Indian, East Indian, Asian, African, Hispanic—whatever race gives you a feeling of warmth and safety, which may not be your own race. It can be any age: very young, middle-aged, or very old. It can be an older, wiser part of you, your own higher self. *You* are imagining this, so you can make up anyone you want.

Now imagine yourself being surrounded with the unconditional love that is emanating from this being of light and love. Imagine that you can relax and rest as you are being supported and held by this loving being. If this being is other than your own higher self or other than someone you know, ask this being for a name. Or make up a name you like or listen for a name to pop into your mind. Any name will do. If no name comes to mind, let that be OK.

Take a few minutes to be with this loving being of light, knowing that you can go back to this beautiful place whenever you want and speak with this being. Let yourself feel and know that you are not alone, that you are never alone, for this loving being is always with you and has always been with you. This being wants nothing more than to love you and guide you toward your highest good. Relax and know that you are never alone.

When this feels complete, open your eyes, and come back into the present.

When I work with people from a Christian background, some of them feel afraid of opening to their spiritual guidance for fear that Satan will come in disguised as light. They have asked me if this can happen when they open to their imaginations and create a guide. Certainly darkness can appear in the guise of light. But since both darkness and light *come only by invitation*, you can be assured that you are drawing only light when you are truly in the intent to learn to love. Your deep desire to love protects you from darkness.

This issue came up in one of my workshops in Missouri, and a Christian woman sent me these quotes from the Bible.

Anyone who claims to be in the light but hates his brother is still in the darkness. *Whoever loves his brother lives in the light and there is nothing in him to make him stumble.* But whoever hates his brother is in the darkness and walks around in the darkness; he does not know where he is going, because the darkness has blinded him. (1 John 2:9–11; *emphasis mine*)

But you, my friends, are not in the dark, that the day should overtake you like a thief. You are all children of light, children of day. We do not belong to night or darkness, and we must not sleep like the rest, but keep awake and sober. (1 Thessalonians 5:4–6)

By choosing to love rather than hate, by staying in the intent to learn about loving, you stay "awake and sober." In other words, you are "woke," as Jesus was. When this is the case, you "do not belong to the night or darkness."

If you practice dialoguing with the guidance you just created—or with whatever or whomever feels loving and comforting to you—asking questions and "imagining" the answers, eventually you will *feel and know* through your own experience that a spiritual being is actually helping and guiding you. You will develop a relationship with this light being, and you will find answers to your questions coming more and more easily.

My guidance has said to me, "We, your spiritual teachers, are funnels for the vast wisdom and truth that is God, and we help you to access the compassion, love, strength, peace, and joy that is God. We came to you even before your birth and are with you always. *You are never alone.* We are always embracing you, holding you within the soft light of love. When you imagine us in any form with an intention to learn about becoming a more loving human being, you access the comfort, power, love, compassion, peace, joy, and wisdom that is here for you."

Imagining a being of light, or light itself, surrounding you with love, can energize your being and bring you great comfort. Being connected with spirit is like being connected with an infinite source of power. It is the difference between trying to light your way with a small flashlight and rundown batteries or with a huge lamp plugged into an industrial-strength wall socket. Our wounded self is exhausted from running on batteries. We have only to plug into the infinite source of love and strength that is God to energize our beings.

## Trust the Process; the Answers Will Come

The universe is filled with the energy of love and truth. It is filled with all the information there is, and it has the answers to all our questions. Just because you cannot see this energy does not mean it is not there. When you turn on your TV, a picture shows up, even though you cannot see the waves coming through the air. We are like TVs. We are receivers, and our intent to learn about loving is the "on" button. When we ask a particular question, we tune in to a particular channel.

In your dialogue with your guidance, you might ask:

- What is the truth about this belief (which you discovered in Step Three) that is causing me pain?
- What will happen if I give up trying to control this person or situation?
- What actions can I take that will show me my belief is false?
- What does my inner child need right now to feel safe and loved?
- What would the loving action be in this situation?

There are numerous examples of dialogues with spiritual guidance in some of the chapters to follow.

Often when I work with people, they say, "I don't know how to take care of my inner child. I don't know how to be a loving adult." It's true. Many of us *don't* know how, because we haven't had any role modeling. The good news is that you do not have to know how to do it; you just need to be willing to ask. That's why Step Four includes asking your spiritual guidance what loving actions you can take.

Asking your guidance questions about the truth of your beliefs and what is loving toward your inner child will eventually result in answers, although often they do not come immediately. They may pop into your mind when you least expect it. They may come to you in a dream or when talking to a friend, in meditation, or when you are in the shower. They may come verbally or in pictures or feelings. You may open a book and find your answer or meet someone who says the exact thing you need to hear. Whatever form your answers come in, know that they will light the way for your next step.

When you sincerely ask, "What is the truth about this belief?" and "What is the loving action in this situation?" you open the channel for this information to come through you. We have long been told, "Ask and you shall receive." Try it. It really does work.

## What the Dialogue Process Looks Like

I am going to give you a brief example of a man working with Steps Three and Four so you can see what the process looks like in action. There are many more examples of dialogues in the chapters to follow. Although the purpose of this book is to teach you how to do the Six Steps on your own, many of these examples show me acting as a facilitator. I am including them because I think that when you have a chance to observe my role in these dialogues, you will best learn how to do them for yourself.

## Hans

I am on Zoom with Hans. It is his third session with me. A successful businessman in his late thirties, he was brought up in a rigid religious household and has continued to practice that religion. He has a strong belief in God, but little personal experience of Divine love and guidance.

Hans knows that an emotional wall protects him from getting hurt. He has just realized that having the wall means that his heart is closed to loving, and this is why his wife, Tonya, wants to leave him.

"I want to open my heart. I want her to stay. I love her. But I'm scared to take down this wall."

"What do you think you could do to make it safe to take the wall down, Hans?"

"I don't know. Can't you do something?"

"Hans, I am doing everything I know to make it safe for you right now, but you're not open. You want me to do it for you, and I can't. Even if I could, wouldn't I be making you dependent upon me instead of helping you learn to do this for yourself?"

Hans gets angry at me. He yells that this is what he pays me for. Then he starts to cry in deep, racking sobs.

"Oh God, please help me," he pleads. The sobs continue. When no help comes, Hans's sobs are stifled by anger. He shouts, "God, what the hell am I supposed to do? I am asking you. Now give me the answers!"

"Hans, you can't hear God's answers until you are ready to risk opening your heart. God can't help you any more than I can until you decide you want to learn about loving more than you want to protect against getting hurt."

"No!" he yells. "That won't work! God is too busy for me! God has better things to do than talk with me. I'm not important enough for him to take his time with me. If I open my heart, then I will really know that God isn't here for me, and that's too scary! Besides, I'm not what God wants me to be. I'd have to be a different person. I'd have to give up me, give up my freedom, give up being who I am and be what God wants me to be. God doesn't love me the way I am!"

When people have this concept of God, I help them get around these limiting beliefs by creating a personal guide. In a subsequent session, Hans was able to visualize a spiritual mentor. He created a guide he called Horatio. Hans discovered that Horatio was never too busy for him. As he opened to Horatio's unconditional love, Hans gradually healed his own false beliefs about the unconditional love that is God. With Horatio's consistent guidance, he was able to begin to see his own inner light—his true soul self, his beautiful inner child.

Here's an excerpt from an early dialogue that Hans had with Horatio to give you an idea of what it's like to work with your spiritual guidance.

Hans: Margaret, I'm afraid to ask Horatio a question. What if he isn't really there? What if I have just made him up, and I get no answer? What if he is too busy for me?

Margaret: A young part of you is really afraid that Horatio doesn't exist or is too busy for you. Can you imagine having compassion for this part of you, the part of you that is so scared? Can you imagine comforting this young part of you?

Hans: Yes. I can feel how scared he is. I feel sad that he is so scared.

Margaret: Do you feel willing to take a risk for this frightened part of you?

Hans: Yes, I do.

Margaret: Then take the risk of asking Horatio what your inner child needs to start to feel safer. But before asking, tell your inner child that even if no one answers, you will comfort him and let him know that you care about him.

Hans: OK. Little Hans, I will be here to comfort you if Horatio isn't really real . . . (Takes a deep breath.) Horatio, what do I need to do to help my inner little boy feel safer?

Margaret: Now, Hans, just open to seeing or hearing or feeling the answer. Notice whatever pops into your mind.

Hans: Well, I just got an image of holding this scared little boy. But I think I am just making this up.

Margaret: Have you ever had this thought before?

Hans: No.

Margaret: Then let's assume that Horatio gave you this image. If you imagine holding your scared little boy, what do you feel?

Hans: I feel . . . good. Kind of filled inside.

Margaret: Safer?

Hans: Yes!

Margaret: Now ask Horatio what you do that makes your inner child feel so unsafe.

Hans: (Asks and listens for the answer.) Another picture just came to mind. I see myself sitting and waiting for Tonya to hold me.

**Margaret:** Now ask your inner child how he feels when you make your wife responsible for his feelings of safety and comfort. Ask him how he feels when you give him away to Tonya.

**Hans:** Little Hans, how do you feel when I give you to Tonya for comfort?

**Child Hans:** I feel scared that she is going to go away and leave me alone, and I feel mad at you for leaving me. I don't think you like me. You never hold me like this.

**Hans:** I can really feel how scared and alone he feels when he's waiting for Tonya to hold him. That's why Horatio told me to hold him! That's really what makes him feel safe!

**Margaret:** So do you think you just made up these images, or do you think Horatio is really here helping you?

**Hans:** Margaret, I really don't think I could come up with this myself. I'm not totally convinced Horatio really exists, but I feel so much better right now and not so afraid of asking him questions. Something or someone seems to be answering them!

By being willing to take the risk of asking questions of Horatio and imaging the answers, Hans stopped relying on Tonya or me to make it safe enough to open his heart, and he learned how to do it for himself. Moreover, through repeated contact with Horatio, Hans eventually had a direct experience of the love that is God. This enabled him to move beyond having a belief in God to *knowing and experiencing* Divine love. He talks with Horatio regularly now and keeps his heart open to loving. Tonya no longer wants to end their marriage.

## Step Five

*Take the loving action learned in Step Four, putting the love that is God into action.*

A major part of healing is about moving out of your false belief system and into living in truth. Although bringing through the truth from your spiritual guidance (Step Four) is essential in healing your false beliefs, it is not enough. Nor is it enough to gain understanding and release your old pain and fear. *Unless you, as a loving adult, take new loving action on your inner child's behalf, nothing really changes, nothing heals.* For example, if your daughter came to you and told you she was scared by your yelling, and you listened and understood but made no attempt to change your behavior, your daughter would not feel heard. She would not feel loved. Likewise, if your inner child is hungry for love, attention, safe boundaries, the end of an intolerable situation at work, a fit and healthy body, or just plain fun, and you listen and understand but take no action, your inner child will continue to feel unloved, unlovable, alone, and unfulfilled. And your wounded self will continue to protect itself against these painful feelings with addictions.

You can tell yourself the truth all day. You can stare into the mirror and affirm over and over that you are a beautiful, wonderful child of God, but if you do not treat yourself that way, your inner child will not believe your affirmations. Words mean little without action. A loving adult acts on behalf of the inner child.

Paradoxically, many people begin doing Step Five by *failing* to take loving action. And that's OK. Your opportunity to begin taking loving action comes when you choose to observe rather than condemn yourself, to be compassionate with yourself, for example, when you slip up and indulge in addictive behavior. This is part of Step Five because nonjudgmentally observing yourself choosing the intent to control rather than love is in itself a loving action.

It may be hard for you to make new choices until you watch yourself making your current choices. As I said in the discussion about resistance in chapter 4, you will never know that you can choose to learn about love until you observe yourself choosing to try to control. You cannot choose to be compassionate with your wounded self until you notice it. If you are not willing to nonjudgmentally notice yourself acting out controlling, self-abandoning behavior, you cannot make new choices.

Taking loving action means learning to be loving with both your inner child and your wounded self. It means releasing judgment and accepting the angry, hurt, shamed, and frightened parts of yourself with love and compassion, understanding that your wounded self has been doing the best it can to take care of you and help you feel safe. Loving action means understanding and having compassion for all the parts of yourself that you have hated or judged as inadequate, unlovable, and unworthy. You heal your false beliefs when you learn to be loving to both your inner child and your wounded self.

The love that is God does not hate, resist, or judge. As long you hate even one person on the planet—*including yourself*—you will limit your ability to be a loving adult. Becoming one with the love that is God means expressing and releasing your anger in the anger process in Step Two, or as part of your dialogue process in Step Three so that you can move beyond your resistance to loving. A good place to start might be with your parents or other caregivers. If you are angry at them, you can express and release your anger and judgments towards them so you can love the part of you that *is* them—your wounded self.

Clients have often asked me, "Are you saying we need to love our parents or caregivers who were abusive to us? Why would we want to do that?" Loving them does not mean you need to like them or condone what they did, any more than you have to like your own unloving behavior. But if you hate, resent, or resist loving your parents, you will continue to hate, resent, or resist loving your own wounded self, who is exactly like them. We all absorbed our parents' wounded selves into our wounded self. Until you can see your parents as wounded children, you will have trouble having compassion for both yourself and them.

Here are some examples of loving actions you might take with the help of your spiritual guidance.

**Set appropriate boundaries within yourself.** For example, if health and/or addiction is an issue for you, you might need to set a boundary for yourself against smoking, drinking, taking drugs, or overeating. You will not be able to follow through on this boundary, or any loving action, without the help of your spiritual guidance. It's not about willpower; it's about tapping into the strength of your higher guidance.

**Set a boundary against someone violating you.** This could range from something as minor as not staying on the phone with an overly talkative friend to something major, like telling a colleague that you will not tolerate their stealing your ideas anymore.

**Leave a relationship** when someone is abusing themselves or you, or when they consistently refuse to open to learning.

**Speak your truth** in a situation where the truth is painful for another to hear.

**Risk being yourself** and owning your personal power even if your partner finds it threatening.

**Leave a lucrative job that you hate.**

**Express your true soul self** by offering your gifts to the planet.

**Invite the love, compassion, truth, and strength of your guidance into your heart,** *even if you don't believe in the love that is God* (or you don't believe that Divine love is here for you personally).

Frequently, taking loving action on your own behalf means risking loss of a relationship, a job, or your illusion of control. Are you willing to go on abandoning yourself in order to maintain "control," or are you willing to risk losing someone or something to gain your true soul self? Are you willing to lose your sense of self to avoid pain? Are you willing to face pain in order to fully manifest your true self?

You are not bad or wrong if you are unwilling to face the pain of loss and loneliness. But you should accept that your present pain is the result of your protective, controlling, self-abandoning actions: it will not go away until you are willing to risk feeling the pain of loss when you let go of "control." You will not experience the light and grace of the love that is God until you are willing to take these risks.

If you find that you cannot take loving action because too much fear or anxiety comes up when you think about it, you need to learn an energy release technique, such as the emotional freedom technique (EFT), to deescalate the feelings. Feelings that are deeply programmed into the body can often be released through this technique, allowing you to take loving action without triggering overwhelming fear or anxiety.

## Step Six

*Evaluate the effectiveness of your action.*

Once you have taken loving action, you will need to evaluate whether it is working for you. Ask yourself what you are feeling. Do you feel happier, relieved, less alone, more connected with Divine love? Is your shame diminishing? Do you feel freer and less afraid? Are you less interested in pursuing your addictions? Next, look for other evidence that you are healing your wounded self and accessing your soul self. Here are just a few of the signs that healing is taking place:

- Increase in personal power
- Improved sense of self-worth
- Increased gratitude and generosity
- Increased playfulness, spontaneity, and creativity
- Compassion for self and others
- A deep sense of inner knowing
- Truthfulness and trust
- More joy and laughter
- Feeling one with spirit and others

If the answers to your self-evaluation show you that healing is *not* occurring, go back to Step Four and ask your spiritual guidance to help you discover another loving action. For example, perhaps your inner child needs even more time with you, more time in prayer, or help with the process. Perhaps he or she needs to be held by someone who can bring through unconditional love and help heal the wound of not having been held this way as a child. Or your inner child may need you to spend more time having fun with others, or it may need more time alone to pursue passions, hobbies, and creativity.

Learning to do what really satisfies the needs of your inner child is an essential aspect of effective loving action. Until your inner emptiness is filled in satisfying ways, your wounded self will continue protecting you with addictive behavior, which only leads to more emptiness. Step Six takes you back, in a sense, to Step One, because to do it properly, you need to tune in to your feelings, both physical and emotional.

Here are some questions that you, as a loving adult, can ask your inner child in Step Six; then listen carefully to the answers.

- Are you feeling more loved by me and more important to me?
- Do you feel you can trust me to be there for you and resist the urge to act out addictively?
- Do you feel you can trust me to not harm others with my anger?
- Do you feel you can trust me to set good boundaries with others? Or are you still afraid I will give in to them or allow them to violate you?
- Are you feeling safe inside, or are you still feeling alone and afraid?
- Am I defining you, or am I still allowing others to define you?
- Do you feel a deep sense of worth that cannot be shaken by others' disapproval, or are you still afraid of rejection?

When you evaluate your actions, you cannot look merely at how you feel in the moment. Acting out addictively generally feels good in the moment: that's how it got to be an addiction. Often a loving action, such as cutting out sugar or junk food, stopping drinking, taking drugs, smoking, not acting out sexually, no longer taking responsibility for another's feelings, or no longer dumping your anger on others, feels awful in the moment. Your wounded self doesn't like being deprived of something that gives momentary relief. Your addictions worked to make you feel better for the moment, so when you stop them, you will likely go through a period of feeling much worse. You may go through both physical and emotional withdrawal. Often what works for you in the short term undermines you in the long term, while what works in the long term may not feel good in the short term.

Even though loving action may not always feel *good* in the moment, if it is truly in your highest good, it will feel *right*. You will experience a sense of inner rightness when you act in a way that is in harmony with your soul. There is a sense of lightness, freedom, and power that comes from taking good care of yourself, even when it feels difficult, frightening, or painful at first.

When you check in with your inner child, you must be sure you are talking to your soul self and not your wounded self. Your wounded self will often tell you that you are making a mistake in giving up a cherished addiction. It has many rationalizations for keeping addictions, especially as you start to feel withdrawal symptoms. You might hear something like this:

- Life is too short to give up these pleasures. What's the point? Why not just enjoy life while I can? So what if I cut a few years off my life? It's worth it.
- Oh, this is not working. Maybe this isn't the right day to start eating differently. I *really* want that doughnut. I'll start eating well tomorrow. One more day of eating junk won't hurt me.
- Life just isn't worth living without cigarettes. I love smoking so much. Not everybody who smokes gets lung cancer, so why go through this hell? Anyway, the stress of not smoking is worse for me than the cigarettes.
- The anxiety and guilt I feel when I don't caretake my husband is too hard, and he hates it. I'll probably end up alone if I keep this up.

If you fall for these rationalizations and give in to the wounded self, you will be giving your inner child a pacifier rather than the real thing. You will force him or her to be satisfied with the illusion of nurturing rather than the true sense of joy and well-being that comes from the loving adult.

If you look inside to evaluate your loving action and find that you are still feeling genuinely, not momentarily, depressed, frightened, hurt, angry or powerless, you need to go back to dialoguing with your spiritual guidance (Step Four) to see what else you need to do regarding a particular situation. This process may go on for days, weeks, or sometimes even months (with very difficult issues) before you discover the loving action that really works for you.

Let's look now at an example of a woman, Natalie, moving through all six steps of Inner Bonding.

## Natalie

Natalie started to work with me because she felt stuck with grief and rage over the breakup of her relationship. She had recently ended a two-year romance with Alan after discovering that he was involved with another woman and had been lying to her about it. She was having trouble concentrating at work because she was obsessing about him. This was not the first time Alan had been unfaithful to her, and Natalie knew she needed to move on, but she couldn't seem to stop thinking about him.

In our first Zoom session, I helped her create her spiritual guidance, whom she named Analee. The following dialogue occurred a few weeks after we started to work together. By that time, Natalie was fairly comfortable with the Six Steps of Inner Bonding and had been dialoguing on her own with Analee.

We started with breathing in to connect with her feelings in Step One, and Natalie immediately told me about her anger.

**Natalie:** Margaret, I am still so furious at Alan. How could he do this? He said he loved me and wanted to marry me and have children with me. How could he lie to me like this? How could he throw away everything we had?

(I could see that Natalie could not yet open to learning about her own self-abandonment, so I asked her to do the Inner Bonding Anger Process.)

**Margaret:** Natalie, I'd like to do an anger process with you that I find helpful to people in moving through anger and opening to learning. First grab a pillow (which Natalie did). Now imagine that Alan is sitting in front of you. Then allow your inner child to tell him in detail everything you are angry at him about. You can yell and scream and hit the pillow with your fists. You can say whatever you want to him. Be very detailed. Say *everything* you wish you could say to his face. Now start by welcoming your angry inner child and giving her permission to do this.

**Natalie** (holding her teddy bear and imagining her angry inner child): Hello, little Natalie. I want you to know that it's OK to get angry. I want you to let it all out. You can say whatever you want to say to Alan.

**Angry little Natalie:** Damn you, Alan! What is the matter with you? How could you be such a jerk? You promised me the last time that you wouldn't lie anymore and that you really didn't want anyone but me. How could you have said those things to me when you didn't mean them? How could you have talked about getting married and having children and then go off with someone else? We even talked about what we would name our children. (Sobbing.) I thought you had changed. You told me you had. I want you to change. I want you to come back to me and tell me this isn't true, that you really haven't been with someone else all this time. Damn you! You're not even fighting for me! Why aren't you getting some help? Why don't you want to straighten yourself out so we can be together? Why don't you care about how much you are hurting me? How can you just let me go without even trying to change things? I thought I was important to you. (Natalie continues in this vein for several minutes, sobbing and yelling until her anger runs down.)

Margaret: Natalie, who does this remind you of from your childhood? Who betrayed you when you were a little girl?

Natalie: Oh my God! My dad. You know I was four when my parents divorced. My dad would tell me he was going to take me great places, and then he wouldn't show up when he was supposed to pick me up. I'd sit at the window for hours, waiting for him. Sometimes he would finally come and sometimes he wouldn't, but almost always he had a woman with him. I never felt important to him.

Margaret: Imagine that your dad is sitting in front of you and let your angry little child get angry at him.

Angry little Natalie: Your women were always more important to you than I was! How could you let a little girl sit and wait like that? How could you lie to me like that? You never really cared about me. I was nothing more than something to show off to your women. I always had to look pretty for you. The only time you ever bought me anything was if you wanted me to dress a certain way for you or for your friends. You never wanted to get to know me. You never talked to me. I was just a thing to you, not a person. You used me, you used me! I hate you! (Natalie again goes on sobbing and yelling for a while until her feelings subside.)

Margaret: Now imagine that your wounded self is sitting in front of you, the aspect of yourself that has also betrayed you by keeping you in a relationship with a man who had lied to you before. This wounded child or adolescent is obsessing about Alan and wanting him back. Let your hurt little girl be angry at the wounded self, who has not taken care of you and let you be in this position. (Here is where the anger process succeeds in moving her into an intent to learn.)

Angry little Natalie: You don't take good care of me. You lied to me. You told me he had changed when he hadn't. You never listen to me. I knew the truth, I could feel it, but you never listen to my feelings. You're just like Dad: you never listen to me. You don't want to know me and what I feel about things. I feel like I'm still waiting at that window. Don't I deserve more? You tell me you love me, but I don't believe you. If you loved me, you wouldn't keep thinking about someone who doesn't love me, who doesn't care about me. I want you to let him go and find me someone who is honest and loving. I want you to listen to my feelings. I want you to stop looking for a daddy to take care of me. I want *you* to be the mommy and daddy I never had. I want *you* to let me know I am important to *you*. You're the one who loves him, not me! I think he's a jerk, but you don't listen to me. I never felt loved by him, not from the beginning. Stop ignoring me! I want you to care about what I want!

Natalie: Wow! I do ignore her. I knew from the beginning that something was not right with him, but I didn't listen to myself. I thought if I was loving enough to him, everything would be all right. I thought I could make him love me so much that he would never think of another woman. After the first time he lied about another woman, I thought if I got angry enough and made him feel guilty, he would never do it again.

Margaret: Yes, you have some false beliefs about being able to control how another person chooses to be. Ask your guidance, Analee, about this belief (Step Four). Ask her whether it's possible to use love or anger to make another person change.

Natalie: Analee, I've always thought that if I loved someone enough, they would love me back, or if I showed them they were wrong, they would change. Could you tell me the truth about this? (Listening inward.) She is telling me, "People change only when they want to. You can't make them change. Some people don't want to change, no matter how much you love them and want them to." So . . . Alan doesn't want to change, and I haven't accepted this.

Margaret: That's right. He apparently is not unhappy with how he is. He probably feels that his way of being is working for him, so there is no reason to change.

Natalie: He was always blaming me for our distance, and I thought if I changed enough, he would change.

Margaret: Part of not taking care of your inner child is being with someone who blames you for his behavior and feelings. As long as you keep picking men like your father and trying to get them to love you, you will end up unhappy. If you want a loving man, you need to pick one who is already loving. You can't make him so, and trying to only creates pain for your inner child. Your inner child will never feel important to you as long as you pick unloving and narcissistic men and try to control them into loving you. And you won't be able to attract a loving man until you are loving yourself. Like attracts like. Like frequency attracts like frequency. As long as you abandon yourself, you will attract men who are also abandoning themselves. When you learn to love yourself, you will start to attract men who are loving themselves and are capable of sharing love with you.

Natalie: I understand that now. And I see that obsessing about Alan is also abandoning and hurting my inner child. I think I'm ready to really let him go (Step Five: taking the loving action).

Margaret: Imagine that your inner child is sitting with you right now. What can you tell her about your commitment to her?

Natalie: You have really been hurt, but you just wanted love, and I haven't been loving you. Underneath all that anger you are a sweet, loving, wonderful little girl, and you deserve to be with a man who loves you. I'm going to listen to you from now on. I'm going to stay tuned into you and not make you be with another man like Alan. When our wounded self starts obsessing about Alan and wishing he would change and come back, I'm going to give you the love you need. I'm going to spend time with you getting to know you before looking for another relationship ... Ah! That feels good! (Step Six: evaluating the effectiveness of the loving action.)

Margaret: Your wounded self has been addicted to trying to get a man like your father to love you. Your loving adult needs to continue to bring through the truth from Analee about how impossible this is, while being compassionate toward your controlling wounded self. Only by staying connected to little Natalie and to Analee will you be able to break this addiction. Your trust in Analee will strengthen you through this process, and you will no longer need a man to fill you. Eventually you will feel the love that is God filling you, and then you can look for a man with whom to share this love.

Natalie: I really don't want to go through this again. I'm tired of it. I'm going to dialogue with these parts of me and with Analee every night. I want to feel Divine love in my heart. I'm tired of feeling empty and trying to get Alan to fill that.

Margaret: Good! But it's not enough to do Inner Bonding every night. Don't forget that this process is ongoing. To stay tuned in, you need practice being present with your feelings in Step One until this feels natural to you, and then practice Inner Bonding whenever you feel anything less than peace and fullness inside. After a while, this process will become natural to you. When your deepest desire is to be a loving human being, first with yourself and then with others, you will be motivated to practice this throughout a day. If your deepest desire continues to be to get love from others, this practice will go by the wayside.

Natalie: I really do want to be loving. I'm going to do this.

Natalie had been stuck in her relationships her whole adult life, believing that her best feelings came from getting love from others. Until she saw the truth—that her best feelings come from being loving to herself and sharing love with others—she was not motivated to learn to be a loving adult.

## Practicing All Six Steps

When you have been doing the Six Steps of Inner Bonding for a while and you are bringing through the love and taking the action to give your inner child what he or she really needs, you will find that more and more frequently, you feel a wonderful lightness of being, a sense of fullness in your heart, and joy that bubbles up from within your soul. This is grace, a great gift of spirit. Fear gradually diminishes and is replaced by peace and joy. The gnawing aloneness that led to addictive behavior no longer exists when you stay in contact with your inner child and meet his or her deep need for love through connection with your spiritual guidance. You will often feel a sense of aliveness, wholeness, and integration. Imagine a figure eight, a perpendicular infinity sign, that starts from Divine love, crosses through your heart, and circles down into your solar plexus in a never-ending flow of love. This is your inner family.

Gradually the experience of separation that so pained you will diminish, and you will feel a sense of oneness with yourself, others, and spirit. You will be unwilling to behave in any way that hurts yourself or others; you will discover your integrity. You will experience a deep trust in yourself and your higher guidance. You will discover that you no longer have to strive to believe in the love that is God, for now you *experience* that love.

No longer will you experience others in terms of "us" and "them." There is no judgment, no enemy. No one is left out, no one is less than you or more than you, regardless of race, religion, ethnicity, gender, or sexual orientation. No one is judged as "saved" or "not saved." All are "saved" without distinction by becoming one with love, no matter what religious or spiritual path they choose. You will come to understand that all ways of learning about love are one way; all paths that are intended to unite with the love that is God lead to Divine love.

These feelings of unity are available to all of us when we open to learning with our inner child and our spiritual guidance and are willing to take loving action on our own behalf and on behalf of others.

However, you will not consistently practice these steps until you accept responsibility for your own feelings and needs: until you adopt your inner child. Many people resist the idea of personal responsibility, believing it is too much work and too confining. Both of these objections are false beliefs. In truth, it is far less work to open to learning and let spirit guide and empower you than to have to do everything yourself or to try to control getting others to give you what you want. Your wounded self may feel overwhelmed at the thought of taking care of the inner child, but this is not the job of the wounded self. It is the loving adult's job, and, far from being overwhelming, it is a joy and a sacred privilege to bring through Divine love and strength and wisdom to your inner child. Personal responsibility is not confining; it is *freeing*. Moreover, you will not consistently practice these steps as long as you hang on to the false belief that your happiness comes from being loved and taken care of by another. Only when you embrace the truth—that *only you in connection with your spiritual guidance can heal you, fulfill you, and provide your safety and security*—will you commit to the process. And when you do commit to doing your inner work, you will discover the astonishing power of Inner Bonding.

When you operate as a loving adult, you never have to wait for someone to fill your emptiness. You never have to feel alone. You have the complete freedom to fill yourself with love and peace whenever you want. You never have to wait for someone to come along to take loving action for you. You have the freedom to take that action for yourself. Taking responsibility for ourselves is a delicious privilege.

The following chart is a detailed summary of the Inner Bonding process. You can refer to it when you are doing the process.

# THE SIX STEPS

## STEP 1

Choose to be MINDFUL of your feelings, ATTENDING to your feelings with the WILLINGNESS to feel your core pain, learn about and take responsibility for how you are causing your wounded feelings, and take responsibility for creating your peace and joy.

## STEP 2

Choose the INTENT TO LEARN with Spirit/God about loving yourself, which opens the heart and creates the loving Adult. Invite love and compassion into your heart. Utilize any meditative/spiritual practices or anything else that helps you to surrender and open the heart to connection with spiritual guidance—such as being held or doing the anger process.

## STEP 3

Choose to WELCOME and LEARN with the wounded self and the core Self.

- EMBRACE and DIALOGUE with the many aspects and feelings of the wounded self: Victim, Defender, Fixer, Blamer, Critic, Martyr, Pleaser, Caretaker, Taker, Predator, Avoider, Resister, Obsessor, Perfectionist, Addict

  Explore with love, compassion and curiosity the feelings, behaviors, false beliefs, and memories of these wounded selves.

  —Possible feelings to welcome, embrace and explore:

| | | | | |
|---|---|---|---|---|
| Fearful | Angry | Empty, Numb | Inadequate | Jealous |
| Anxious | Trapped | Depressed | Unimportant | Disrespected |
| Insecure | Desire to kill | Guilty, Shamed | Damaged | Excluded |
| Terrified | Helpless | Unworthy | Hurt | Disappointed |
| Panicked | Alone | Unlovable | Needy | Abandoned |

- Ask: "How am I behaving and/or thinking that is causing these feelings?"

  —Possible behaviors to welcome, embrace and explore:

| With self and/or others: | Lecturing | Attached to outcome |
|---|---|---|
| Criticizing, shaming, judging, lying, angry, blaming, violent, violating, withholding, having expectations | Obsessing | Acting out addictively |
| | Pleasing | Making others responsible for defining my worth and lovability |
| | Complaining | |
| | Defending | |
| Denying | Resisting | |
| Pulling | Caretaking | |
| | Procrastinating | |

—Possible false beliefs, underlying the above behavior and resulting pain, to embrace and explore:

| | | |
|---|---|---|
| I am a victim. People and events cause my feelings and behavior. | I am selfish if I take care of myself. | Resisting control is essential to my integrity. |
| I am flawed, bad, inadequate, unimportant, unworthy, unlovable. | Others' approval and disapproval define my worth. | I won't survive if someone I love disconnects from me. |
| I can and must control outcomes, people, feelings. | I am alone. God has abandoned me or doesn't exist. | I can't handle pain. |
| | I'm responsible for others' feelings. | |

- EMBRACE, DIALOGUE with and LEARN ABOUT the core Self, the essence

| | | |
|---|---|---|
| Intrinsic goodness | Calling | Loneliness |
| Intrinsic worth | Creativity | Sorrow |
| Intrinsic lovability | Heartache | What brings joy? |
| Intrinsic competence | Heartbreak | What fulfills the heart? |
| Talents | Sadness | What fulfills the soul? |
| Passions | Grief | |

Forms of Intelligence

| | | |
|---|---|---|
| Linear | Spatial | Spiritual |
| Creative | Physical | Intuitive |
| Relational | Practical | Abstract Emotional |

## STEP 4

**Utilizing imagery, DIALOGUE with SPIRITUAL GUIDANCE/HIGHER POWER**

- Ask for truth about the false beliefs and about others' intent.
- Ask for the loving action toward the wounded self and the core Self.

## STEP 5

TAKE the LOVING ACTION(S) learned in Step 4. Examples:
- Set loving boundaries within self and with others.
- Care for the body, the house of the soul.
- Pursue the calling of the soul.
- Create balance between work and play.
- Spend time holding your inner child and getting held.
- Help others, do service, give to others.
- Practice mindfulness.
- Choose the intent to learn each moment with self and others.
- Practice these Six Steps throughout the day.
- Make amends.
- Define own worth and lovability daily.
- Reach out for help when help is needed.

## STEP 6

EVALUATE THE ACTION(S). What are you feeling and experiencing? If healing is not occurring, go back to Step 4 to discover another loving action.

Evidence of healing of the wounded self and release of the core Self

| | | |
|---|---|---|
| Personal power | Spontaneity | Understanding |
| Self-esteem | Connection | Gentle, kind |
| Peace, serenity | Wisdom | Trusting |
| Joy, laughter | Knowing | Have integrity |
| Gratitude | Intuition | Intimacy |
| Freedom | Vision | Conflict resolution |
| Integration | Oneness with Spirit | Respectful |
| Authenticity | Oneness with others | Truthful |
| Transparency | Compassionate | Honoring of self/others |
| Playfulness | Loving | |

# 8

## Dialogues with the Shadow Side

The wounded self is our dark or shadow side, not because it is bad but because it is cut off from the light of God. It lives in the darkness of the fear created by false beliefs instead of in the light of love and truth. Moving toward "enlightenment" is moving into the light of truth. When we heal our false beliefs and resulting fears, our energy lightens. We may even hear from others, "You seem so much lighter!"

### Doorways to Darkness

Just as the light of God enters our heart when we open to love, the darkness enters when we to close our heart and act from the false beliefs of our wounded self. I love the example in *Return of the Jedi* (the last of the original Star Wars series) of Luke refusing to go through the doorway to darkness. In this movie, the Emperor, who was the epitome of darkness, was trying to get Luke to join the dark side. He knew if he could get Luke angry or frightened enough, he would want to kill his father, Darth Vader; then the Emperor would own Luke as he owned Luke's father. The Emperor knew that anger and fear were doorways to darkness.

Anger, fear, shame, judgment, and hurt are the cracks in our energy field through which the darkness enters. It can also enter when we cloud our energy with drugs, alcohol, nicotine, sugar, and processed nonfoods.

In one of my dialogues, my guidance challenged me about darkness: "Margaret, you have worked for many years to be physically healthy. Not only that, you have strived to be immune to illness. Likewise, for many years you have sought to become a more loving person. Now your task is to become *immune to darkness.*"

I was blown away. Becoming immune to darkness means *never* acting out of my wounded feelings, but *always* moving into an intent to learn about them as soon as they come up. I can tell you, it's quite a challenge! I don't know if I will ever fully accomplish this, but I continue to evolve toward this goal.

Through being loving to ourselves on the physical and emotional levels, each of us can reach a place where our frequency is high enough that we can hear our spiritual guidance most of the time. Being in conscious connection with both our inner guidance—our feelings—and our higher guidance, is a goal of Inner Bonding. By doing the dialogue processes with a true intent to learn and taking loving actions (Steps Three and Four), we begin to heal the cracks in our energy field through which the darkness enters, and we shine the light of truth into the wounded self's false beliefs.

When you have been operating most of the time as your wounded self, you cannot suddenly become a loving adult in order to do the dialogue process. Often your early dialogues may be between one aspect of your wounded self (for example, the part that judges you for your weight), and another aspect (the part that is resistant to being controlled and indulges in junk food). Since dialoguing between two aspects of your wounded self won't get you anywhere, you might conclude that Inner Bonding doesn't work for you.

Here's what's really not working: we cannot bring light to darkness with darkness. In other words, we can't heal our darkness by judging it, trying to control it, or being resistant. We can transform darkness into light only by compassionately learning about our good reasons for controlling and resisting—our false beliefs. We heal darkness only with the light of learning, compassion, love, and truth. Our challenge is to compassionately open to learning as a loving adult with the wounded self. It's a challenge that we can meet only as a loving adult.

But how can we have a dialogue between our inner child, our wounded self, and our loving adult when we haven't yet developed a loving adult? Here is where your imagination comes into play. Imagine that the dialogue is between your inner child or wounded self and the spiritual guidance that you imaged, whether it be God, Jesus, Buddha, a personal teacher, a guardian angel, a Divine light, or the oldest, wisest part of yourself. You ask questions and offer comfort and help, not from your own thoughts, but from what you would *imagine* your loving, wise, and powerful spiritual guidance would say and do. (You will see two examples of how this works in the dialogues later in this chapter.) Or, if you know a person you feel is loving, wise, and powerful, imagine that person in dialogue with your inner child and your wounded self. Either one is a good stand-in for your undeveloped loving adult.

Susan Sarandon's character in the movie *Dead Man Walking* is a wonderful role model for loving behavior. She plays a nun who has been asked by a murderer on death row to help him avoid execution. The murderer, played by Sean Penn, is a despicable human being. Not only did he rape and murder in cold blood, but he is also a racist and he continues to avoid responsibility with his blame, lies, and manipulations. Almost no one in the nun's life supports her efforts on his behalf. They accuse her, blame her, shun her, yet never once does she lose her connection with the love that is God. She tells the murderer that he is a son of God and therefore greater than his worst acts. While never condoning his acts, she never condemns him as a person. She lovingly confronts him with himself. Although she does not like him—just as we might not like our wounded self—she is loving with him. She becomes the face of love for him, and through her love, he opens his heart and is redeemed. Penn's character is very dark, the worst of the wounded self, while Sarandon's is very light, the best of the loving adult.

I have had many clients who are loving parents with their children, yet they say they have no idea how to love themselves. I tell them it's exactly the same thing. I encourage them to imagine that their inner child is a baby or toddler who needs them in the same way their children do, and that they need to attend to their own feelings and needs with the same caring and compassion. Their actual parenting becomes their role model for their inner parenting.

Since you might not have role models of loving behavior in your daily life, you can use your spiritual guidance as your role model. Eventually, when you do this long enough, you begin to take on the qualities of your guidance. This is how you develop your loving adult. Just as exercise is the workout for developing strong muscles, Inner Bonding is the workout for developing your strong loving adult. It takes time and practice to trust what you hear.

When clients first start to do this, I generally hear them say, "How do I know this is real? It feels like I'm just making this up, that it's *just* my imagination." Many of us have been brought up to believe that when we create—whether it be poetry, a painting, a song, a musical score, a book, a screenplay, a theory—we bring these things forth from our own minds. We may believe that we have the capacity to be creative all by ourselves. The truth is that creativity flows when we are open to our inner soul and our higher guidance and use the gift of our imaginations.

I no longer believe that my theories, my writing, my paintings, or even the words that flow from me when I am working with clients come from my own individual mind. I experience my mind more as a receiver of Divine information, which I can transmit through my work. Love, compassion, truth, peace, and joy are not feelings we generate from within our own small selves but are gifts from spirit. The same is true of imagination and the creativity that flows through us. We all have the capacity to learn to access our Divine source of wisdom and creativity.

## The Need for Practice

It has taken me time and practice to trust the information that comes through me. I have learned over the years that when I do not, bad things happen. This hit home for me many years ago when I was leading an Inner Bonding five-day intensive in Missouri. It was the fourth day, and I was pouring some tea from a pitcher during one of our breaks. I heard my guidance say, "Do not drink that; it is contaminated." I decided I was being paranoid and drank it anyway. The next morning, I woke up with a terrible sore throat—the first time I had been sick in years—and so did a number of other people, all of whom had drunk the tea. Even with all the years I had been listening to my guidance, I still lacked trust and needed another lesson in humility: my individual mind, unplugged from spiritual guidance, doesn't know much.

Although it takes a lot of practice, practicing seems to be difficult for many people. If you were determined to become accomplished at a particular skill, for example playing a musical instrument, you would think nothing of practicing every day. You would know that you needed to practice daily in order to become skillful and maintain your skill. Becoming skilled at Inner Bonding is no different. You will become skilled only by ongoing practice, and you will continue to reap the benefits only by ongoing practice. Only this way will you learn to consistently hear and trust guidance from both your higher self and your inner self. The problem is that the wounded self won't practice, so unless you pray daily for help in shifting your deepest desire from getting love to being loving, you will not have enough of a loving adult to override the wounded self and make the moment-by-moment decision to practice.

Many clients who come to me find that they start to feel better within days of starting to practice Inner Bonding. Then, as soon as they feel better, they stop practicing and go right back to feeling bad. Sometimes they then conclude that Inner Bonding doesn't work. This is like saying that if you have a young son and you give him love one day but ignore him for the next few days, he should continue to feel happy because of the one day you did give him love. This doesn't work with your inner child any more than it does with actual children. Just as babies need you to be constantly tuned in to them, your inner child needs you to be constantly aware of your feelings and needs. Becoming aware and maintaining this awareness takes ongoing practice.

Because our brain has neuroplasticity and develops new neuropathways regarding what we consistently focus on, the good news is that practice really pays off. Clients of mine who have been practicing Inner Bonding for an extended period of time (it varies for each person) find that eventually they do it naturally most the time. They naturally stay tuned in to their inner child and their spiritual guidance, and they dialogue with them whenever they feel anything other than peace and fullness inside. They find themselves doing it in the shower, while preparing meals, doing chores, waiting in line at the market, or stuck in traffic. After much practice, they are delighted to find that they no longer allow themselves to feel bad for any length of time. They are gratified that they are progressing toward wholeness and oneness with the love that is God.

## Dialoguing with the Wounded Self

Here are several examples of dialogues where people are struggling to move into the light of love and take loving action.

## Jennifer

Jennifer, whom I introduced in chapter 2, came to see me for Inner Bonding because she was unhappy with some of her relationships, especially with her husband, Mark, as well as with her best friend and her mother. She was often very angry, even enraged, at seemingly minor incidents, and she seemed to have no control over her rage. While her relationship with her two sons seemed pretty good, Jennifer noticed that as they grew older, she was occasionally angry with them too. She blamed those around her for her anger. If only other people would be more caring, she told me, she wouldn't get so angry.

As Jennifer and I explored her history, she told me that when she was around two years old, she had fallen off an outside flight of stairs and fractured her skull on the concrete below. For a while, she hovered near death and had to remain in the hospital for a long time. During the most critical period, she had been strapped to her bed, and her parents weren't allowed to see her. Jennifer was told not to cry: crying would make her worse. She spent terrible weeks alone and terrified, feeling completely abandoned. She unconsciously decided that no one cared about her. Then she sank into her core shame: no one cared about her because she was bad. By the time she got out of the hospital, these beliefs were deeply imbedded in her wounded self.

Uncovering the root of Jennifer's painful feelings took time, but even understanding all this did not reduce her sudden outbursts of rage. Awareness itself is rarely enough to alter behavior. As long as Jennifer still believed she was bad, that people didn't care about her, and that it was other people's responsibility to change so she would feel safe, her wounded self's behavior would persist. She would continue trying to control getting love by getting angry and blaming others for her feelings of abandonment. As long as Jennifer did not have a loving adult caring for her inner child, she would continue to feel abandoned, no matter how loving others were. There would always be something that would touch her deep childhood abandonment wound until her inner child no longer felt abandoned by her loving adult.

While Jennifer had not yet developed a solid loving adult, she did have excellent access to her spiritual guidance, Teresa. Below is a composite dialogue between her guidance, her loving adult, and her wounded self during a number of sessions. In this dialogue, Jennifer uses a doll to represent her inner child.

**Wounded Jennifer** (crying and angry): I'm so angry at Mark. He just doesn't care about me. He never wants to spend time with me, and he criticizes me all the time. And he doesn't help me when I really need it. We had company over Sunday, and he got so involved with the kids and our guests, he didn't even notice when I needed help with things. (Blaming, feeling like a victim. She is not yet in Step One.)

**Margaret**: It sounds like you felt really abandoned again.

**Wounded self**: That's right. He always does this to me, and I'm sick of it. I didn't get married to be treated like this. (She has no intent to learn. Her anger and her blaming serve to protect her from the feelings of aloneness and loneliness that she fears.)

**Margaret**: Jennifer, would you be willing to go a little deeper and see what is under this anger? Are you willing to pray and ask Teresa for help right now? (Asking her to move into Steps One and Two).

Jennifer is reluctant to give up her anger and blaming. She is addicted to it, and once she starts, it is hard for her to stop. She finally winds down when I refuse to participate in her blaming. She closes her eyes and takes some deep breaths. Then she speaks with quiet sincerity.

Jennifer: OK . . . God, please help me open my heart. Please help me want to learn. Teresa, please help me right now. I really need your help.

After a few minutes, Jennifer calms down and is able to access her guidance. As her heart opens, she is moved to tears, not from feeling abandoned or victimized, but from the love that enters her heart. She now essentially becomes Teresa, speaking as Teresa, allowing the words to come through her.

Teresa (speaking through Jennifer): Jennifer, I am here, and I love you. You are not alone.

Margaret: Jennifer, please imagine that your little child is with Teresa, and so is your three-year-old wounded child. Ask Teresa first to show you who your true soul self—your inner child—is. See if you can see her through Teresa's eyes rather than through your mother's eyes and see why Teresa loves you. (This is part of Step Four. Steps Three and Four can be done in reverse order. Often you can go back and forth between Steps Three and Four.)

Jennifer: OK. Teresa, please tell me who I really am as my inner child. (Jennifer smiles as she sees an image in her mind's eye.) Oh! She is showing me a beautiful shining little girl, so innocent, so loving, so smart!

Margaret: Is there anything bad about this little girl?

Jennifer: Oh no! There is nothing bad about her at all!

Margaret: Does she deserve to be loved by you?

Jennifer: Yes!

Margaret: Now ask Teresa to show you your inner child in the hospital.

Jennifer: Oh, I see her. She is so frightened. She feels so alone. (Starts to cry again.)

**Margaret:** Jennifer, ask her what your wounded self is telling her that leads to her getting so angry. (Step Three.)

**Jennifer** (in a soft and compassionate tone of voice): Jenny, why do you get so angry? (Jennifer now allows herself to drop down into her wounded self and speaks from that part of her.)

**Wounded Jenny:** It's not my fault. Mark makes me so angry!

**Margaret:** Ask her what she hopes for by getting angry at Mark. (She asks the question of Jenny.)

**Wounded Jenny:** I hope he will see that he is hurting me and change.

**Margaret:** So you hope your anger will have control over Mark? You hope he will change and take away your pain?

**Wounded Jenny:** Yeah, I guess so.

**Margaret:** Is it working?

**Jennifer:** No, not at all. He is moving further away from me. I'm scared he's going to leave me.

**Margaret:** Jennifer, where did you learn to use anger to try to control? Who used anger in your family to control?

**Jennifer:** Both of my parents, but especially my mother. She was always yelling at us and at my father. Oh my God! When I was a kid, I vowed never to be like my mother and here I am, just like her.

**Margaret:** Did her anger work to control you?

**Jennifer:** Yes. I was always trying to please her. Until I was a teenager, and then I rebelled.

**Margaret:** So now you believe that because it worked to control you when you were little, you can use it to control others?

**Jennifer:** Yes, I see that. I do think I can get people to stop hurting me with my anger. I see that it is not working. But I feel so awful when people are not caring about me. I don't know what to do.

**Margaret:** You feel awful when you *believe* people are not caring about you, and then your wounded self tries to protect you from this *perceived* threat of abandonment. What is really happening is that *you* are not caring about you. You are abandoning your inner child and then projecting this onto others, thinking that they are abandoning you. Imagine that you as a loving adult are with your inner child and with Teresa. Can you go over and put your arms around your inner child? (Step Five.)

**Jennifer:** Yes, I can hold her. She's so frightened. She feels so alone ... I see her again in the hospital bed. She wants her mommy. She doesn't understand why her mommy isn't with her.

**Margaret:** Now go over to the hospital bed and pick her up and hold her. Let her know that you and Teresa are here with her, that she is not alone anymore ... Jennifer, is she alone in that hospital bed because she is bad?

**Jennifer:** No. She isn't bad. Well, I don't know. Maybe she is bad for falling off the stairs. She wasn't supposed to be playing there, so maybe this happened because she was bad.

**Margaret:** Ask Teresa if this happened because she is bad. (Step Four.)

**Jennifer:** Teresa, did all this happen to me because I am bad? Was I bad for playing on the stairs?

**Teresa** (speaking through Jennifer)*:* My dear, you are that sweet innocent child I showed you. That is who you really are. You were not bad for playing on the stairs; you were just being a naturally curious child. You did not fall because you were bad. It happened because your mother allowed you to play there, and you were too young to be there alone. You were not left alone in the hospital because you were bad. It had nothing to do with you being bad. Sometimes bad things happen to people, but it doesn't mean *they* are bad. It's just part of life.

**Margaret:** Jennifer, you have a very frightened little girl inside who thinks she is bad and needs love in order to know she is good and that she is not alone. She keeps trying to get that love from others and gets furious when she thinks they are not giving it to her. Her rage is covering the awful fear and aloneness, stemming from your hospital experience, that comes up when you can't get someone to love you and when you are not loving yourself. Your inner child needs you to go in that hospital room in your imagination and pick her up and hold her every time you feel angry. She needs your love and compassion, not your judgment when she is angry, blaming, and judgmental.

Jennifer: I think I can do that. I feel so much better right now.

Margaret: Now, ask Teresa if Mark loves you. (Step Four.)

Jennifer: Teresa, I really want to know if Mark loves me or not ... Oh, I see. Oh, poor guy! (She is finally able to have some compassion for Mark. Compassion is impossible when the wounded self is in charge of the person's feelings and behavior.) He really loves me. He hurts when I get so angry. He's pulling away from me, but not because he doesn't love me. He just doesn't know what else to do.

Margaret: Do you love him?

Jennifer: I do. But it probably doesn't look like it when I'm blaming him and yelling at him.

Margaret: You feel love and compassion for Mark right now, but as soon as you feel alone and frightened, your compassion leaves, and you just feel angry. It will be hard for you to maintain your compassion for Mark until you develop compassion for the hurting child within you. Every time you feel angry, would you be willing to imagine your little child in that hospital bed and go and pick her up before you start to rage? This will be a challenge, since you are so addicted to the anger, and it happens so fast. Maybe you could try just holding your doll for about ten minutes every day, imagining it is you as a frightened little child. (Step Five.)

Jennifer: I really want to do that. I feel happy inside holding her. I'm going to practice that and see what happens.

One characteristic of the wounded self, which we see in this dialogue, is narcissism: wanting others to be responsible for your feelings and needs and having no compassion for theirs. The wounded self, operating from narcissistic rage that originated from an abandonment wound, does not care about the effects of that rage on others. In the moment, he or she cares only about getting someone to take away the pain.

As Jennifer worked with Inner Bonding, she saw that as her wounded self, she was always trying to get love from Mark and others and had never wanted to give love, either to herself or to them. In the same vicious circle we talked about earlier, Jennifer's controlling behavior perpetuated her core shame belief that she was bad. Once she shifted her intent from trying to control to wanting to learn and love, she started liking herself. Each time she was able to offer love to her inner child, healing occurred. Each time she offered love to Mark, her mother, her friends, and her children, she felt joy, which further healed her core shame.

It is very helpful when dialoguing with an abandoned part of yourself to think of specific times when you felt alone and afraid. For Jennifer, this was the time she was in the hospital. For you, it may have been an afternoon on the playground, or one night lying in bed alone after being yelled at by one of your parents or having been physically or sexually abused. Imagine yourself feeling alone and afraid in that specific situation. Then imagine that you as a loving adult, along with your spiritual guidance, walk in and pick up, hold, and comfort your inner child. You will find this extremely healing.

## Matthew

Matthew had been consulting with me for quite some time and had made a lot of progress in his relationships with his coworkers and his wife, but he still felt empty and alone much of the time. He couldn't seem to get himself to do much dialoguing. He felt stuck.

Matthew was brought up in a fundamentalist religion with many erroneous concepts about God. He believed in a higher power, but he rarely prayed. Through a number of explorations in our sessions together, it became apparent that Matthew's fears about God and his anger at his concept of God were keeping him stuck. The following is an excerpt from one of his sessions exploring his inner child's feelings and his wounded self's beliefs about God. Matthew was already in Step One when we started this exploration. He had also already created, through his imagination, a guardian angel he called Roy.

**Margaret:** Matthew, I'd like you to imagine that Roy is here, surrounding you with love . . . and ask him to help you explore your feelings and beliefs about God (Step Two. Matthew does this.) Now welcome and embrace your inner child and ask him to tell you how he feels about God. (Step Three.)

**Child Matt:** I'm afraid of God.

**Margaret:** There must be some very good reasons your inner child is afraid of God. Please open to learning with your wounded self and ask what God is to him and why he doesn't want you to connect with God.

**Matthew:** OK. (Breathing inside, opening to his wounded self.) Please tell me about how you see God and why you don't want to connect with him.

**Wounded Matt:** God is a big man with a white beard in the sky. He sees everything you do, and when you do something bad, he punishes you. He can get really, really mad.

**Margaret:** God sounds just like your father.

**Matthew:** That's right! That's how my wounded self sees God! An angry, punishing, righteous, and judgmental father.

**Margaret:** Well, I can see why you don't want to connect with God. Move back into your wounded self and talk more about not wanting to connect with God.

**Wounded Matt:** It will hurt. God will make me do things I don't want to do: I can't be me. It's too much work; God wants too much from me. He wants me to suffer. You have to suffer if you connect with God because God wants us to. And I'll end up alone. God will separate me from everyone.

Margaret: Was your father like this too?

Matthew: Yes. I couldn't be me with my father. It always felt like he wanted me to suffer, that suffering meant you were good. And one of the ways he punished me was making me be alone a lot, telling me that God wanted me to contemplate my sins.

Margaret: It sounds like you are angry at God the Father.

Wounded Matt: Yeah, but I can't be angry at God. He will punish me if I am angry at him. I am supposed to love God.

Margaret: Like you were supposed to love your father? And not get angry at him?

Matthew: Yes. Margaret, I know in my head that all this isn't true, but this is what I feel inside. I don't know how to change these beliefs. I know they aren't accurate, but they *feel* true.

Margaret: These beliefs will not change through your own mind. The truth needs to come to your inner child from a higher source of truth; it needs to come *through* you, not *from* you (Step Four). And after it does, you will need to act on this information (Step Five). So, let's move into Step Four. Imagine that Matt has just said all this to your guardian angel. What does Roy say about what God is?

(Matthew moves into connection with Roy by imagining him.)

Roy (speaking through Matthew): God is spirit—the spirit of kindness and gentleness. God is nothing like your father. You can even be angry at God, and God will understand. God helps you to feel a part of everyone. God takes away your feelings of aloneness and loneliness and helps you share love with others. (Matthew starts to cry.) Being disconnected from the love that is God is what's causing you to feel so alone and empty.

Matthew (Sobbing): I know this is true, but my wounded self doesn't believe it. What do I do?

**Margaret** (gently): Respond to Roy from your wounded self.

**Wounded Matt**: If God is so kind, why did he let my father be so mean to me?

**Margaret**: Now answer as Roy.

**Roy**: Your father's heart was closed to Divine love and kindness. But I have always been here helping you, as I did through your dog, who had the same name as I do.

**Matthew**: My dog Royboy! Oh, I never made the connection! (Smiles.) He was a huge old golden retriever. I loved him so! He was always there when I felt alone.

**Margaret**: So because the love that is God could not come through your father, he came to you through the big loving heart of your dog.

(Matthew pauses and thinks over what he's been learning.)

**Matthew**: OK, I can see that my fear of God is really just my fear of my father. That makes sense. (Smiles again.) When I think about Royboy, I can feel my heart open. It feels so good.

**Margaret**: That good feeling is Divine love within your heart. Maybe spirit gave us dogs so we can directly experience love. They certainly bring through more love than many people do. How are you feeling now? Do you feel more open now to praying to and connecting with God?

**Matthew**: Yes, I really want to. (Laughing.) I think I can feel closer to God if I think of Him as my dog instead of my father!

**Margaret**: Good idea! Maybe that will also change your concept of yourself. One of my clients prays, "God, please let me be the person my dog believes me to be!"

## Jeremy

Jeremy came to see me because he had just been diagnosed with heart disease and his doctor had insisted that he quit smoking. He had tried through the years to quit but had never been able to. Now his life was threatened, yet he was still unable to quit and was quite distressed over this.

Jeremy came from a very lonely background. His father died when he was around three years old, and his mother had to work. He was left with baby sitters who didn't have much time for him. Once he started school when he was five, he was left alone each day after school while his mother was at work. He had a hard time making friends at school and spent much of his time feeling very alone. He got into trouble as an adolescent, but he went on to college and did well. In college he drank, smoked, and ate poorly. When he came to see me, he had cleaned up his diet and stopped drinking in an attempt to control his heart disease, but he was still smoking. Jeremy's wife, Carolyn, loves him very much, yet he continued to feel alone.

The following dialogue is a composite of some of the work we did. Jeremy was already in Step One—open to his feelings—when he came in to see me, and in the work we did before the conversation that follows, he had imaged a spiritual guide named Joseph.

**Margaret:** Jeremy, take a moment to connect with Joseph, asking him for help in opening to learning about your false beliefs. (Step Two; he does this.) Now, coming from your curiosity and compassion for the part of you that is so addicted to cigarettes, ask him why it is so important to him to smoke. (Step Three.)

**Jeremy:** Little Jeremy, why do you smoke? Why is it more important to smoke than be healthy?

**Wounded Jeremy:** Smoking is the only thing that calms me, makes me feel less alone. While I'm smoking, I feel like I am with my best friend. I can always rely on this friend to be here for me. I can turn to it whenever I want. I feel too anxious and alone when I don't smoke. Nothing makes me feel as good as a cigarette.

**Margaret:** So smoking is the way you have learned to take care of your feelings of stress and aloneness?

Jeremy: Yes. The stress I feel when I don't smoke is awful. That can't be good for my heart either.

Margaret: That's right, it isn't, but it sounds like you believe that either you smoke or you feel stress.

Jeremy: Yes, that is the way it has been.

Margaret: I'd like you to ask Joseph what you are doing that causes little Jeremy to feel so alone and stressed. (Step Four.)

Jeremy: Joseph, how do I cause my inner child to feel so alone and stressed? . . . He is showing me that I ignore him most of the time. I don't listen to him or take time with him.

Margaret: That sounds like what happened to you when you were a child.

Jeremy: That's right! My mother didn't listen to me or spend time with me. I just got left alone all the time. I hated it.

Margaret: But now you leave your inner child alone, just like your mother did.

Jeremy: I guess I do.

Margaret: And you depend on Carolyn to fill that aloneness, don't you?

Jeremy: Well, she always tells me I'm trying to control her. I do want her with me all the time. I hate it when she goes out and leaves me alone.

Margaret: So you try to use her in the same way you use the cigarettes—to take away the feelings of aloneness?

Jeremy: I guess so.

Margaret: What could you do about this?

Jeremy: I don't know.

Margaret: Ask Joseph.

Jeremy: OK . . . He's saying, "Your inner child's aloneness needs to be healed by loving him. Only love feels better than a cigarette."

Margaret: How does your wounded self feel about that?

Jeremy: Actually, I can hear him right now. He is saying to me, "This will not work. This is bullshit! As soon as we can end this session, let's just chill out for a few minutes and have a smoke. This is making us feel tense, and tension is not good for us. So let's just calm down with a cigarette."

Margaret: Now imagine that you are with Joseph. What would Joseph say to this?

Jeremy: Joseph is saying, "Little Jeremy, I love you very much. You are a very wonderful, bright, and caring little boy. I love you too much to let you harm yourself with smoking. I know you believe that it helps you, but it is hurting you. It could kill you. I love you very much, and I will not allow you to harm yourself in this way."

Margaret: Now respond as your wounded self.

Wounded Jeremy: I don't care if it kills me. I'd rather be dead than feel this way. Life isn't worth living if I can't feel good some of the time. Anyway, a few cigarettes won't hurt me.

Margaret: Now answer as your own loving adult, pretending you are talking with a child you adore.

Jeremy: I am here for you, little Jeremy. I won't leave you alone any more, like mom did. You are not alone. I am here. Joseph is here. God is here. And Carolyn really loves you and is very worried about you. It deeply upsets her that we continue to smoke. A few cigarettes *will* harm you, and I will no longer allow that. I know I haven't treated you well and that you don't know what a wonderful little boy you are. I will start to spend time with you and learn more about who you are. That will help you to feel less alone. I see that we smoke because of feeling so alone for so long, and I will no longer leave you alone.

Margaret: I would like you to agree to attend Nicotine Anonymous. You need some support with this, and you need to strengthen your connection with your higher power.

Jeremy: OK. (When he takes this action and the one suggested below, he will be doing Step Five.)

Margaret: Also, you need to commit to dialoguing every day with your inner child, especially when you want to smoke. Instead of turning to the cigarette to fill the emptiness, you need to consciously turn to Joseph and the love that is God. Instead of smoking, ask Joseph what you can give to your inner child and to Carolyn. Start to think more about what you can give to yourself and to others. You also need to start being conscious of the voice of your wounded self, luring you toward the cigarette. Now ask Joseph what you can give to Carolyn.

Jeremy: Joseph, what can I give to Carolyn? What would be loving to her? . . . He is saying to stop and pick up some flowers for her. She loves flowers, and I hardly ever buy them for her. She would really love that! She'll be so surprised!

Margaret: How do you feel now? (Step Six: Evaluating the effectiveness of the loving action.)

Jeremy: Much better! I feel good.

Margaret: Jeremy, as soon as you asked how you could love Carolyn, your heart opened, and the love that is God entered your heart. This is why you feel good. Do you need to smoke right now?

Jeremy: I can still feel my wounded self wanting to smoke, but right now I want to go get the flowers. I can't wait to see Carolyn's face when I give her flowers!

Jeremy didn't give up cigarettes for good that day. In fact, he struggled with this issue for a number of months. But with the help of Inner Bonding and his Twelve-Step group, he was able to strengthen his connection with his higher power and develop a more powerful loving adult. His adult was then able to stop smoking, not through willpower, but through filling his emptiness with the love that is God and bringing that love to his inner child and sharing it with Carolyn.

The wounded self tries to use willpower to control behavior such as alcohol, drugs, overeating, smoking, anger, TV, video games, social media, pornography, gambling, and spending. When you strengthen your connection with your higher guidance and learn to love your inner child, you no longer operate from the wounded self. You tap into the infinite strength and power of love to help you take good care of yourself and be caring to others. *True willpower uses your will to open to the love and strength of your higher power.*

Many people spend their lives in denial about their shadow side. Not only are they unwilling to explore this aspect of themselves, they do not even admit that it exists or that it is a problem. As they disown their darkness, the darkness is allowed to grow unchecked and often results in unloving, violating, or even violent behavior. Until you are willing to learn about your own darkness—about the good reasons you have for the beliefs that keep you stuck—you will stay stuck in denial and its consequences: aloneness and loneliness, hurt, depression, anger, shame, guilt, fear, and anxiety. Until you are willing to learn about your shadow side instead of denying it or shaming yourself for it, you will continue to suffer.

The inner child contains all the memories of your past experiences that led to the false beliefs that you absorbed as a result of these experiences. When you have done the dialoguing of Steps Three and Four for a number of months, your inner child will let you in on these memories, and the connection with your spiritual guidance will enable you to heal the spiritual abuse that disconnected you from Divine love. Through this process, you will experience the unconditional love that is God. You will know through your own direct experience that you are never alone and are always being guided and supported in your highest good.

# 9

# Healing with Vessels of Love

One day I was discussing with Erika the fact that some of the people I was working with were stuck in their wounded self, especially in anger and blame, or in resistance, withdrawal, and numbness. All of them understood the concepts of choice and intent. All truly desired to be loving and connected with their higher source of love. But they couldn't seem to stay open to learning about loving. Some couldn't even pray for openness. As soon as something scared them, either coming from their own thoughts and beliefs or from someone else's unloving behavior, their wounded self was instantly in charge, and they turned to their usual controlling behaviors.

This happens for many people until they have developed new neural pathways in their higher brain for the loving adult. It takes time and practice to recognize when the moment of choice is at hand and act on it by making a new choice. The more you practice the Six Steps, the more you see that you have choices when fear comes up. Most people who devote themselves to practicing Inner Bonding slowly gain this awareness and are able to make new choices.

But there are always those who can't seem to make a new choice even after lots of practice. I wondered why and asked Erika what she thought.

"They can't self-nurture until they get that nurturing from someone else," she replied. "They need mothering. They can't feel the love that is God until someone brings Divine love through to them. They don't know that their higher power is there for them until they experience Divine love through someone else. They will stay stuck until they get the nurturing they need."

She was right. Because of traumas they suffered as small children, some people can't see their lovability and worth on their own. They need to receive love through another before they can receive Divine love. I call people who can do this for others *vessels of love.*

## Mothering

Mothering is the experience of unconditional love that we all should have received from our parents. Mothering happens when we are touched or held with no agenda: the other person has no outcome attached to the nurturing. They do it purely from the desire to love. Mothering lets us receive love without having to do anything to get it or owing anything for it. Mothering gives us the experience of the love that is God.

Mothering comes from the loving adult in both men and women. The loving adult must be both mother and father to the inner child. The mother aspect of ourselves—the upper right-brain, feminine aspect, the yin—is the part that chooses to learn when we are upset and brings through love from spirit to the inner child. The father aspect—the upper left-brain, masculine aspect, the yang—is the part that takes loving action for us in the world. We all have the capacity to mother and father ourselves and others.

As we heal, we become more and more capable of being instruments of Divine love. As we clear out the fears and false beliefs, we become clear channels through which this love can flow. We can then serve the love that is God by being vessels of love, offering this unconditional love to others, sometimes through mothering or fathering them.

Babies receive this love when being held and gently stroked by parents who are capable of bringing Divine love through to them. If you missed out on this as a child, you may need to have this experience. When I was doing in-person intensives, I often held or touched my clients when they were in deep pain. Sometimes they needed to curl up like a baby in my lap; other times they just needed me to hold their hand or touch their shoulder. I have found that most people receive much-needed comfort when they are held or gently touched. I strongly disagree with the traditional psychotherapeutic injunction not to touch clients, just as I strongly disagree with the rule that teachers should not hug their students. Unfortunately, therapists and teachers fear being sued and often hold back from giving the healing touch that the client or child needs. Sometimes a child gets the message that they are lovable only when a kind and caring teacher hugs them. How very sad that teachers are not allowed to give in this way!

The laws against holding and touching have come about because some people have abused touch, allowing their wounded self with a sexual agenda to do the touching. As professionals and/or parents, it is incumbent upon us to do our own inner work so that we *always* come from our loving adult when offering comfort and touch to others. Unfortunately, too many parents, therapists, and educators, as well as clergy, operate from their sexually addicted wounded selves.

Mothering can help people who have an intent to learn about their own intrinsic lovability. Holding an angry or withdrawn person who does not have the desire to take responsibility for themselves, however, will only foster their dependence. If their anger or withdrawal is a tactic (conscious or unconscious) to get someone else to take responsibility for them, it is inappropriate to hold them.

Since that discussion with Erika, I have put this idea into practice, with wonderful results. I have encouraged people to recognize their need for mothering and seek it from loving friends and partners. Sometimes this is very challenging. It is often difficult for women to ask for mothering from women and for men to ask for it from men. It may be equally difficult to get it from the opposite sex without sex becoming a part of it, or from the same sex in gay relationships for the same reason. Occasionally people turn to gay relationships because they erroneously conclude that because they want to be held by someone of their own sex, it must mean they are gay. Sometimes they sexualize their need for mothering, believing that the only way they can get held is to have sex.

Sex is not mothering and does not have the healing quality that mothering has. *Mothering never has sexuality attached to it.* While sex with a loving adult is a way to bring through the love that is God, two people cannot reach this kind of expression until both have done their inner work and know their own lovability. Sexuality does not heal the wounded self's shame; it can perpetuate it.

Do you remember Jennifer, who felt so out of control with anger and blame? She is a good example of someone who needed mothering in order to know she is lovable. Jennifer was stuck in an inner system that kept wounding her inner child. Because of the shame that became deeply imbedded when she was alone in the hospital for weeks as a small child, Jennifer believed she was unlovable. Whenever she thought someone was uncaring toward her, she got angry, thus abandoning her inner child (by blaming someone else for her feelings instead of taking responsibility for them) and perpetuating her belief that she was unlovable. She could not feel lovable while she was behaving so unlovingly. Each time Jennifer became angry and blaming, she wounded her inner child again with her self-abandonment.

Jennifer often came to her in-person sessions already angry at me. While driving to my office, she would project her own self-judgments onto me, and by the time she arrived for the session, she was convinced that I really didn't like her. She would then find something that I would do—maybe I didn't smile brightly enough, or I was a minute late—that verified for her that I didn't care about her and was judging her. She would start off the session defensive and closed. If I gently commented on this, she would say I was attacking and blaming her. This let me know that Jennifer was operating from her wounded self: it is a hallmark of the wounded self that it always hears information about oneself as an attack, as opposed to the loving adult, who hears it as a gift. Being stuck in her wounded self with no intent to learn at that moment and convinced that I was judging her, all Jennifer could do was get angry and blame me for how she felt.

After my conversation with Erika about mothering, I interrupted this cycle by going over to Jennifer and holding her, bringing through Divine love and compassion to her. The first time I did this, it stunned her. Her mind couldn't understand why I would want to hold her if I thought she was a bad person. But Jennifer could not hold on to her anger while she was receiving love through my gentle touch. Her skin took in the message of unconditional love, even when her mind couldn't grasp it. Since the inner child communicates through the body, her child received the communication directly, bypassing the mind. I made sure I touched Jennifer's skin—her arm or hand or cheek—and stroked her hair, as I often had with my children, so that her inner child could directly feel Divine love coming through me to her.

When her inner child *felt* that I wasn't judging her and that I felt loving toward her, even when she was angry, Jennifer's belief in her own unlovability started melting away. It was miraculous to experience the progress she made once she received some mothering. She didn't need a lot of it. Jennifer received mothering from me a few times in individual sessions, then joined a women's group and received mothering from some of the women in group. She was soon able to give it as well as receive it. As Jennifer shifted out of her belief that she was unlovable, she became less reactive when her abandonment issues were triggered. Soon she was more consistently able to bring through love to her inner child when she felt alone and unwanted. She was no longer stuck in the vicious circle of feeling rejected and acting out in anger, thereby confirming her own unlovability.

If Jennifer's true intent had been to get someone to fix her instead of taking responsibility for her own feelings, my mothering would not have helped her. Instead, it would have perpetuated her addiction to having others fill her up. I have found that when someone has a true intent to learn to love themselves, mothering may begin to help immediately. Holding people who want to heal themselves is an energizing experience for me, while holding those who have no intent to learn is very draining. They are a bottomless pit of neediness; holding them only enables them to continue in their addiction to getting others to take responsibility for them.

## Giving to Get

Holding someone will not be healing if the person doing the holding is giving to get, that is, if the holder has an agenda attached to the holding, such as to get love back, to be seen as a loving person, to get sex, or to manipulate the other person into not being angry. In these instances, the person being held will not feel that they are receiving Divine love. Instead, they will feel used in some way. This is especially dangerous if the person who needs to be held has sexual abuse in their background. Children who have been sexually abused end up feeling objectified: instead of feeling worthwhile in their own right, they feel like objects that are used for other people's benefit. Later on, if as adults they are offered comforting by someone with an agenda—especially if the agenda is to get sex—the holding will feel invasive and wounding instead of loving, comforting, and healing.

This can become confusing in a marriage when a husband puts his arm around his upset or crying wife ostensibly to comfort her but secretly hoping this closeness will lead to sex. If she pushes him away, he may become hurt or angry, accusing her of being cold and rejecting his help. She may not even know why his touch feels so bad, so she might take his accusations as true, thus confirming her core shame. Only when couples understand the concept of intent can they begin to make sense out of these interactions.

Intent cannot be concealed. It is always manifested through the energy that we unconsciously transmit to the other person. We can act nice, but if our intent is to get something in exchange for what we are giving, the energy will feel bad to the other person, who will feel pulled at instead of loved.

Understanding the intent behind your action is the only way to untangle the complex interactions that follow. It can get to be a mess if an angry or crying person is trying to get love to fill up his or her emptiness, and the person's partner responds with the kind of holding that comes from the wounded self, which also is trying to get love. Then they are two empty, needy, codependent people, each making the other responsible for filling them up, and both getting hurt or angry when they don't get what they want. Couples who have not done their individual healing work are often stuck in this dynamic. They may eventually separate or divorce, each blaming the other for the marital problems, only to find themselves in similar situations in future relationships. We always take our unresolved wounded strategies with us into future relationships.

The tangled mess of codependent interactions becomes clear when both people embrace a desire to learn about their intent regarding each other. As both people do their inner work, each is more frequently able to maintain an intent to learn.

Then they become true instruments of Divine love, capable of helping each other heal.

## Fathering

Fathering is taking loving action for our inner child, as well as for others when they are unable to act for themselves. While our mother aspect does Steps One through Four of Inner Bonding, our father aspect does Step Five: taking loving action.

All truly loving action that you take for yourself is also loving toward others, since it brings through Divine love. Needy people may not feel loved by the loving actions you take for yourself, but people who do take responsibility for themselves will applaud them. Likewise, all truly loving action taken for others is also loving toward yourself.

Any action that brings through Divine love to yourself or others is loving action and therefore enhances your sense of self-worth. Giving and receiving mothering and fathering lets you know you are important, lovable, and worthy.

During my in-person five-day intensives, I often worked with men and women who had been physically and sexually abused by a parent. In many cases, the other parent either did nothing to protect the child or even encouraged or participated in the abuse. Allowing the inner child to express his or her hurt and rage is a crucial part of healing, but it is equally important for the individual to express themselves as an outraged loving adult, letting the abusive parent and everyone else know that they will never again allow anyone to abuse them. Sometimes the person is afraid of their own anger, fearing that by expressing it they will become like their abuser and hurt others. When this is the case, they need someone to do it for them. Here is an example of how fathering helped both the giver and receiver.

Kimberly was a teacher in her late twenties, plump and dark-haired, with enormous green eyes. She was timid and quiet, with a very sweet and loving nature that she rarely expressed.

Kimberly had memories of being repeatedly sexually abused by her father, who was both a sex addict and addicted to raging. She was terrified of her own anger and allowed others to walk all over her. The only way she knew to protect her inner child from being taken over and controlled by others was to avoid relationships entirely. She had no loving adult to set appropriate boundaries. All her wounded self knew how to do to be safe was to isolate.

As a result, Kimberly was very lonely, but she preferred that to giving herself up to others. She had left her marriage because she had lost her sense of self. She had become a caretaker and was completely controlled by her husband, fearing his anger and ridicule. Since Kimberly was new to Inner Bonding and had not yet done the work necessary to create a loving adult capable of setting boundaries, her inner child still felt fearful and unprotected.

Max, who was also in this intensive, was a man I had worked with for some time. Max was in his early forties, a tough, wiry engineer. He too had uncovered extensive physical and sexual abuse at the hands of his father. However, his father was also the only one who had ever showed him any caring and affection. His mother was cold, hard, and brutal, while his father occasionally showed some tenderness. Because Max had hung on to this tenderness as his only link to love, it was extremely difficult for him to express any anger toward his father, who was now dead. Instead, Max himself had become a violent man, taking his anger out on other men in hundreds of fights.

Max feared that if he got angry at his father, he would lose his feeling of love for him. If I ever encouraged him to express his outrage at his father for hurting him, his anger turned on me. Max was stuck in his rage, which is why he decided to come to the intensive. He was unable to express his love and creativity because he was so afraid of his anger and pain. And as we saw earlier, love, joy and pain are all carried by the inner child. If we can't access pain, we can't access love and joy.

At one point, while Kimberly was working on herself, the air was tense with her unexpressed anger at her father. I asked her if she would like someone else to express her anger for her. She said yes, she would love that. She turned to Max and asked him. Max grinned, then got up, picked up a plastic bat, and proceeded to yell at, threaten, and pound on a pillow that represented Kimberly's father. Kimberly loved it. Finally someone was standing up for her and protecting her. Max had taken the role of the loving father, acting on her behalf.

In doing this for Kimberly, Max opened the door to the possibility of being a loving adult for his own inner child. The next time Max worked, he was finally able to express his outrage toward his father for hurting him so much. He saw that he could do this and still maintain his love for his father. It was a huge breakthrough for Max, enabling him to move out of his stuck place and begin moving on with his life. He began expressing his creativity through painting, something his inner child had longed for most of his life, but which he had been unable to do. Through reaching out and fathering Kimberly, Max found the father within himself who could take loving action for his own inner child.

Six months later, Kimberly attended another intensive. This time she was able to stand up for herself with her father, hitting a pillow with the bat and yelling at him for hurting her so badly. Much to Kimberly's surprise, she discovered that after standing up for her inner child, her food addiction began to subside. She had struggled with her weight for years, but as soon as her inner child knew that there was a loving adult within to stand up for her, she no longer needed the weight to feel safe.

I have found that no matter how many blocks to loving I heal, spirit always presents me with new challenges regarding giving and receiving love. I used to feel upset when difficult situations came my way, but now I actually invite these challenges into my life. They hone us, and when we choose to walk a spiritual path, we experience this honing for the rest of our lives. *This is what we are here for.* This is why we were born. Challenges present themselves whenever we have relationships with others—friends, partners, parents, teachers, therapists, physicians, neighbors, coworkers, employers, employees. We can use each situation to learn to bring Divine love through to ourselves and to others.

As you do your own inner work, you will find that more and more often you can reach out for help rather than to get fixed, and you can reach out to help rather than fix others. Being able to give and receive love is very satisfying and healing to both people involved.

## The Importance of Receiving

When you connect with both your inner child and your spiritual guidance, your heart is open and you are available to give and receive love. When your wounded self is in charge, your heart is closed to both giving and receiving. The wounded self only knows how to give with an agenda attached; it knows how to take but not to receive.

*Not receiving love is as unloving as not giving love.* When we do not receive others' love, we rob them of the joy of giving to us. When your heart is closed and you are unavailable to receive, you rob spirit of the opportunity to give you the love, compassion, truth, and power that is God. True giving is a way of expressing the love we receive from our higher power. When two or more people have open hearts, they create a circle of love, which is the highest experience of life. They each bring Divine love through to themselves and send it out to others. They connect with Divine love, with themselves, and with others. When two or more people are able to do this, there is joy, there is love—there is the love that is God.

Parents sometimes do not receive their children's love, giving them the message that their love is meaningless. One of my clients remembers being devastated as a toddler when her love wasn't received. She had offered her father a crayon because she loved him and wanted to give him something that was of value to her, and he brushed her off with a shaming comment: "I don't want *that*." When what you offer to your parents appears to have no value to them, you may go into core shame, concluding that *you* have no value. When a parent receives what a child tries to give, the parent is also giving *to* the child. Receiving children's gifts tells the children that their lovingness has value and that they have value.

Giving and receiving occur simultaneously, so when you give and receive, you receive the experience of your worth and your lovability. When you mother or father someone or are being mothered or fathered yourself, both of you give and receive. When you cannot receive, you cannot truly give.

Slater was stuck. He had been working with Inner Bonding for about two years and had uncovered memories of intense shaming and criticism by his father. His mother had been weak and needy and had never provided any safety for her quiet, withdrawn son. Slater deeply desired to connect with his higher power, but whenever he tried, all he experienced was criticism. He tried to imagine an older, wiser part of himself, but his higher self would turn into his father criticizing him. Without a connection with his higher guidance, he could not create a loving adult to take care of his inner child, and he couldn't connect with Divine love because of the images of verbal abuse.

Slater had never had an experience of receiving unconditional love. He did not believe it existed. As lonely as he was, Slater did not want to be in a relationship, because he did not want to take responsibility for another's feelings or suffer rejection if he didn't comply with the other person's desires. Yet he could not break through his block and receive the unconditional love that is God until he could receive it from another person. The whole situation felt hopeless to him.

In one of our in-person sessions, I asked Slater to let me be an emissary of the love that is God and bring love through to

him. He closed his eyes as I stroked his arm, imagining myself
to be a vessel bringing through the love and light that is God.
After fifteen minutes or so of this, he opened his tear-filled eyes
and said, "That is the first time I have ever felt love." After this,
Slater was able to begin experiencing Divine love for himself.
Compassion for his inner child filled his being, and this compassion extended to his family and friends. For the first time in
his life, he was able to give and receive love.

## Caring and Caretaking

It is important to understand the huge difference between
*caring* and *caretaking*. You are caretaking when you give to
someone out of fear, obligation, or guilt. You are caretaking
when you have an agenda attached. For example, you may want
to be seen as good and loving, or you may want to be loved back
or avoid anger. You are also caretaking when you do for another
what they need to do for themselves. Giving that harms you—
physically, emotionally, financially—is caretaking. Caretaking
is draining. You are not bringing through Divine love; you
are giving in the hopes of getting something back or avoiding
something you fear. When you don't get what you want, you feel
drained and resentful.

On the other hand, you are caring when, out of your love,
empathy, and compassion, you do for others what they cannot do for themselves, with no strings attached. You are caring
when you take care of babies, children, the elderly, the disabled,
and the ill (provided they are not using their illness as a way out
of personal responsibility). You are caring when you are mothering, bringing through Divine love to others who cannot yet
do this for themselves. You are caring when you are fathering,
acting for others when they cannot act for themselves.

You are caring when you give something to another as a
gift with no strings attached. You may give money or time that
comes from your heart and brings you joy to give. You might

make a lovely dinner for someone, even though that person is fully capable of making dinner, because it gives you joy to give to him or her in this way. There are many little things you might choose to do for others because it makes their life easier, not because you expect anything in return, but because it gives you joy to do so. This is caring. This is love. This is being an instrument of Divine love.

Caring is giving from the loving adult, being an emissary of the love that is God. Caretaking, by contrast, is giving from the wounded self: giving to get, or giving out of fear, obligation, or guilt.

## Taking and Receiving

It is also important to understand the difference between *taking* and *receiving*. You are taking when you have expectations about what another person "should" be giving you. You are taking when you expect others to do for you what you can and need to do for yourself. You are taking when you try to control what others choose to give. You are taking when you do not take responsibility for your own health and well-being, expecting others to give themselves up for you by taking care of you physically, emotionally, financially, sexually, or spiritually. Whenever you expect someone to sacrifice themselves for you, you are taking.

You cannot be giving when your intent is to take. This is the true definition of *selfish*: wanting only to take from other people, wanting others to sacrifice themselves for you, and giving to them only with the intent to get something in return, and not caring about the effect your unloving behavior has on them.

You are *receiving* when you accept help when you need it. You are receiving when you allow others to mother or father you, to bring through Divine love to you. You are receiving when you lovingly take in what is offered from the heart: compliments, appreciation, validation, gifts. It is the loving adult who allows the inner child to receive. It is the ego wounded self who blocks out receiving, who just wants to take and have control over what is given.

There is no sense of obligation when you are caring and receiving—only when you are caretaking and taking. Feeling obligation can alert you to the fact that the other person is caretaking rather than caring. When there are strings attached to giving, you will probably feel obligated. When someone gives to you from the heart and obviously receives joy in the giving, you will not feel obligated. When someone is caretaking, an invisible scorecard is kept, and eventually the caretaker will get angry if you do not even the score by giving him or her something back. Many people automatically keep this invisible scorecard. In addition to feeling that you owe them something when they caretake you, they feel that they owe *you* something when they take from you. This scorecard ruins many relationships.

In a session with Connie, we explored her difficulty reaching out for help when she needed it and receiving help when someone offered it to her. Connie had been on a committed spiritual path for many years, yet the peace she sought eluded her. As we explored the beliefs of Connie's wounded self, she discovered an old and deep false belief: "Receiving from others puts you into your ego; it diminishes your spirituality because it makes you rely on others instead of relying on God. Receiving from others also makes you vulnerable to being controlled, because now you owe them." Connie had not realized that the love she could receive from others would be, in fact, the love that is God, which is a free gift with no strings attached.

Receiving and caring come from the loving adult. Taking and caretaking come from the wounded self. The wounded self in all of us is narcissistic. It is driven by fear, and its most important priority is to protect us with controlling behavior. This creates a lack of empathy and caring for others. We become centered on ourselves, unable to give from the heart or receive love. It is a very lonely and isolated state.

The wounded self may fear being controlled if we open to our natural empathy. You may have grown up with an empathic parent who allowed himself or herself to be controlled by his or her spouse. From seeing this, you may have concluded that empathy makes you vulnerable to control. The real culprit here is lack of appropriate boundaries. Conversely, if you have a partner whom you are able to control through his or her empathy, you may fear that the same will happen to you if you open to your natural empathy.

When you fear being controlled if you are empathic, you may act empathically from your wounded self as a form of control, rather than from your loving adult. For example, you know your partner wants your empathy, so you act empathic to get something (maybe even empathy) back. This eventually creates distrust in your partner, who learns that your empathy is not heartfelt, has strings attached, and is not something he or she can count on.

When trying to feel safe by protecting against rejection or control is more important than creating true inner safety by loving yourself and others, you are in your wounded self. In this case, mothering and fathering will not help you. They will only help when your true desire is to become a loving human being.

Through practicing Inner Bonding, you can learn to tell the difference between your own and others' wounded self state and loving adult state. This important information lets you know whether it is appropriate to give mothering or fathering. Giving mothering and fathering can be great gifts to both the giver and the receiver when the other person is truly open to receiving.

# PART III

## *Putting Love into Action*

It is not enough to understand and release your old pain and fear. It is not enough to recognize and reject your false beliefs and learn truth from your higher guidance. Unless you take new, loving actions based on this truth, *nothing changes*. This section expands upon the two final steps of Inner Bonding: Step Five, which is taking the loving action inspired by your guidance, and Step Six, evaluating the effectiveness of that action.

# 10

# Food for Your Soul

Your body is a sacred temple that houses your soul while it does the work of evolving in your ability to love. That's why caring for your body is one of the most important ways that your loving adult puts Divine love into motion in your life. You need a clear and healthy body to keep your frequency high enough to hear your spiritual guidance.

The body is also a vehicle through which our higher soul and our inner soul communicate with us by giving us feelings that offer us vital information. A loving adult takes the loving action of keeping the body physically and emotionally healthy, clear, open, serene, free of toxicity, and fit so that you can clearly experience your feelings and access your higher guidance.

Do you see taking care of your body as a burden or as a sacred privilege? Do you even think about taking care of your body? Or do you take it for granted, thinking it will continue to serve you without any special care? We live in a time where our environment does not support us well in caring for our bodies. Our air, water, food, food containers, cleaning products, and cosmetics are often contaminated with many toxins. Electricomagnetic fields (EMFs, also known as *radiation*) bombard us through kitchen appliances, TVs, computers, cell phones and other electronics, lights, and power lines. Many of us have sedentary jobs. The stresses in our society are numerous, and stress, both physical and emotional, erodes the immune system. To have a healthy body, we need to pay attention to it and embrace the sacred privilege of taking care of it. Through Inner Bonding, taking care of your body can be a joy rather than a chore.

When you do not know that your body is a temple that houses the precious being of your inner child—your soul—you may abuse it in order to numb your pain and find momentary pleasure. Weight and health issues abound in our society, which would not be the case if we were loving adults who experienced caring for our bodies as a sacred privilege. As a loving adult, you would set loving inner boundaries for your body: you would get enough exercise and sleep, you would set appropriate limits regarding what you put into it, and you would create a healthy balance between work and play to prevent constant stress. You would not devote yourself to working all the time, which gives your inner child no time to play, create, or relax. You would learn how to create inner safety in relationships by not taking others' behavior personally and by setting loving boundaries with them. You would do your best to provide financial security for yourself so you would not be overly stressed about money, and you would set appropriate boundaries on what you spend and what you spend it on, so as not to overextend yourself and create more stress.

Taking loving care of ourselves involves the limits we place or do not place on ourselves. As a loving adult, you set inner boundaries that empower you, creating an inner sense of safety and enhancing your sense of self-worth. These are the same boundaries you would set if you were taking loving care of an actual child. Loving parents do not indulge their children by allowing self-destructive behavior such as eating junk food, smoking cigarettes, using drugs and alcohol, or getting little sleep, nor do they create such rigid limits that the child has no choice or flexibility.

Inner Bonding provides a process for learning to love, honor, and respect your inner child so that you naturally and joyfully provide the best for him or her. Eating well, exercising, and eliminating stress become your natural way of being—not something you force yourself to do, but something you do from love. You focus on the health of your body rather than on the number of pounds you weigh or the measurement of your hips. The self-discipline to accomplish this aim comes from your higher guidance when you accept the powerlessness of your wounded self to control your lifestyle.

Let's say your anxiety is building, which usually leads you to binge. Your wounded self wants to eat everything in sight, especially the pint of ice cream in the freezer and the muffins you bought on the way home. This time, however, you remember your decision not to live like this anymore. Instead of eating, you move into the Six Steps of Inner Bonding. You choose to feel your anxiety and take responsibility for it. You state your intention to learn from the anxiety, which opens your heart. Then you dialogue with your inner child. Your dialogue may start like this:

"Little one, I love you, and I know you are feeling very anxious. I want to know how I'm treating you, or what I'm telling you, or what I'm doing or not doing from my wounded self that is creating your anxiety. I want to nurture you and fill you with my love, not just with food. Your health and well-being are important to me, and I'm no longer going to let our wounded self harm you with bingeing."

You listen to what your anxiety is trying to tell you, dialoguing with your inner child, your wounded self, and your spiritual guidance until you understand the feelings, false beliefs, and unloving behavior that are causing the anxiety, and what loving action you need to take. Finally, you take that action and evaluate whether it was effective. If you took a loving action, you will feel calm rather than anxious.

As you move deeper into Inner Bonding, you will find that the more you see, feel, value, and cherish your precious inner child, the more motivated you are to behave in ways that create health, safety, and integrity. In addition, the more you choose to take loving care of your inner child by creating a healthy home for your soul to live in, the more loved and cherished your inner child feels. It's win-win all the way around!

## Guidelines for Loving Self-Care

Sometimes we have gotten so off track in caring for ourselves that we need help recognizing what healthy actions are. Below is a guide for being a loving adult to your inner child by caring for your body physically and emotionally. It includes information about what may be appropriate for you in terms of food, substances, sex, money, work, time, and feelings.

There are two important caveats about this guide, however.

First, it has come from my personal guidance for myself. That means *it is not definitive.* If some of the recommendations do not feel right to you, cast them aside and dialogue with your own spiritual guidance to discover what will enhance *your* health, safety, self-worth, and inner integrity.

Second, do not read these guidelines and feel that you have to start following every one of them right away. If you view my suggestions that way, you will feel overwhelmed and be tempted to turn to your addictions to soothe your feelings. Instead, regard the actions listed below as *information* about what loving self-care might look like for you. If you have not taken much loving care of yourself, you may find some things that surprise you.

## Food

The loving adult:

- Tunes into the body's signals, eating when you are hungry and stopping when you are full. It neither overeats nor undereats.
- Puts mostly healthy food (preferably organic) in your body. Limits the amount of junk food, sugar, caffeine, and chemicals (such as preservatives, artificial sweeteners, and other food additives) that you consume, allowing these only occasionally. If you have a severe reaction to substances like sugar, gluten, or MSG or various food allergies, your loving adult makes sure that you never eat them. In cases like this, strict boundaries are enforced.
- Gets a balanced diet of fresh fruits and vegetables, proteins, sprouted grains, and good fats, containing essential fatty acids. If you are not sure what foods contain these substances, look at a nutrition book or go online and learn about them.
- Makes sure you eat foods you like (except for those that are self-destructive), so you do not feel deprived.
- Reads about health and nutrition so you can make healthy choices instead of leaving this important area up to others.
- Moves into Inner Bonding if the wounded self wants to eat too much or too little, wants to purge, or craves unhealthy foods. Explores the feelings and false beliefs that are triggering the addictive behavior and takes loving action to fill the inner child's needs in healthy ways.
- Learns about the microbiome—your gut bacteria—and what to do to create a healthy gut, which is the major seat of the immune system.
- Learns about antinutrients such as lectins, phytic acid, and oxalates, which are in some fruits and vetetables, and experiment to see if these are having a negative effect on your health.

## Weight and Grooming

The loving adult:

- Decides what weight is normal and healthy *for you as an individual* and makes sure that you maintain that weight through proper diet and exercise. The loving adult does not allow the wounded self to make this decision, since the wounded self's view is often very distorted, as is the case in anorexia.
- Does not comply with or resist other's views on how to dress or wear your hair, but makes these decisions based on what makes you feel best.

## Smoking

Just as a loving parent would not give a child cigarettes, so a loving inner adult does not buy cigarettes for the inner child. If the wounded self is addicted to cigarettes, the loving adult does whatever is necessary through Inner Bonding to break the addiction and heal its cause. Addiction to nicotine is one of the hardest to break. It is often related to deep levels of loneliness and grief and a profound need for nurturing.

Cigarettes are both physically and emotionally addictive. They become a person's best friend, something a person can turn to when feeling lonely or stressed and there is no loving adult to handle these feelings. A loving adult understands this and does not judge the wounded self. Instead, the loving adult continues to learn with compassion about what the inner child needs and develops a solid connection with higher guidance so that the addiction can eventually fall away. In addition, the loving adult does the research necessary to discover how to best handle the physical addiction to smoking. A loving adult also prays for release from this and other addictions and asks others for help as well. This applies to all substance abuse. A loving adult might also seek support through Twelve-Step groups.

## Drugs

The loving adult:

- Does not allow the inner child to consume recreational or psychoactive drugs on a regular basis, except medical marijuana in the case of pain or other challenges that are helped by marijuana. Occasionally allows guided use of plant medicine.
- Explores and heals through Inner Bonding whenever drugs are desired addictively and are being used to avoid emotional pain. Learns to lovingly manage pain rather than numb it.
- Does not use prescription drugs to avoid taking responsibility for and exploring feelings of anxiety and depression. Prescription drugs can sometimes provide much-needed relief and a window of opportunity to do inner work. However, they become a Band-Aid instead of a support when they are used *instead* of inner work rather than *in addition* to it. Many people find they no longer need these medications after consistently practicing Inner Bonding.
- Reads books on nutrition to learn to balance the body chemistry nutritionally so that the need for prescription drugs recedes.

## Alcohol

The loving adult:

- Drinks no alcohol if you are addicted to it. Explores and heals the addiction through Inner Bonding and Twelve-Step programs.
- Allows light drinking when no alcoholism is involved and you are not driving. A loving adult *never* drives when you are under the influence of alcohol or drugs or rides with someone who is.
- Never allows you to be put in a situation where alcohol or drugs can compromise your health, safety, or emotional well-being.

- Does not use alcohol as a social crutch, to deal with sex, to unwind when you haven't been taking a care of yourself, or in any other addictive way.

## Exercise

The loving adult:

- Makes sure you get enough exercise.
- Finds forms of exercise that are enjoyable for you. It's very important to do exercise you really like; otherwise you will probably drop it.
- Does not place rigid demands on you to the point of exhaustion, underweight and stress.
- Does not exercise addictively. Overexercising can often cause as many problems as underexercising. A loving adult finds a healthy balance that can be maintained over a lifetime.

I love to walk out in nature and do Inner Bonding while I walk. I exercise and connect with myself and my guidance. I talk out loud during my walks (I live rurally, so no one hears me). If you walk where people can hear you, just put earbuds in your ears and people will think you are on the phone! I keep my phone with me because some of my best ideas come while I'm walking and dialoguing, and I can record them on my phone. I seem to hear my guidance best when I am moving and out in nature. Much of what is in this book came from my guidance talking with me while I was on my walks.

## Activities

The loving adult:

- Makes sure you wear a seatbelt in a car.
- Makes sure you wear a helmet and protective clothing when riding a motorcycle and makes sure that you drive safely or ride with someone who drives safely.

- Makes sure you wear a helmet when biking, and a helmet and protective padding when in-line skating.
- Makes sure you wear protective clothing or goggles when participating in work or hobbies that could injure your eyes, skin, or internal organs.
- Requires that you either are competent or have a competent person with you when participating in hobbies, sports, or activities that could be life-threatening. These include flying, gliding, boating, race car driving, rock climbing, backpacking, sky diving, paragliding, hang gliding, and so on. However, the loving adult does not refrain from trying these activities if this is what your inner child desires. A loving adult does not prevent the inner child from taking risks but does everything possible to minimize the risk.

## Money

The loving adult:
- Sets appropriate inner boundaries to make sure you are financially secure, while allowing you to enjoy the fruits of your labors.
- Does not allow you to addictively use spending and the accumulation of clothes and toys to fill your emptiness, take away your pain, or give you a feeling of worth (even if you are wealthy). Rather, the loving adult uses Inner Bonding to help you fill your emptiness and define your worth.
- Does not engage in social or financial competitiveness. Does not make purchases for image, status symbols, or social standing.
- Never allows you to addictively get into debt by accumulating clothes or toys or from expensive activities such as vacations, dining, gambling, or beautifying.
- Allows debt under specific circumstances, such as buying a house, starting a business, attending school, or getting other training that can lead to personal growth and security.

- Does not give away or lend money that you cannot afford or buys expensive gifts that you cannot afford.
- Does not give away your personal power and choice regarding money (or anything else) to a leader or guru.
- Lets your inner child know that when you have extra money, you deserve to spend it on things that give you joy and pleasure, such as clothing, vacations, activities, gifts for those you love, tithing, and donations to charity.
- Finds ways to donate to charity, even if very minimally.
- Provides fiscal planning and establishes consistent savings patterns when possible.

## Sex

The loving adult:

- Always uses a condom (when he and/or the partner is a man) or makes sure the partner wears one in all situations other than with a long-term, monogamous sexual partner.
- Does not allow the wounded self to use sex addictively. Explores and heals the causes of the desire to act out in sexually addictive ways and seeks help for sexual addiction, such as joining Sex and Love Anonymous.
- Allows appropriate masturbation. If the masturbation is addictive, that is, if it is being used to bolster worth, fill emptiness, or avoid intimacy and rejection, the loving adult uses Inner Bonding and seeks help to explore and heal the source of the addiction.
- Does not allow the wounded self to act out addictively through exhibitionism, voyeurism, or sexual violence. The loving adult recognizes the need for healing when these desires are present, moves into Inner Bonding, and seeks therapeutic help.
- Never objectifies other people sexually or uses sex to harm or have power over another human being. Does not engage in sadomasochism or bondage.

- Makes no sexual demands on partners. Allows sex to emerge from love rather than neediness.
- Does not impose others' rules on your sexuality. Allows you sexual freedom within emotionally and physically safe limits.
- Listens to the inner child and spiritual guidance about decisions concerning birth control and abortion rather than following external value systems.
- Listens to and honors your inner child regarding your sexual identity instead of allowing others to define what is right and loving for you.

## Time and Work

The loving adult:
- Does not procrastinate. The loving adult does what has to be done in time to avoid negative consequences.
- Puts forth your best effort at work. Desires to do things well.
- Does not use work or busyness addictively to avoid facing pain.
- Creates a balance between work, personal growth, play, creative time, time with others, time alone, and time to do nothing.
- Makes sure that both work and free time are fulfilling.
- Gets enough sleep but does not allow the wounded self to sleep away the time.

## Feelings

The loving adult:
- Intends to learn about the inner child's feelings.
- Allows the inner child to release upsetting feelings in appropriate ways—crying when sad, screaming and pounding when angry—without dumping these feelings on others or blaming and/or physically harming others.

- Allows the inner child free expression of joy and excitement.
- Does not allow the wounded self to wallow in self-pity, worry, or obsessive or negative thinking.
- Thinks thoughts that create peace, love, safety, and joy within.

## Healing Addictions

When people come into traditional psychotherapy to deal with their addictions, they often find that they make no progress. Twelve-Step programs have proven more helpful for substance abuse and process addictions because they rely on a higher power to give people the strength to abstain. But even these do not go far enough. They do not show you how to develop a loving adult to heal the underlying cause of the pain that has led to your addiction. In a sense, the program itself becomes the loving adult, and people find themselves dependent on it to maintain their abstinence. While I highly recommend Twelve-Step programs for the wonderful support they give, I also recommend that individuals practice Inner Bonding so that at some point they can also rely on their spiritual guidance and their own loving adult.

Barbara consulted with me after having been in Overeaters Anonymous for three years. Barbara was very slender and maintained her weight by following a rigid food plan. Her inner child was unhappy with the rigidity, but her wounded self would binge as soon as she went off her food plan. She had no loving adult capable of eating in a less rigid and more natural way. Highly motivated, Barbara took to practicing Inner Bonding with a deep determination to succeed. It took her about a year of consistently practicing Inner Bonding before her loving adult was solid and connected enough to her higher power to allow her to safely stop her rigid diet. Barbara now eats normally.

Adam consulted with me after deciding to quit smoking pot. He had been addicted for ten years and had made the firm decision to quit but was really struggling with it. He had never been able to follow through on this decision before. This time, however, he started practicing Inner Bonding so that when his pain came up—the pain of heartbreak from the loss of a job he loved—he was able to deal with it in a new way. By opening to his pain with an intent to learn and bringing through the love and compassion of his spiritual guidance, Adam finally did quit smoking marijuana addictively. In addition, he discovered a new depth and passion within himself that eventually led to a new and satisfying career.

## Practicing the Six Steps

Below are examples of dialogues to help you understand how to practice the Six Steps of Inner Bonding to develop your loving adult and create a healthy body for your soul.

Caitlyn was driving home at six o'clock in the evening, and all she could think about was picking up a quart of chocolate ice cream. She knew that if she bought it, she would eat it. She had promised herself for the millionth time that she would not do this again, but she seemed to have no control as she pulled into the parking lot of the market. She had a huge sense of inner agitation and conflict as one part of her, her wounded self, desperately wanted the ice cream and another part, her inner child, was screaming "No! Don't do this to me again!"

This was Caitlyn's moment of choice. She could choose to avoid responsibility for her feelings by trying to soothe her underlying agitation with ice cream, or she could move into Inner Bonding and find out what her inner child really needed to feel safe and comforted. She turned off the engine, took a deep breath, and chose the intent to learn. Then she addressed her inner child.

Caitlyn: I can feel your agitation. How am I abandoning you right now?

Inner child: You paid no attention to me all day. You don't even know I'm here. I don't matter to you at all.

Caitlyn: Tell me more.

Inner child (angrily): You don't love me. You never pay any attention to me. You never talk to me. You never listen to me. You never stand up for me. Just today at work, when Jim criticized me, I felt shamed and alone. Where were you?

Caitlyn: So when Jim criticized you and I didn't say anything, you felt alone?

Inner child: Yeah, just like I did with Mom. She always let Dad criticize me, and she never stood up for me. I wasn't important to her, and I'm not important to you. Then you shove food down me, just like Mom did.

Caitlyn (gently): Not this time. I don't want to ignore your feelings and just pacify you with food. I want to learn to love you. Tell me more about how you feel.

Inner child: How I feel is pissed at you! You're such a wimp! I hate you! You let everyone treat me the way Dad treated me. And you criticize me the way Dad did. I never do anything good enough for you. I know you hate me.

Caitlyn: I understand why you feel this way. I have been treating you the way Mom and Dad treated you, and I don't blame you for being angry. You must be very hurt inside. I can feel that you are in a lot of pain

Inner child: (Starts to sob).

Caitlyn: It's OK to cry. I'm here. I'm not going away. I want to understand your pain.

Inner child (sobbing): I feel so alone. I have to do everything myself. Most of the time I just feel overwhelmed. It's too much for me. I don't know what to do when people criticize me. I always feel like everything is on me. I feel so afraid and alone and empty. I need you, but you are never around. I have always felt alone. Mom and Dad were never there for me. At home no one is there for me. I just feel alone. I never feel like I'm good enough. (The false belief behind the feelings.)

Caitlyn: My dear sweet little one, I am so sorry that I have not been loving with you and that I haven't let you know what a precious child you are. I want you to know that I am going to learn how to love you rather than stuff down your feelings with food. You are a wonderful child, but you won't know this until I pay more attention to you and learn to stand up for you. How are you feeling now?

Inner child: I feel a little better. I like it when you talk with me. I don't feel so alone.

At this point in the dialogue, Caitlyn's craving for ice cream started to ebb, and she was able to drive home without agitation.

Often eating disorders and smoking are symptoms of an underlying mothering issue. The inner child did not receive adequate nurturing and uses the food, cigarettes, or drugs to fill the emptiness. Many clients tell me that cigarettes comfort them when they are feeling alone. Do you remember Jeremy, the smoker with heart disease, in chapter 8? Through dialoguing with his inner child, he discovered that he was smoking in order to fill up the loneliness he had carried since childhood, when he was left alone a lot by his mother.

Sometimes smoking or eating provides physical as well as emotional comfort. Madeline did the following dialogue in a session with me.

Madeline: I'm struggling again to get control over my eating. I can't seem to regain the control I had last year. Everything is going well—my work is great, and I'm getting more time to play—so I can't figure out why food is still such a big issue for me.

Margaret: Madeline, when was the last time you did not have to struggle with your weight and with eating?

**Madeline**: I was fine until I broke up with Todd. In fact, I was at my thinnest the day I broke up with him. Right after that I started eating again.

**Margaret**: Maybe food is the only comfort your wounded self has when you are lonely and have no physical contact with anyone. Let's ask your inner child about that.

**Inner child**: Yeah! Food is hugs!

**Madeline**: That's right! It is! I haven't had hugs in ages. I mean *real* hugs, the kind you have when you lie naked in bed with someone you love.

**Margaret**: Do you ever hold and hug your doll next to your skin while bringing love through from your spiritual guidance?

**Madeline**: No.

**Margaret**: Try that. Some people find that it brings them the physical feeling of comfort along with the spiritual comfort that their spiritual guidance provides.

Again, this client is dealing with a mothering issue. Madeline was not held often as a child, and she still needs that. When she has no one in her life to hold her, she turns to food for the feeling of the physical comfort she craves. Until Madeline learns to self-nurture and to ask for nurturing from others, she will continue to turn to food for the comfort.

Food is a difficult addiction to deal with because, unlike other substance addictions such as nicotine, drugs, and alcohol, you cannot be totally abstinent. And food works so well to temporarily fill the feelings of emptiness that come from not being loved. Chocolate and bakery items especially feel comforting to the body, so it feels as if you are loving and nurturing your inner child when you eat them. In fact, it may be the only form of nurturing you have. You may not be able to give up using food to emotionally nurture yourself until your need for love and nurturing is filled by being a loving adult with your inner child.

Weight often serves as a buffer to keep the inner child safe when the adult does not set loving boundaries. In fact, the wounded self often uses substance abuse in general for this purpose.

Margo had been an alcoholic for seventeen years when she consulted with me. She had tried everything, including AA, to stop drinking, but nothing had worked. Instead of addressing the drinking directly, Margo and I worked on her boundary issues: she was letting everyone in her life—her husband, her son, and her business partner—overrun and control her. Using Inner Bonding, Margo diligently started to set loving boundaries. About two months into the process, she came in all smiles and announced that she hadn't had a drink in a week, nor had she wanted one. It turned out that her desire to drink had come from her inner child feeling deeply abandoned when Margo let people run over her. As long as she took care of herself, speaking up for herself and setting appropriate boundaries, she had no desire to drink.

People often have a great deal of difficulty making the choice to dialogue when an addiction is involved. It seems much easier and more satisfying in the moment to go shopping, have sex, turn on the TV, play video games, scan the Internet, glue oneself to social media, or grab for food, alcohol, drugs, cigarettes, or coffee than to find out what their inner child really needs. Many of my clients put dialoguing off for quite a while before deciding to try it. With addictions, the wounded self is so much in control that it takes a well-developed loving adult to start dealing with them. This is why Margo and I first worked on her setting boundaries, an action of the loving adult.

## The Vital Importance of Boundaries

Creating a healthy home for your soul is about creating an environment of safety for your inner child. Your child feels safe when your loving adult sets responsible inner and outer boundaries and recognizes your inner child's intrinsic worth so that you can handle rejection.

During an Inner Bonding group session, Betsy did the following dialogue with her inner child:

**Betsy** (speaking to her inner child): I know we are both tired of being so overweight, yet we just can't seem to do anything about it. There must be a good reason that we keep this weight on.

**Inner child**: I don't like being fat, but I'm afraid to be thin.

**Adult**: Why are you afraid?

**Inner child**: Because when I'm thin, Jack [her husband] is always after me for sex. And I don't like sex with him.

**Adult**: Can you tell me more about why you don't like sex with Jack?

**Inner child**: He is not nice to me. He criticizes me all the time. He yells at me a lot. He withdraws from me a lot. I don't feel loved by him. He wants to have sex with me for his own needs, not because he loves me. I feel used by him. He wants me to dress up in sexy things and act in weird ways that I don't like. He wants me to watch porn movies with him and fantasize yucky things with him. I hate it. When I'm fat, he stays away from me.

**Margaret**: It sounds like when you are thin, your adult does not protect you from being used by Jack.

**Inner child**: That's right! She gives in to him all the time and makes me do yucky things I hate to do. I don't feel safe when I'm thin.

**Betsy**: She's right. I don't know how to say no to Jack. I've been taught that it's a wife's job to satisfy her husband and that if I say no, I'm being selfish and being a bad wife. But I don't have to deal with this much when I'm fat, because then Jack is not attracted to me.

**Margaret**: Are there other areas in your marriage where you give yourself up to Jack?

Betsy: Oh yes. I do it all the time. Many times I don't do things I want to do because he wants me to do something with him. I let him decide how we handle our money and where we go on our vacations. Sometimes I even let him overrule me on what to do on my own birthday.

Margaret: So your inner child is certainly not going to trust you to take care of her by setting boundaries about sex until you start taking care of her in other areas, is she?

Betsy: I guess not.

Margaret: So it seems pointless to keep trying to lose weight until your inner child trusts you to protect her by setting loving boundaries against being used sexually. Are you willing to start taking care of her and setting boundaries in some other areas, rather than keep putting your wounded self in charge?

Betsy: Yes, I am. I'm tired of feeling like this. Sometimes I think I'd rather be alone than be married to Jack, that it would be easier and feel better.

Margaret: Well, that is an option. But if you ever want a relation-ship, you will still have to learn to care of your inner child as a loving adult. Any relationship will challenge you in this area. If you just leave, you miss an opportunity to grow into a more loving adult. This marriage is challenging you to show up for yourself. Who knows how Jack would be if you set loving boundaries and treated yourself with respect? He might even start to respect you. And if he doesn't, you can always leave then. But why not take a chance on setting boundaries for yourself with Jack and see what happens? You might be surprised.

Betsy: OK. It feels scary, but I'm willing to try.

Margaret: What are you most scared of?

Betsy: I guess of Jack thinking I am a bad, selfish person.

Margaret: Do you believe you are bad and selfish?

Betsy: I don't know. I've been told that so much that I'm afraid I am.

**Margaret:** So one of the things you need to do as a loving adult is embark on the journey of discovering the beauty of your inner child, of who you really are, instead of letting others label you "bad" or "selfish" or whatever. Are you willing to take on that job?

**Betsy:** Yes.

**Margaret:** Let's start right now by moving into Step Four. Betsy, put your focus into your heart and move into an intent to learn with your spiritual guidance. (Betsy closes her eyes, sits in silence for a moment, then nods.) Ask your guidance for the truth about who your inner child really is, about whether or not you are bad or selfish if you set loving boundaries for yourself. Ask your guidance to speak through you to your inner child, telling her the truth about who she is.

**Betsy:** OK. (She breathes into her heart, silently asking for the truth. Then she opens her eyes and looks directly at the doll that represents her inner child.) Little one, you are a treasure. You are a good, kind, loving little girl. You would never deliberately hurt anyone. You have such a loving heart, and you just want everyone to be happy. You are not at all a selfish person. You never have been. It is Jack who is being selfish by expecting you to take care of him instead of taking care of his own feelings. He expects you to make him feel like he's lovable and worthwhile by doing what he wants, especially sexually, but that is not your job. It is loving to say no to him and give him the opportunity to learn to take care of his own inner child.

**Margaret:** Now ask your inner child how she feels.

**Betsy:** How do you feel right now?

**Inner child:** I like that you said that to me, but I'm not sure that you mean it. I will know you mean it when you start to say no to him and listen to me instead.

**Betsy:** OK. I'm willing to do this. I have felt so desperate about this that I've sometimes felt like killing myself. I wouldn't really do it, but I have felt like it. I guess that's how unhappy my inner child is about this situation of my not standing up for her. I'm really going to do this.

It took a great deal of courage for Betsy to face this issue, because it related to childhood issues of rejection. But as she slowly started standing up for her inner child, she was gradually able to create a truly healthy home for her soul, inside and out. As Betsy healed and became a loving adult, it became apparent that Jack was not willing to take responsibility for his own feelings. Eventually Betsy left the relationship and is now dating.

Boundaries that we set within ourselves are also important for self-care. Below is a brief dialogue between Joanna, her inner child, and her higher guidance. Joanna would very much like to get out of debt but finds herself shopping and spending even when she doesn't need anything.

**Joanna:** What are you needing from me when you want to shop and buy things?

**Inner child:** I don't like shopping and buying things.

**Joanna:** Oh! That's a surprise!

**Margaret:** It's not your inner child who shops and buys things; it's your wounded self. It's an addictive way your wounded self has learned to pacify the stress when you are abandoning yourself.

**Joanna** (to her inner child): What do you need from me that I'm not giving you?

**Inner child:** I want your attention. I want you to care about my feelings. I want reassurance that I'm not all alone.

**Joanna** (to her spiritual guidance): My inner child wants attention and reassurance from me. What does it look like to give her this?

**Higher guidance:** Spend some time each day holding your bear, rocking her in the rocking chair, caressing her, and telling her how wonderful she is, reassuring her that she is a very lovable little girl and that you are here for her. Pin a picture of yourself as a child onto the bear and concentrate on seeing the beauty within you as a child. As you begin to see your beauty, feel the loving energy from me coming through you into her. Also, seek out friends who can hold you with unconditional love. And practice staying present for your feelings and learn to take responsibility for them rather than go shopping to avoid them.

**Adult**: And this will help my spending addiction?

**Higher guidance**: Yes. Real love feels far better than buying things, so if you are consistent, your wounded self will no longer take over to pacify your feelings. But you must give her this *every day*, especially when you are stressed. As soon as your inner child starts to feel a lack of nurturing energy from you, she will feel alone, and your wounded self will want to take away the feeling of aloneness by buying things. It takes attention and consciousness to reach for your bear instead, but if you do it, your addiction will heal.

Joanna was blown away by the experience of having so much wise information come directly through her. This is not unusual. My clients often tell me they are astounded at the information they are able to access.

As loving adults, our job is to learn as much as we can about creating and maintaining our physical and emotional health. It is our job to stay tuned into our bodies and find out what creates our greatest sense of well-being. But we cannot take care of ourselves unless we are well informed. We cannot leave it up to doctors to lead the way: we must take responsibility for our own health and well-being. We need to explore the many different theories of nutrition, as well as the connections between the mind, body and spirit, and the healing power of prayer.

To maintain a stress-free inner environment, learn to set loving boundaries in relationships with others. When you allow others to control you with criticism, anger, sarcasm, or with-drawal of love, and when you allow others to shame and blame you for their unhappiness, you are not setting loving boundar-ies. (We'll discuss how to take care of yourself in relationships in chapters 12 and 13). Allowing your inner child to be abused in any way will make him or her feel alone and unsafe. That is when your wounded self will most likely turn to substance and process addictions to numb the fear and fill the emptiness. *Tak-ing loving action means doing what you have to do, without harming others, to create a sense of safety, peace, and fullness within.* By consistently dialoguing with your inner child and your spiri-tual guidance, you will discover the loving actions you need to take.

You can affirm over and over that you are lovable and wor-thy, but if you ignore your pain and fill your emptiness with addictions instead of dialoguing with your inner child, explor-ing what you are doing from your wounded self to cause the current pain, and giving yourself what you really need, your affirmations are just empty words. If you tell an actual child that she is a precious being and that you love her very much, then ignore her, discount her, sit her in front of the TV, or give her a cookie when she comes to you in pain, she will not feel loved. Spending time with her laughing and playing, bringing her Divine love, gazing at her with love and being there when she's in pain will let her know that, in her innermost self, she is lovable and important to you. *The same is true on an inner level.*

I have seen people struggle over and over to lose weight or stop drinking, smoking, using drugs, spending, or stressing out. Over and over, when they shift from the intent to protect against their pain with addictive behavior into the intent to learn to love themselves, they develop a powerful, loving, spir-itually connected adult who is able to follow through on their decisions easily and naturally.

*Intent is the key.* As long as your primary desire is to pro-tect yourself against your painful feelings, you will not be able to stop hurting your body, no matter how much willpower you exert. As soon as your primary intent is to be a loving person, you will begin taking responsibility for your pain, connecting with your guidance, and healing the false beliefs of the wounded self. *Intent is a major key to creating a healthy home for the soul.*

The goal is to attain and maintain a high level of physical and emotional health that gives us the energy to do all the things we want to do and have what we want out of life. When we feel energized and healthy, we know we are taking appropriate loving action for ourselves. This translates into a higher frequency that enables us to more easily stay in direct communion with our higher guidance.

# 11

# Defining Your Soul and Expressing Your Gifts

The loving actions that we take in Step Five are about the health and safety not only of the body but also of the soul. Taking loving action for the soul means allowing ourselves to act from the truth of who we are. It means letting our true soul self express all the beauty that we are: our gifts, talents, creativity, and passions.

As you practice Inner Bonding and take loving action, you gradually liberate yourself from the fears and false beliefs that limit you. As the wounded self heals, the soul self is revealed, and you remember, define, and experience who you really are. You discover that spirit supports you in being all you came here to be. This is why our soul came to this planet: to share our unique expression of God that is our soul.

## Defining Ourselves

How do we define who we really are and discover our gifts? When we operate from the wounded self, we hand over the job of defining our worth to others. We attach our worth to how we look and perform, and we attempt to control getting others' approval through looking and performing "right." Not only is this exhausting, it puts us in a nearly constant state of performance anxiety. Instead of doing things *well* for the satisfaction of it, we try to do them *right* to win approval, which leads to the rampant incompetence that permeates our society. When we are doing things *right*, we tend to do them just enough to get approval or money. We will do them *well* only when doing them is an expression of our soul self.

When we define our own worth internally through our connection with our spiritual guidance, we open to the truth of who we really are, and what we do becomes *an expression of who we are instead of a definition of who we are.* This is summarized in the following chart.

As you can see from the chart, you cannot accurately define yourself without connecting with your spiritual guidance. *The truth of who you are comes from your higher guidance*, not from others or your wounded self. That's why healing begins with establishing a spiritual connection, then bringing that truth down to your inner child. As you learn to see yourself through the eyes of Divine love rather than through the eyes of your parents or your wounded self, you gradually remember and define yourself from truth rather than from false beliefs. The more your inner child feels seen and loved by you, the more it will let you access your gifts, for your gifts are in your inner child. Then you can experience the joy and sacred privilege of expressing who you really are.

## Bringing Through the Truth of Who You Are

Here is an exercise you can do as part of Step Four of Inner Bonding. In this exercise, you bring through the truth of who you really are. Imagine your spiritual guidance is here with you right now. Imagine that you as a young child are here as well. Now imagine that you are looking at your inner child through the eyes of your spiritual guidance, which shows you your

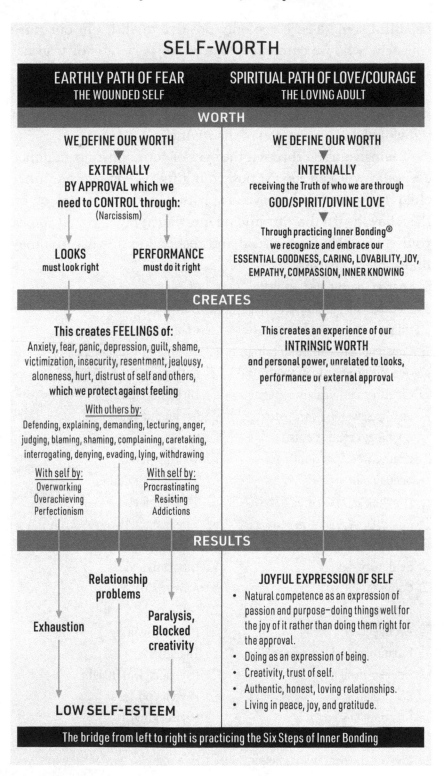

# SELF-WORTH

| EARTHLY PATH OF FEAR<br>THE WOUNDED SELF | SPIRITUAL PATH OF LOVE/COURAGE<br>THE LOVING ADULT |
|---|---|

## WORTH

**WE DEFINE OUR WORTH**
▼
**EXTERNALLY**
**BY APPROVAL which we**
**need to CONTROL through:**
(Narcissism)

**LOOKS**
must look right

**PERFORMANCE**
must do it right

**WE DEFINE OUR WORTH**
▼
**INTERNALLY**
receiving the Truth of who we are through
**GOD/SPIRIT/DIVINE LOVE**
▼
Through practicing Inner Bonding®
we recognize and embrace our
ESSENTIAL GOODNESS, CARING, LOVABILITY, JOY,
EMPATHY, COMPASSION, INNER KNOWING

## CREATES

**This creates FEELINGS of:**
Anxiety, fear, panic, depression, guilt, shame,
victimization, insecurity, resentment, jealousy,
aloneness, hurt, distrust of self and others,
**which we protect against feeling**

With others by:
Defending, explaining, demanding, lecturing, anger,
judging, blaming, shaming, complaining, caretaking,
interrogating, denying, evading, lying, withdrawing

With self by:
Overworking
Overachieving
Perfectionism

With self by:
Procrastinating
Resisting
Addictions

This creates an experience of our
**INTRINSIC WORTH**
and personal power, unrelated to looks,
performance or external approval

## RESULTS

**Relationship**
**problems**

**Exhaustion**

**Paralysis,**
**Blocked**
**creativity**

**LOW SELF-ESTEEM**

**JOYFUL EXPRESSION OF SELF**
- Natural competence as an expression of
  passion and purpose–doing things well for
  the joy of it rather than doing them right for
  the approval.
- Doing as an expression of being.
- Creativity, trust of self.
- Authentic, honest, loving relationships.
- Living in peace, joy, and gratitude.

The bridge from left to right is practicing the Six Steps of Inner Bonding beautiful soul. (There are only positive qualities in our pure soul self—who we came in as before we were hurt or traumatized.) What do you see? Do you see your innocence, beauty, lovingness, playfulness, curiosity, honesty, generosity, creativity, kindness, integrity, light? Do you see that you are a perfect individualized expression of the Divine?

Seeing yourself through the eyes of your spiritual guidance every day will lead you to know your gifts. As you see your inner child through the eyes of your spiritual guidance, check off on the following list the gifts and talents that apply to you. If you let your spiritual guidance read and respond to this list, you may find some surprises.

- ☐ Sports: coordinated, athletic
- ☐ Mechanical: can make or fix things
- ☐ Construction: can build things
- ☐ Green thumb: can grow things
- ☐ Clothing: can design patterns and/or sew
- ☐ Cooking; creative cuisine
- ☐ Crafts: weaving, quilting, needlepoint
- ☐ Drawing
- ☐ Painting
- ☐ Ceramics
- ☐ Sculpture
- ☐ Commercial art
- ☐ Landscape design
- ☐ Architecture
- ☐ Furniture design and making
- ☐ Interior design
- ☐ Set design
- ☐ Costume design
- ☐ Jewelry design and making
- ☐ Playing musical instruments
- ☐ Singing
- ☐ Dancing
- ☐ Choreography
- ☐ Writing music, composing
- ☐ Acting
- ☐ Directing films
- ☐ Producing films
- ☐ Screenwriting
- ☐ Writing fiction
- ☐ Writing nonfiction
- ☐ Writing poetry
- ☐ Science; creative research
- ☐ Inventing
- ☐ Innovative ideas
- ☐ Advertising
- ☐ Selling
- ☐ Public speaking
- ☐ Teaching
- ☐ Psychological insight
- ☐ Psychic powers
- ☐ Networking
- ☐ Humor
- ☐ Healing

☐ Healing touch

☐ Eye-hand coordination

☐ Social interaction

☐ Leadership

☐ Organizing

☐ Business: creating, running, and/or fixing

☐ Languages

☐ Typing

☐ Computers; creating new programs

☐ Computer software

☐ Computer hardware

☐ Raising money

☐ Making money

☐ Parenting

☐ Remembering details (excellent memory)

☐ Sharing warmth, love, caring, and understanding

☐ Inspiring others

☐ Helping others

☐ Listening

☐ Empathy and compassion

☐ (Add your own.)

## Expressing Your Soul

Remember the image from the guided meditation where you imagined love as being the color violet? Let's continue the metaphor. When we participate in an activity, we are either in our wounded self—trying to get bits of violet from people and activities to fill the emptiness within—or we are in our soul self and our actions express the violet that overflows from within us. When we offer our gifts from love, we express our souls.

Life provides numerous arenas through which we can express our talents, creativity, and passion. These include work, service, parenting, creativity, play, relationships, and sexuality. It is our privilege as loving adults to explore these arenas and discover the most joyous ways of expressing our love and the beauty of our souls.

## Work

Each of us comes into this life with special God-given talents. In a loving family, these talents are allowed to develop so that we can discover what we came here to contribute. Too often in our society, however, we don't know or use the talents we were given, especially in the workplace. Work becomes drudgery, something we have to do before we can relax and have fun. But in many indigenous societies, work is a fully satisfying part of life as each person contributes their special talent to the whole. When you discover your talents and express them through work, you will experience work as a joy and a privilege rather than as a burden. Your job will become a loving action to express and evolve your soul rather than just something you have to do to survive or to get love.

In *The Continuum Concept*, Jean Liedloff wrote about her experiences living with the Yequana Indians of South America. She discovered that the Yequana have no word for *work*. They have words for various activities that we consider work, but they do not distinguish work from other ways of spending time. What we call work is something they do because it expresses who they are, and it fulfills them.

Liedloff described an unusual situation that occurred in the village while she was living there. One of the men had been taken away as a child and had lived in the city for most of his youth. He came back as a young man and had no desire to work. The rest of the community happily supported him for five years, and no one ever tried to make him work. Then one day he decided he wanted to work and started to lay out his garden. The chief thought it was hilarious that it took this man five years to discover that he wanted to work. Everyone brought up in the community naturally desired to work, and none of them could fathom why anyone would not want to.

In our society, we tend to ignore our special talents and choose our careers according to what will give us a sense of security. Too often, however, what makes us feel safe does not fulfill us emotionally or spiritually. I work with many people who, after doing what they believed they should do to earn money, change their minds in midlife and seek to discover their gifts. When they experience the joy of sharing their talent with the world, they generally find that they can earn enough money to support themselves. Even if they earn significantly less than when they worked at something they disliked, they find they are far happier.

The false belief that earning a lot of money will bring you peace and joy often leads to anxiety and depression when you achieve your financial goals and discover that you still feel empty, insecure, or alone.

Roger worked for many years as an attorney, but he never enjoyed it. He made lots of money, yet when he consulted with me, he was suffering from anxiety and depression. He had become an attorney because his father had been an attorney and wanted him to follow in his footsteps. Roger had gone along with what his father wanted for him because he didn't know what else he wanted. now, in midlife, he was miserable. He yearned to discover his passion.

A few months after starting to practice Inner Bonding, Roger remembered that he had really wanted to be a teacher. He had never seriously considered teaching because he felt he couldn't make enough money, but now he was willing to make far less money because he was so unhappy with his present work. Roger went back to school and got his teaching credential and is now a high-school social studies teacher. The last time I spoke with him, he was radiant. He loved working with adolescents, and he felt he was making a real contribution to their lives. For the first time ever, he felt alive and passionate. His wife took up some of the financial slack by doing something she had always wanted to do: design children's clothing. She started her own online business and is thrilled with it. Their marriage and family life are flourishing because both of them are happy and fulfilled within themselves.

Ricki came to see me because she was so unhappy working as a controller of a big import business. Yet she had no idea what else she wanted to do. It took about a year of practicing

Inner Bonding before her inner child told her that she wanted to be a nutritionist. Ricki hadn't wanted to hear her inner child because she didn't want to go back to school. Finally she was so unhappy that she decided to listen. She is now back in school enjoying learning more about her passion.

While it may not always be immediately possible to change your work to something you love, if you follow your passion, it will often lead you there. Even when you have to earn money in ways that do not express your soul, you can seek volunteer opportunities and hobbies to do so. Often these can lead to the work that you will eventually do.

Alfredo worked as a manager of a large supermarket. With his small savings, he decided to start pursuing a hobby that had always fascinated him: restoring old cars. He used all his extra money to buy his first old car and spent many blissful hours restoring it. He was so good at it that he was able to sell his restored cars for a lot of money. Eventually he was able to quit his job at the market and pursue his passion full time. Ultimately, he started a project in a prison teaching inmates to restore cars. Alfredo now loves what he does and receives great satisfaction from helping others.

Your soul has a deep desire for you to express yourself through work, to produce something that is of value to you and contributes to society. It is your job as a loving adult to discover what that is and to bring it about.

## Service

As we heal from spiritual abuse, connecting with Divine love and taking loving action for ourselves, our hearts become so filled that we feel compelled to help others. We may do service not because we think we should, but simply because it gives us great joy. Unfortunately, many people who become involved in service organizations act from their wounded self, who wants to be seen as good and win approval. This is not service: it is caretaking, giving to get. True service springs from a heart so overflowing with love it spills out to others.

There are many forms of service, and we each need to find the way that works best for us. There is no right way. We can serve by helping one person, such as being a Big Brother or Big Sister to a disadvantaged child, or by helping whole groups, such as raising funds for environmental projects. We can offer our time building houses for the poor, or we can offer money. We can be of service to people, animals, or Mother Earth. Your service may be in being a loving parent to your children, helping a friend in need, or being a loving partner who supports the other's highest good in many little ways.

Doing service is a matter of discovering your passion and then offering your time and love. You might have a special interest in social issues, such as protecting the environment, working for racial or gender equality, stopping child abuse, helping the homeless, or animal welfare. You might offer service through your creativity, creating beautiful drawings, ceramics, or quilts to donate to charitable causes or give as gifts. As you practice Inner Bonding and get to know your inner child, he or she will let you in on your passions.

Steve discovered his passion for helping the elderly when his father became ill and was in a convalescent home. A hard-driving businessman, Steve was surprised to find how joyous and fulfilled he felt when he visited his father and brought his humor and compassion to the other elderly people at the home. Being with them was so satisfying that Steve cut back on his work to spend more time at the home. He had discovered what makes his heart sing.

Kurt, the president and CEO of a large and successful company, had a similar experience, which led him to change his life. While reading the paper one day, he came across an article about a privately run school for gang members and school dropouts. He was drawn to visit the school and soon became involved with some of the kids. Kurt discovered that he felt filled with love and joy when he was at the school, helping them. Mentoring them became his passion and his service.

Work, too, can be service. When you experience your work as helping people and you love doing it, it is service, whether you are a hairdresser, a teacher, an auto mechanic, an attorney, or a bus driver. While you get paid for your time, no one can pay you for the love you put into it. Love is a gift that can come through you.

In fact, *anything* you offer that expresses your love is service, including your time, creativity, encouragement, or a warm and caring smile to a hassled store clerk. Service is not only expressed in specific works but also in your intention in each moment. Have you ever smiled at a stranger or offered a compliment just because you noticed something in him or her that caught your eye? When was the last time you said how much you appreciate someone? When your heart is open to others, service can be as ceaseless as prayer.

Service does not have to be done only on an individual level. It is possible for whole families to participate in service projects. Rather than relaxing around the house and watching TV together, you can participate in a local environmental or social project. Families who do service together generally maintain a higher level of values and unity than those who do not.

Erika, along with being the cocreator of Inner Bonding, is a chaplain and founder of Hope America Ministries Foundation, which was an extension of Inner Bonding. Years ago, Erika traveled around the country in a motor home, ministering to the poor, the homeless, and anyone in need. She found jobs and housing, gave first aid, provided sleeping bags, food, and other supplies to the homeless, and even did weddings and last rites when that was needed. When she called me on the phone to tell me of the people she helped that day, she was always filled with incredible peace and joy, knowing that she was offering her special gifts of love and compassion where they were most needed.

## Parenting

Parenting, like work and other forms of service, can be experienced as a burden or a sacred privilege. When your intent in having children is to get something from them—to take away your loneliness, be cared for in your old age, or gain an identity as someone's mom or dad—you are acting from your wounded self, and you may experience your children's demands as a burden. This is when child abuse is most likely to happen.

Child abuse is enacted by an out-of-control wounded self who feels burdened by the demands of the child, wants to control the child in order to avoid feeling powerless, or is projecting its own self-loathing onto the child. When you have not done your inner work to heal your own wounds, you may have deep pain, rage, and feelings of powerlessness. You may take these feelings out on your children. You may expect them to give you what your parents did not and what you are not giving to yourself. You may become enraged when you don't get it.

Loving parenting means being there for our children as well as for ourselves so that we do not expect them to do it for us. Our children need us to take care of them, but we must find a way to do so without sacrificing our own inner child.

I was brought up to be a caretaker—to put myself aside and take responsibility for others' feelings. When I became a mother, I moved right into this caretaking behavior, putting my own inner child aside in order to take care of my children's needs. Often this left me exhausted, because I was there for them but not for myself. When I started doing Inner Bonding, I realized that at least half of good parenting is being a role model for personal responsibility, and I was not providing my kids this modeling. As I learned to take responsibility for myself, I became a far better parent.

As you become a loving adult and discover the beauty of your soul, you will experience parenting as a great gift. Raising your children becomes a wonderful adventure as you bring through Divine love to them, then watch their souls evolve and contribute what they came here to contribute. When you are in an intent to learn, your children become your teachers. They challenge you to further heal and evolve your soul.

I work with many parents who would never have sought help were it not for challenges from their children. A good example of this is Cameron and Celeste, parents of Aaron, fifteen, and Bernard, twelve. Cameron and Celeste consulted with me because Aaron told them that he didn't want to live with them anymore unless they received help. He told them he was tired of always seeing his mother anxious and angry and his father withdrawn. Aaron had recently spent some time with another family that was open and loving, and that was how he wanted to live. It was not his parents' meanness to him that upset him; it was their meanness to each other.

One of the greatest gifts we can give to our children is our own happiness and wholeness. As we explore our true soul self and our unique gifts, we give our children permission to do the same. As we see ourselves as an individualized expression of the love that is God, it is far easier to see and value the uniqueness within children. Often behavior problems occur because children feel they are not being seen for who they really are. Our society tends to pathologize unusual behavior instead of trying to understand it. The drugs we give children for behavior such as attention deficit disorder are often a way of protecting ourselves from knowing who they really are and what they really need emotionally, spiritually, and nutritionally. Let me give you an example of what I mean.

Elliott was born into a quiet, restrained family, one that did not easily express feelings. Elliott came bounding into the world filled with intense and creative energy. To his family, this little boy was an alien, and they went about trying to "fix" him. Through anger and silence, they attempted to mold him into their quiet, restrained way of being. Elliott reacted to this unloving behavior by becoming even more intense and getting enraged. He became the "bad boy" of the family, and he acted out his assigned role to the fullest. When, as an adult, Elliott sought my help, he was convinced that he was a bad person and a hopeless rageaholic. He had overcome alcohol and drug abuse, but he was addicted to getting approval and to raging when he didn't get it. His marriage was falling apart as a result.

Through Inner Bonding, Elliott discovered the intense, caring, and highly creative little boy who had never been acknowledged by his family. He discovered that his "bad boy" had been a protection against the agonizing pain of being so unseen. As he learned to see himself and give himself the approval he had sought from others, the creative genius within him soared, and his intense rage gradually subsided.

As you embrace the uniqueness of your own soul, you stop trying to fit your children into a mold. You stop seeing them as dysfunctional when they do not fit the norm. You allow them to discover their passions and learn how they would most enjoy expressing their gifts. Instead of emphasizing getting good grades and getting into good schools, you emphasize support-ing your children in being all they came here to be. Imagine what your life would have been like if your parents had said to you, "I don't care about your grades. I don't care if you go to col-lege or what college you get into. I don't care how much money you end up making. All I care about is that you discover your gifts and your passions that bring you joy and how you can best offer them to the world."

Now imagine saying that to your children, as well as to your own inner child.

## Creativity and Play

While not all play is creative, all creativity is play. In fact, cre-ativity is the highest form of play. Creativity is the experience of being inspired by spirit and bringing that inspiration into some kind of form. One meaning of the Latin word *spiritus*, from which *spirit* is derived, is *divine breath*, and this is what inspiration is—opening to Divine love breathing creativity through you.

Creativity can be manifested through many forms of art, science, and invention, as well as through humor, sexuality, and healing. If you face a canvas to create a painting, but if your primary intent is to paint a "good" painting in order to gain approval, earn money, or avoid disapproval, you shut off the flow of creativity, and painting will not be a joy. It will be a task to complete in order to receive the reward. There is an excellent example of this in our first book on Inner Bonding, *Healing Your Aloneness*:

> Hal used to play the piano as a child; as an adult he had wanted to buy one for a long time. The day the piano was delivered he quickly ushered the movers out the door so he could play it right away. Armed with his only piece of sheet music, a Mozart sonata, he attacked the piano. He found that his hands were stiff, and the piece was difficult to play. But Hal was going to make this fun no matter how hard it was, or what it took to finish the piece. Within a few moments his body was rigid and sweating. His face was tense and frowning, but at last he was the conqueror— he finished it! A little voice within him asked, "Yes, but was it fun?" and he suddenly remembered why he gave up the piano in the first place! Feeling totally bewildered, he decided to throw the music away and just play what he felt. In that moment he set his inner child free and what flowed from the piano was the sound of joy and creativity that he had so long denied. What he learned was that trying to "do it right" was hardly fulfilling. His inner child knew how to play all along, and the sound was magnificent.

When your intent is to be loving to your inner child, the experience itself is the reward as you receive inspiration and bring it into form.

The same is true of sex. If you have sex with a set goal in mind—having an orgasm, getting connected with the other, getting affirmed and validated, getting filled and taking away loneliness, relaxing, or even having fun—it probably won't be much fun. Instead of being in the moment, which is how you receive inspiration, you are focused on the goal, and there is no creativity in the experience. Being sexual with someone in order to express your love is a highly creative experience, a delightful form of play that is immensely satisfying. I will say more about sexuality below.

If you converse with someone, whether or not your discussion is creative again depends upon your intent. Even if you are discussing something about which you disagree, the conversation can be a delightful experience of creativity and play when both people are open to learning. But if one or both of you want to be right or fear being run over by the other, the discussion will be tense instead of free-flowing. You cut off the flow of inspiration when you move into the intent to control. Your wounded self will attempt to make points or hold the line against losing rather than learning, and it will be anything but fun and creative.

Unfortunately, most people act from their wounded self when disagreements arise, especially over hot topics such as abortion, religion, politics, climate change, gender identity, misogyny, racism, money, parenting, and sexuality. Even people on a learning path can move into their judgmental and blaming wounded self over who is right and who is wrong, especially today, with so much polarization about so many topics. Some people move into their wounded self during *all* disagreements, always needing to win (or avoid losing) in order to feel safe. Unfortunately, they miss out on one of the greatest joys in life: learning, discovering, and creating something new with others in conversations. We will not solve our individual or global problems until we can approach one another with a deep desire to learn.

Learning is a form of play because it is deeply creative and brings a profound sense of joy and satisfaction. The more we heal from spiritual abuse, the more we find ourselves bubbling up with joy and letting it explode into deep belly laughs. Eventually the healing process moves out of the realm of drudgery into joy.

This often happens at my five-day intensives. The first couple of days are usually filled with pain and anger, as people release their pent-up tears and rage. This opens the door for exploring and releasing the false beliefs that have kept them locked into pain and anger. This in turn opens up space for truth and love to come in. By the third day, although our work is going even deeper, there is laughter amid the tears. By the end of the intensive, many of the participants leave knowing that the learning process, even though it includes moments of pain and fear, can be fun and joyful.

Part of the action of the loving adult is to make sure you have time to play. We all need time to play, and we each need to discover what our inner child experiences as play. For some, it is a sport such as tennis, swimming, golf, softball, or basketball (provided the goal is playing rather than winning ). Others experience artistic expression—music, art, writing, dance—as play, while for still others, it is social gatherings. Even work can be play when it is a loving and creative process (which is how I experience my work). Whatever play means to you, remember that the child in you loves to play, and it is up to you as a loving adult to make sure you have enough of it in your life.

## Sexuality

While I've already mentioned sexuality as a form of play, it is much more than this, and it is integrally tied to relationship, which we will discuss in the next chapter.

We were born with the gift of sexuality, not only to perpetuate our species, but to express our love through our bodies.

However, too often sexuality is not experienced as a sacred privilege, a gift to be cherished, but as an addiction, a way to fill the emptiness, numb the fear, or satiate the wounded self's need for power. Sex without intimacy generally comes from the adolescent wounded self; it is a momentary fix rather than the divine play it is meant to be.

This has created a huge problem in our society. If we all operated as loving adults who desired to express and evolve our souls, incest and rape would not exist. If we operated from the spiritual rather than the earthly perspective, we would never violate others or allow others to violate us. If evolving our souls towards love were our highest priority, we would never knowingly do *anything* hurtful to another person.

When we embrace the sacred privilege of sexuality, we experience it as creative play, an expression of spirit. Sexual expression between two people who are sharing love is a sweet and passionate experience of grace. Those who allow their wounded self to indulge in the addiction of sexuality may never experience the great gift that has been offered to them.

## The Difference between Connection and Intimacy

Sometimes we confuse connection and/or sexuality with intimacy. Connection with another occurs when we are connected with our own higher guidance and our feelings. When your heart is open, you can connect with anyone else whose heart is open. You can have a momentary connection with the cashier at the gas station, expressing Divine love in that moment through your open heart. You don't confuse that connection with intimacy unless you are operating from your wounded self.

On the other hand, when you meet someone with whom you sense a soul connection—the feeling of having known them before—you might mistake that connection with intimacy and feel drawn to have sex with them. Afterward, you wonder why you feel empty.

Intimacy, by contrast, occurs when people create a safe space to deeply share themselves with each other—their fears and passions, their struggles and creativity, their wounded selves, and their hearts and souls. Intimacy is being compassionately present for each other on the healing journey. True intimacy involves a mutual commitment to tell the whole truth and be in a learning process with each other. When people are intimate, they are devoted to creating a safe space for each person to be all of who they are.

Intimacy may or may not include sexuality. You can be intimate with your friends, your parents, and your children. It is only when you are intimate with a partner that sexuality becomes a part of intimacy, a profound, playful, creative, and fulfilling expression of love.

We cannot be intimate with someone unless there is a sense of equality between us. By this I mean that we are equal in our knowledge of our true soul self, equal in our level of healing, equal in our personal power. People are drawn together by either their common level of woundedness (of self-abandonment) or their common level of healing (of self-love). When one person knows his or her own goodness and another does not, they will not have genuine intimacy.

If you are healed enough to know your own worth and you are with someone who believes they are unlovable or unworthy, you cannot be intimate with them. Because this person feels one down to you, he or she may feel threatened by you. This person may seek your approval, give himself or herself up to avoid your rejection, resist you, or attempt to diminish you. You will always feel a sense of loneliness when you know your own worth and you are with others who do not. You cannot have the ecstasy of play and intimacy without equality. And you cannot *make* others feel equal to you. Their sense of equality has to come from within. You can help them with this, but you cannot do it for them. Helping them may be fulfilling, but it is not intimate. Intimacy occurs when two or more people help each other through mutual sharing and learning.

I was working with a woman named Letty at one of my five-day intensives. My intent was to be fully present for her with my love and support as she did her inner work. I would have loved to play with her in the sense of high play, to share love as she learned about her pain and her joy. However, her heart was closed. Her intent was to figure out how to do her inner work "right" so she could get my approval. She did not know that she already had my love. Because of her closed heart, her inner child felt alone, and Letty wanted to use me to take away her aloneness rather than learn with me. I was aware of *my* loneliness as I worked with her, because she saw herself as less than me.

My feelings of loneliness were valuable to me because they gave me information about Letty. They told me that her heart was closed. Gently, I asked Letty to notice her intent. She realized that she wanted my approval. Grinning, she chose to learn about this rather than judge it. Then her heart is opened, and we could play. Now Letty could learn about the beliefs of her wounded self and discover more of her soul self, and we could move toward equality and genuine intimacy.

When we are devoted to defining ourselves through the eyes of our spiritual guidance, we open the door to expressing the gifts of our soul. Whether we do so through work, service, parenting, creativity, play, sexuality, or relationships, we discover the joy of fully being who we are. The rewards are well worth the time and effort it takes to heal the false beliefs of the wounded self.

# 12

# The Relationship Path to Healing

Just as we all need time to regenerate our bodies (which we do when we sleep), we all need time to regenerate our souls. There are two primary ways of doing this, and *both* are necessary for the soul to feel fulfilled. One way is alone, through prayer and meditation, being with nature, learning, and expressing our creativity. The other way is in relationship with others. Shared love, joy, and laughter are the highest and most fulfilling experiences in life. Learning how to create these with another person is the most sacred, and the most challenging, path to healing and connection with your higher guidance.

Nevertheless, a relationship can stir up our deepest fears of abandonment, engulfment, loneliness, and helplessness. When these fears are activated, choosing to love instead of controlling can feel like a trial by fire. However, as challenging as they are, relationships are a great gift for evolving our souls.

Most of us enter into relationships in the hopes of receiving the love and security we might not have received as children. It is common to pick someone as a partner (or even as a friend, employer, or employee) who reminds us of a parent we had a problem with, and then try to get what we did not get in our family of origin. At the root of this behavior is a deep desire, conscious or unconscious, to heal childhood wounds. With each new relationship, we hope that this time the person will love us or care about us in the way we want.

But as long as we are operating from our wounded self, we will recreate our original scenarios over and over again. Because the wounded self is not whole, we repeatedly seek others to fill us up. It is as if we were each born with an invisible plug to connect to a dependable source of love. If we do not know how to plug into Divine love—the only truly dependable source of love—we walk around empty and unplugged, hoping to find someone who will be our source of love.

When two wounded people meet and plug into each other, they may call this falling in love. But it is not. It is a codependent relationship in which each person tries to make the other a dependable source of love. Because this doesn't work, eventually both people will still feel empty, and sometimes trapped, and will blame each other for the problems between them. Until each takes responsibility for plugging into Divine love, they will continue to feel alone and disappointed in each other.

I remember waking up one morning many years ago in tears. I didn't know why I was crying, but I was willing to feel my pain and find out. I chose the intent to learn, then I asked my inner child why she was so upset. She told me, "Because no one has ever been consistently unconditionally loving to me." When I thought about this, I realized it was true, and I felt very sad. Moving into Step Four, I turned to my guidance and said, "My child says no one has ever been consistently unconditionally loving to her."

"Of course they haven't," my guidance replied. "People cannot consistently love you unconditionally until they consistently love themselves unconditionally, and no one you know has learned to do that yet. Likewise, you cannot consistently love others unconditionally until you consistently love yourself unconditionally, which is something you are still learning. So don't expect this from others. It is your responsibility to give your inner child the consistent unconditional love she wants. You can only do this by receiving it from the love that is God and passing it on to her."

I felt much better hearing this. I had always felt deprived because no one had given me consistent unconditional love. Eventually I learned not to expect it from others but to open my heart and receive it from my higher source instead.

When I tell this story, I am often asked, "If I learn to be a loving adult and take care of my own feelings and needs, why do I need a relationship?"

When you are a loving adult, you seek a relationship, not to be taken care of by someone else, but to share the love in your heart with a partner. You seek someone to learn and evolve with as you each face the opportunities inherent in the relationship path to healing and love. As loving adults, we seek the challenge of being in a relationship in order to become more loving to ourselves and others. Relationships challenge us not only to be one with the Divine within us, but to share that Divine love with others. We also come together to support each other and have each other's back, to have fun together and create together, and to share lovemaking. Just because we learn to love ourselves doesn't mean that we want to be alone or that we will end up alone.

Love means something very different to the wounded self than to the loving adult. In our language we have only one word for *love*, but Spanish has two, *te quiero,* which means, *I want you for me*, and *te amo*, which means *I am love extending to you. Te quiero* is how the wounded self defines love: "I want from you; therefore I love you." *Te amo,* on the other hand, is the loving adult's definition of love: bringing through the truth, compassion, and caring of the love that is God.

The challenge of taking care of ourselves is substantial even when we are not in a relationship. It is not easy to remember to move into an intent to learn, especially when we are stressed.

But a far more complex situation arises in a relationship, especially if we are in conflict or fear conflict with the other person. It is an enormous challenge to take responsibility for our own feelings without violating the other and to care about the other without taking responsibility for their feelings.

## Feeling Victimized

Many of the people I work with feel victimized in their relationships. Angela is a good example. She had read one of my books and scheduled a phone session with me. The conversation went something like this:

"My husband, John, spends most of his time either at work or doing his hobbies. He never seems to want to spend time with me."

"Angela, do you want help with taking care of yourself or getting John to change?"

"I just want things to be better."

"How do you respond when John doesn't spend time with you?"

"I get really angry."

"Why do you get angry?"

"Because he's not paying any attention to me."

"Why do you use anger as your way of dealing with this?"

"What am I supposed to do? It's so frustrating. He's like a brick wall."

"Would you be willing to back off from him and learn to take care of yourself, making yourself happy in whatever ways you would if you were not in a relationship?"

"But then we would *never* spend time together. What kind of a relationship is that?"

"It sounds like John feels controlled by your anger and backs off. If you back off and take care of yourself, perhaps he would find you more attractive and want to spend time with you."

"I'm not the controlling one," she says. "He is."

I could see that Angela was not in an intent to learn, but I tried once more to offer help.

"It sounds to me like you both are trying to control. You are controlling with your anger, and he is controlling with his resistance. You are in a power struggle in which you see yourself as a victim. You can break this struggle by taking care of yourself instead of making him responsible for you."

Angela did not like hearing this.

"Well," she said, her voice tight with anger, "thank you very much." Then she hung up.

Obviously Angela felt victimized by her husband's choices and wanted me to tell her how to get him to change. She had no faith that if she took care of herself, she would be happier than if she continued to see herself as a victim. Controlling was more important to her than learning and loving.

Whenever you expect another person to be responsible for your feelings or you take responsibility for another's feelings, you set up a codependent system. Sometimes you are on the taking end: trying to make the other person responsible for preventing your loneliness. At other times you are on the caretaking end: taking responsibility for preventing the other's loneliness in the hope that when they feel loved, they will return the favor. The "benefit" of this behavior is that trying to control how others feel protects you (temporarily) from your own feelings of aloneness and loneliness.

Whenever we choose to find our happiness, worth, and safety through others, we try to control them to give us what we want. When they don't come through for us in the way we want, we feel victimized. There is no way to avoid this outcome until we are ready to take responsibility for ourselves.

Don and Joyce are in a continual power struggle over how to handle their children. Joyce tends to be authoritarian, while Don is fairly permissive. When Joyce gets frustrated with Don's parenting, she usually yells at him about his permissiveness. Sometimes she goes on for over an hour, and he just sits and listens. When he tries to talk with her, she refuses to listen. Don feels victimized because he has listened to Joyce, but she won't listen to him.

When I asked Don in a session why he sits and listens to Joyce yell at him, he said that he hopes if he listens to her, she will listen to him. I asked him if she ever had listened to him during these conflicts, and he answered, "No."

"Why do you need her to listen to you?" I asked.

"I want to explain to her why I did what I did with the children."

"Why do you need to explain it to her?"

"So she won't be mad at me."

By explaining, Don hopes to control how Joyce feels about him. By letting himself be yelled at, he hopes to control Joyce into listening to him. When this doesn't work, he feels victimized and blames her for being an angry, controlling person.

If Don were willing to take responsibility for approving of himself through his connection with his higher guidance, he would not sit there when Joyce was yelling at him. Instead, he would set a boundary, stating that he will listen to her only when she speaks to him with respect and is open to learning with him. But as long as he needs her to approve of him, he will not set this boundary. Until Don turns to his higher power for confirmation of his worth, he will feel victimized by Joyce's unloving behavior.

## Loving Actions in Conflict

When a conflict arises in a relationship, there are four different loving actions you can take:

1. Offer comfort
2. Open to learning
3. Lovingly disengage
4. Set loving boundaries

## Offering Comfort

If the other person is obviously in their wounded self, maybe acting out with anger or blame, you might assume that they are coming from some fear. If you are able to stay in your loving adult and they are available to being comforted, you can reach out to them with compassion, letting them know you are here for them. Sometimes this will be enough to bring about some calmness, enabling you to open to learning with them.

## Intent to Learn with Others

Being in an intent to learn with someone *without judging yourself or them* is far more complex than doing this with yourself alone. You will likely not be able to do this until you have practiced Inner Bonding long enough so that when you get stressed, you can still remember to be in an intent to learn with yourself.

Being in an intent to learn with another means four things:

- You believe that both you and the other person have very good reasons for your feelings and behavior. There is no judgment, only openness.
- You are willing to share your total truth and hear the other's truth, again without any judgment.
- You are willing to feel your heartache and helplessness rather than protecting yourself by trying to control the other person.
- You have no investment in the outcome. The only way this will happen is if you have done your own Inner Bonding work and discovered the loving action you need to take for yourself in the situation. You must know how you are going to take care of yourself if the other person turns out not to be open to resolving the conflict. If you are invested in the outcome, you will try to control. But learning cannot occur in a controlling environment.

## Lovingly Disengaging

If the other person isn't open to learning with you and keeps attacking, you need to get your inner child out of range of their wounded self. This means taking a time-out, without anger, to do your own inner work and comfort your inner child. It means accepting your lack of control over the other person's intention. You can say something like, "I need a time-out. I'll check in with you in half an hour to see if we can talk about this."

Lovingly disengaging isn't the same thing as withdrawal. Withdrawal is a form of control: withdrawing your love to punish the other person. Lovingly disengaging is a way to take loving care of yourself in the face of the other person's wounded self.

It's a good idea to have an agreement with your partner that if one of you says, "I need a time-out," the other honors this request and doesn't try to reengage until both of you are open.

## Setting Loving Boundaries

Most people have no idea how to set loving boundaries with others. Often, when we first realize that we have the right to set boundaries, we do so with hostility, acting from our wounded self. We violate others with our anger and blame as we lay down the law and attempt to control them into respecting us. In other words, we end up doing the very thing we do not want others to do to us. We act with a modified version of what I call the "gang mentality of the wounded self," which is "If you disrespect me, I will kill you."

In such instances, we are not taking care of our souls. We cannot be loving when we are trying to control. In order to behave lovingly in conflicts, we must be willing to let go of control: blaming, resisting, complying, having to be right, and having to win. This is a tall order. It means letting go of trying to make others understand our point of view or be different than they are. It means letting go of the outcome and simply taking care of our own inner child.

Setting loving boundaries in relationships is not about trying to get others to treat us well. It is about making our own choices about how we are going to take care of ourselves when we are being violated or do not get what we want from the other person. It is about being honest with ourselves about our personal limits and telling others about them and what we will do for ourselves if they don't respect our limits. It is about taking action, verbally or nonverbally, to maintain the boundaries we have set in ways that do not harm, violate or blame others. In order to do this, we have to compassionately listen to the feelings of our inner child, then to take loving care of our feelings from our loving adult rather than from our wounded self. Here are a couple of examples of loving boundaries:

If your partner tends to judge you in front of others, letting your partner know that next time he or she does this, you will speak up in front of the others, saying that you are not available to being treated badly; you will leave the restaurant or event and go home, and they can find their own way home. If this happens at your home, you will speak up and leave the company, either taking a walk, going to a friend's house, or going into another room until the others leave.

If your partner is always late in leaving for an event and you hate being late, you can let them know that the next time they are late, you will take your own car and meet them there.

You can't control your partner, but you can control your own choices. If there is physical or emotional violence, you need to leave the relationship: getting your partner to change isn't an option. Of course, leaving might be very challenging, and you will possibly need much help and support with this, especially if your partner is physically violent.

## The Challenge of Loneliness

Unlike aloneness, loneliness can be an existential fact of life: a part of our existence on this planet. Is there no way to be here on this planet without feeling lonely at times? Isn't loneliness caused by having our hearts closed? Couldn't we just open our hearts and feel better?

It's not that simple. When you open your heart to Divine love, you will not feel alone inside, but you may still feel lonely. But the loneliness can be very brief if you open to the information it is giving you about the other person, embrace it with compassion, and then give it to spirit. It's amazing now quickly you can move through and release loneliness when you show up as a loving adult. The more you feel connected and whole within, the more you will feel your sense of oneness with others, which goes a long way to end loneliness. Although we may feel lonely without a family or close friends with whom to share our love, even this loneliness is quite mild when we deeply connect with ourselves and our higher guidance.

Many people in our society live alone and do not have families. Our modern lifestyle—living in separate houses, with little sense of community—can make it hard to meet other people. Similar to this is the loneliness and grief of having lost a loved one to death, divorce, or some other factor. But I've seen over and over that when the survivor does not abandon their inner child, the loneliness and grief are short-lived and manageable.

A very good friend recently lost her beloved husband of sixty years. When the loneliness and grief come, she is easily able to let it move through her, because she is connected with her spiritual guidance. Her faith is unshakable, and she is a wonderful role model for all who know her.

There is also the momentary loneliness of having your heart open and being with someone whose heart is closed. If this person is someone you meet in passing, you may feel a moment of sadness. But if you have this experience with someone you are close to, you need to attend to what your inner child is telling you about that person and then release the loneliness to spirit. If you are unwilling to feel the loneliness, you may blind yourself to the fact that the other person's heart is closed. Or you may tap-dance around, trying to fix it, unconsciously believing that you have caused the other person to close his or her heart. By attending to your lonely feeling and the information it is giving you, you can allow it to move through you and bring love, peace, and acceptance into your heart.

Feelings of loneliness can be very helpful. They can indicate that either the other person's heart is closed or yours is, or both. You are certainly going to feel both alone and lonely when your own heart is closed. You will feel equally lonely when your heart is open to learning and playing but the person you care about is not. When this happens, you can say something with an intent to learn, or you can accept the fact and disengage. Either way, you can do something loving for yourself rather than battering yourself against another's closed heart. But if you close your own heart, you will feel alone, lonely, and stressed.

While feeling helpless over others is certainly painful, it is no longer life-threatening, because we are no longer children. We are adults who can take loving action and bring Divine love to the frightened child within us. It is very important to remember this, because others' choices can set off our infant fear of helplessness and loneliness in a split second. Unless we are willing to compassionately feel these feelings, we will instantly protect ourselves by becoming controlling. This situation often creates power struggles in relationships.

The fear of setting loving boundaries is also rooted in the fear of the loneliness we are afraid to feel if that person rejects us for not doing what they want. When you fear rejection and loneliness, you may give yourself up to the other person rather than saying no. Or, like Raymond in chapter 4, who frustrated his controlling mother by dawdling whenever he complied with her orders, you may *appear* to give yourself up but secretly engage in passive resistance. You will not feel free to take loving care of yourself in relationships until you are willing to open your heart and compassionately feel your loneliness and help-lessness over others and allow these feelings to move through you to spirit.

Loneliness and helplessness are not feelings that will go away if we change our beliefs. They are existential feelings of life, not wounded feelings being caused by self-abandonment. Opening your heart opens you to these feelings, but you cannot open to loving without opening to the pain of loneliness, grief, heartbreak, and helplessness concerning others. Remember, love, joy, and pain are in the same place in the heart. When you do not open, you stay empty, unable to connect with your essence or your higher guidance. When you bring love to your inner child instead of protecting yourself in the face of these feelings, the door opens to rapidly releasing these feelings and receiving the spiritual lessons of loneliness. You discover that there are lights within the darkness, and each light is a new soul lesson.

## The Lessons of Loneliness

Loneliness may indicate that you need to change something in your life. You will be motivated to make these changes only when you have the courage to feel your loneliness and see what it is telling you. While operating out of your addictions, you are not seeking to truly give and connect with others; you are just trying to take away your loneliness and aloneness. But feeling your loneliness can motivate you to see what is happening with your relationships.

For me, one of the major lessons of loneliness has been learning that I no longer have to protect myself against feeling lonely; it is a very manageable and short-lived feeling when I am connected with my higher guidance. Until Inner Bonding, I used my addictions to anger, work, busyness, judging, food, and caretaking to protect myself from feeling lonely. I couldn't see that these were addictions until I was willing to feel the loneliness that they were covering. I now find that the addictions feel much worse than the brief feeling of loneliness.

Now I welcome the feeling of loneliness because it gives me information about whether my heart is open or closed and whether others are open or closed. The feeling of loneliness in my personal relationships lets me know that I might need to open to learning with the person or to lovingly disengage and do my own inner work.

The feeling of loneliness with a client lets me know that they are closed, and I'm lonely with them because I can't connect with them. This is vital information for me. I can help them to explore the good reasons they are closed—the false beliefs they are operating from—which can help them to feel safe enough to open to doing their healing work.

Before I was willing to feel my loneliness, I would close my heart when others closed theirs, and I would become irritated or judgmental. Now I am compassionate with myself and others when this happens. Embracing my own loneliness enables me to understand and feel compassion for the fears that drive people to close their hearts.

Loneliness can also teach us gratitude for our journey here on this planet. Since loneliness, heartbreak, grief, and helplessness concerning others are among the most difficult feelings, they provide us with profound opportunities to evolve in our ability to love. When we embrace these feelings as challenging gifts rather than as something to be avoided, we can feel grateful for the opportunity to be here on this planet and learn the lessons of love.

Gratitude opens our heart, opening us to receiving a direct experience of our guidance. When we open to our guidance, we can love ourselves, which then enables us to have wonderful loving relationships with others. The more we lovingly manage loneliness, grief, heartbreak, and helplessness, the more we will be able to stay open to learning with others, even in the face of fear. We will learn how to take loving care of ourselves rather than attempting to control others. We will become who we were meant to be, in all our fullness and glory.

# 13

# Loving Actions in Relationships

Now I want to give you some role models for taking loving
action in relationships. Because we have few role models
for this, the information about loving actions during conflict
with another needs to come from our spiritual guidance. We
access this in Step Four of Inner Bonding, and we take the loving action in Step Five.

What works in one situation may not work in the next. New
situations always come into our lives to challenge us and help
our souls grow. Below are some ideas about loving ways to handle different types of conflict. The suggestions offered here, as
with the guidelines for a healthy body in chapter 10, come from
my own spiritual guidance. *They are not definitive.* By opening to
your spiritual guidance and asking, "What is the loving action
in this situation?" and paying attention to what pops into your
mind, you will discover what action is right for you.

When you can stay open to compassion and can lovingly
disengage and set loving boundaries for yourself, you can keep
the energy between you and the other person open to sharing
love. These skills are the basis of creating loving and caring
relationships, both at home and at work. They take much prac-

tice. When you master them, you will have taken a huge leap in the evolution of your soul's journey toward love. Through practicing the Six Steps of Inner Bonding and practicing these skills in your relationships, you create new neural pathways in your brain. And the more you practice, the more you will directly experience Divine love and wisdom, as well as a deep sense of worth.

## A Case Study of Loving Action

Let's start with a common situation that couples often encounter. It's Friday night, and Robert wants to tinker in his shop, but his wife, Linda, wants him to watch TV with her. When he says what he wants, Linda gets angry and yells that he never wants to spend time her.

In this situation, Linda is being a victim, blaming Robert for her feelings. If Robert gets angry back at her or withdraws, he is also being a victim, blaming her for his feelings. If he chooses to be a loving adult, he first tunes in to his inner child (Step One), acknowledging how sad he feels when Linda gets angry and blaming. He opens to his spiritual guidance, to learning and bringing compassion into his heart (Step Two). He welcomes and embraces his sad inner child, reassuring him that he is not wrong or bad for wanting to work in his shop and that he is not responsible for Linda's unhappiness (Step Three). He accepts that he is helpless over Linda's intent to control him.

By accepting this helplessness and opening to his spiritual guidance (Step Four), Robert embraces this conflict as an opportunity to learn more about taking loving care of himself. He is then able to move into compassion with Linda, recognizing that when she yells, she may feel alone and afraid, and she has no loving adult in that moment to handle these feelings. Then he moves into the intent to learn with her and sets a loving boundary (Step Five). All of this takes only moments if he has spent enough time practicing Inner Bonding.

Let's see what this looks like in action.

In a soft, open, compassionate, and caring tone of voice, with the true curiosity of the loving adult and no investment in a certain outcome, Robert says, "Honey, I really don't like being yelled at. But there must be a good reason that you are angry at me. Do you want to talk about it?" Knowing that Linda generally responds to touch, he reaches out and takes her hand to help her young, wounded self feel safe and loved.

Robert knows that his being in a compassionate intent to learn does not guarantee that Linda will open. If she does, they can explore the fears and beliefs under her anger:

**Robert**: Why do you believe that my not wanting to watch TV means that I don't want to spend time with you?

**Linda**: It just seems like you always find other things to do rather than be with me. I feel shut out a lot.

**Robert**: Maybe you are right, but it would be much easier for me to look at this if you were interested in understanding rather than yelling at me. And I would like to understand why you yell. Do you know what that's about?

There is much to explore here: the fears and false beliefs behind Linda's yelling and Robert's withdrawal from Linda. Linda can explore her abandonment issues and the ways she tries to control Robert rather than taking care of herself. Robert can explore his engulfment issues and the ways he withdraws. Their intimacy grows when each speaks their truth and is open to learning about themselves with each other.

"What," you might ask, "does Robert do if Linda *doesn't* open to learning with him?"

If she doesn't open and continues to blame him, Robert can set a loving boundary by saying, "I'd like to explore this with you when you are open to it, but I'm not available for being blamed. Let me know when you are open to talking." Robert accepts his helplessness over Linda's intent and lovingly disengages from the conflict rather than trying to get her to open. Then he acts on the boundary by leaving the room *without anger* (also Step Five). Once he is alone, he goes through the Six Steps to make sure his inner child is OK, and he explores the issue that Linda brought up: his withdrawal from her.

"But" you might object, "what if after he leaves the room, she won't leave him alone? What if she follows him around yelling at him and blaming him?"

When that happens, Robert may need to go into a room with a door he can lock, or to his shop, or leave the house for a while. If he goes into a room and locks the door and Linda continues yelling at him from outside the door, he can play music loud or wear earbuds. Robert cannot actually make Linda stop yelling at him without violating her in the same way she is violating him— yelling at her, threatening her, even hitting her—but he can take himself away from her until she is open to learning. What he can also do—which is very helpful to both of them—is to send her love, visualizing the light of spirit around her, and pray for her to remember that she has the choice to open her heart.

It is vital for Robert to reassure his inner child that Linda's behavior is not personal: it is not about him. It comes from her own wounded self. If he takes her yelling personally, he will revert to his wounded self and will probably end up punishing her if she does finally open. Then the tables will be turned: she will be open while he is closed. They can repeat this cycle ad infinitum if they keep taking the other's behavior personally.

When we are responding as victims, we desperately need others to feel compassion for our pain, because we are not feeling compassion for our own pain. We are not being loving adults. We are trying to get others to be the adult for us. When someone is pulling on you to be the adult for them, you need to have compassion for both of you. If they are open to exploring their choice to be a victim, it is loving to stay and help. It is loving to be a vessel of love if you know they really want to learn but are stuck. It is loving to be a loving adult *with* them, but not *for* them. If you know they have no desire to get unstuck—that they just want you to fix them—it is not loving to stay and "help." You would simply be allowing them to plug into you as their source of love instead of plugging into their higher guidance as their source of love.

## Creating a Safe Relationship Environment

Relationships thrive when both people take responsibility for their own sense of safety within and for their openness and honesty with each other. These actions create a safe space for both. We all need to feel safe in order to open our hearts, be vulnerable, and risk loving. Often we find ourselves relying on our external environment to create this sense of safety: that is, if others accept us, we feel safe. Yet this safety vanishes in a flash the moment someone becomes judgmental, critical, nonaccepting, or angry. Is our safety really such a fragile thing?

The answer is, yes and no.

There are two kinds of safety: safety within and safety without. Safety within, unlike safety without, can become very reliable.

We create safety within when we have a consistent loving adult who stands up for us, speaks our truth, sets loving inner and outer boundaries, helps us to not take rejection personally, and takes loving care of our bodies. We experience safety within when we stay connected with our spiritual guidance, bringing love and compassion to ourselves and others. We feel safe within when we act on the guidance we receive.

Doing all this will make us feel safe to be spontaneously ourselves, except in an intimate relationship that is very important to us. Then it takes *both people* to create the safe space to be open and vulnerable. A safe space is created when:

- Each person not only takes full responsibility for his or her own feelings, but also for behaving in a way that does not deliberately hurt or violate the other.

- Each person takes responsibility for staying open to learning with themselves and the other person. The intent to learn creates a clear, safe energy. Most of us are very sensitive to energy, even if we don't realize it, and the relationship space feels unsafe when the energy is tense because of an intent to avoid and control.
- Each person sets inner boundaries for their own behavior when their issues are triggered. They do not indulge themselves and act out their fears by yelling, blaming, shaming, threatening, physical violence, smothering, resisting, or withdrawing.
- Each person learns to truthfully tell the other (without blame and with an intent to learn) when they feel afraid, rejected, unheard, unseen, engulfed, disrespected, misunderstood, or pulled on, as well as when they feel loving and grateful.

When we act out our fears, we damage the safety of the relationship. When one partner is afraid to speak their truth because the other usually reacts with controlling or avoidant behavior, love slowly dies. When we are committed to loving ourselves, we may eventually leave a relationship where we cannot be completely truthful without encountering blame or resistance. It takes both partners to create a safe external environment where love and passion can flourish.

If you begin relationships by trying to create a safe space for others but not yourself—that is, if you take responsibility for their feelings instead of your own—they may become dependent upon you for their sense of safety. They are likely to blame you if you later pull back and focus on taking loving care of yourself. Caretakers tend to start relationships this way, then feel burdened by it and pull back, wondering why their partner is upset with them. When you take responsibility for someone else's feelings while ignoring your own, you may feel victimized by their anger.

## Boundary-Setting Opportunities

One Sunday years ago, when Erika and I were both living in Los Angeles and before we had our own horses, we decided to go horseback riding. We had heard about a place in Malibu Canyon where we could rent horses and ride along the beach, so we called and made an appointment. We arrived there on time, and an elderly man named Luke greeted us, telling us he was the owner.

Instead of getting our horses ready, Luke started talking about himself, telling us in great detail about his war days. He went on and on, controlling the time and the conversation. After a while, I told Luke we wanted to go riding, but he kept right on talking. I didn't know what to do. I kept glancing at Erika and could see that she too was bored stiff, yet neither of us said anything. We both felt trapped. We didn't want to hurt the man's feelings by saying anything, and we didn't want him to get angry and not let us ride, so we spent a miserable hour listening to him. We did finally get to ride, and it wasn't worth it. The horses were nags. In fact, one of them was a donkey!

On the way home, Erika and I discussed our feelings about letting ourselves feel trapped by Luke and how upset we were that we hadn't known what to say or do. We each tuned in to our higher guidance and asked what we might have done differently. This is a composite of what they said:

> You had a problem because you made Luke's inner child more important than your own, and you made riding more important than taking care of the boredom and agitation you both felt. You each needed to pay attention to your inner child and realize that it was not worth feeling so trapped. If you had been willing to take responsibility for your *own* feelings and needs instead of taking responsibility for *Luke's* feelings, you could have spoken your truth and dealt with the consequences. You could have said, "Luke, we would like to ride

now," and walked away toward the horses, effectively cutting off the conversation by setting a boundary and taking action. If Luke had become upset with you, you could have told him that either he get the horses ready or you would leave, again setting a boundary and taking action to maintain it. To take this loving action for yourselves, you needed to be willing to feel sadness if Luke got angry as well as the sadness and helplessness of not being able to ride. By allowing yourselves to feel victimized, you tried to control Luke's anger and blame, and your own potential sadness and helplessness.

We asked our guides why they did not advise us to move into an intent to learn with Luke, and they explained:

It is not always appropriate to move into an intent to learn. You do not attempt to learn with people whom you know from past experience are sure to stay closed. This would be abusive to yourself, like hitting your head against a wall. Other times, as in the situation with Luke, it is appropriate to just set the boundary and act on it. You move into an intent to learn with others when they are people with whom you want to continue to have a relationship. Since Luke was not someone with whom you wanted to continue a relationship, you just needed to take care of yourselves in a way that did not violate him.

Since that time, I've learned how to take loving care of myself with overtalkers. In such situations, I smile kindly, gently touch their arm or hand, say "Excuse me," and walk away. I don't worry about what they think of me leaving the conversation. I don't worry about being rude. My responsibility is to take loving care of my inner child rather than allow them to suck the energy out of me.

When my clients overtalk, I interrupt them and move them into an Inner Bonding process to explore why they are doing this. What are they trying to control? What are they avoiding?

What are they trying to get from me? How are they abandoning themselves? There is much to learn!

## Boundary Examples

Here are some other boundary examples:

It is always painful to be ridiculed by a parent. Janelle experiences this with her father, who shames her for her spiritual beliefs, telling her that she is crazy for going to a nonsectarian church instead of following the family religion. He denigrates her in front of others at family gatherings, laughing at her, and ridiculing her for her beliefs. She has tried to talk to him about it, but he won't discuss it. He just goes into more shaming. He has no caring about her feelings and no intent to learn about her beliefs.

In this situation, it is crucial for Janelle to show up as a loving adult and not allow her inner child to be annihilated. As in dealing with all conflicts, Janelle would first need to be in Step One of Inner Bonding: willingness to accept her feelings of helplessness over her father's choices and heartache over his not caring about her. She would need to attend to her inner child's heartache by connecting with her spiritual guidance in Step Two, so her inner child does not feel alone. She would need to accept this as an opportunity to evolve her soul, rather than continue to give herself up to her father. Janelle could then to go through Step Three, talking to her wounded self and exploring her beliefs about her right to take care of herself around her family. Once she accepts that she has the right to take care of herself, she can ask her guidance in Step Four for the loving action to take.

There are two ways Janelle can set a loving boundary in Step Five: she can confront her father publicly or privately. If Janelle decides to do it publicly, the next time she is at a family gathering and her father shames her, she can say, "Dad, I love you very much, but I'm no longer available to being shamed and ridiculed by you. If you keep this up, I'm going to leave." She might fear doing this because she believes it is her responsibility to protect her father's feelings, but her true responsibility is to take care of her own feelings. She needs to know that she isn't doing this to hurt or control her father, but to take loving care of her inner child.

Her father might get angry in response, or he might go into denial or shame her further, saying she is too sensitive and he is only joking. In this case, she would have to follow through on the boundary she set and leave. If her father repeated his behavior at the next family gathering, she could leave again after another public announcement, and she could tell him that she won't attend any more family gatherings until he agrees to stop shaming her. Then she would need to follow through on that.

If Janelle decides to confront her father privately, she could tell him (and all her other family members individually) that she will no longer attend family gatherings until he agrees to stop shaming her about her spiritual beliefs. If her family values her presence at family gatherings, they will become her allies in dealing with her father, unless they too are afraid of him.

In order to set this boundary for herself, Janelle has to decide, as is so often the case, that she is willing to lose her father or other family members rather than lose herself. Of course, she always has the option of mentally ignoring him instead of setting a boundary. Her choice depends on what feels truly loving to herself. If she can ignore him without feeling a loss of self, that might be the most loving step. But if being publicly shamed feels more abusive to her than the possibility of losing her family, she would need to set the boundary. To do so, she needs to be willing to attend to the heartbreak and helplessness that she will likely feel if her father refuses to deal with the issue and her family members do not support her. If Janelle does not take loving action on her own behalf, she will continue to feel victimized by her father. If she does take loving action, then she needs to evaluate the action in Step Six, tuning into her feelings to see if she is feeling empowered and more peaceful.

Natalia's best friend, Janice, is angry at her a lot. When Natalia asks why, Janice says it's because Natalia judges her all the time, and she feels shamed by her. Natalia acknowledges this, knowing that she tends to be judgmental, and is open to learning about it, but she does not want to be blamed or judged in turn. She does not want to be told she is responsible for Janice's choice to use her anger as a way to deal with it.

After dialoguing with her inner child and reassuring her that she is not responsible for Janice's anger, even when Natalia *is* being judgmental, Natalia would need to ask her spiritual guidance how to approach Janice in a loving way that takes care of her own inner child without blaming Janice.

Two explorations could occur here. One is about Natalia's being judgmental; the other is about Janice's anger. Natalia could say, "Janice, I really care about our friendship, and I want to know when I am being judgmental. I would really appreciate it if you could point it out. But I feel judged when you get angry about it and blame me for your anger. Can you point it out to me without getting angry? I know that you have good reasons for getting angry, just as I have good reasons for being judgmental." (Remember, both anger and judgment are forms of control and means of protection against our pain, often heartache or helplessness over others). If you are willing to, we could explore them together."

If Janice continues to be angry and is unavailable to explore, Natalia would need to set a boundary: "Janice, I am not available to talk with you when you are angry at me and want to blame me for your behavior. Let me know when you are done being angry at me." Then she would need to disengage until Janice lets go of her anger. She would need to do this each time Janice gets angry until Janice either stops being angry or Natalia decides that the friendship is on hold until

Janice is ready to take responsibility for her own behavior. Meanwhile, Natalia could explore her tendency to judge people on her own.

Renee's husband, Donald, has a habit of coming up behind her and grabbing her breasts. She hates this. It makes her feel like an object. She feels that Donald is acting from his needy, wounded adolescent self and is trying to take something from her rather than coming from love and wanting to give to her. She has asked him over and over to stop, yet he keeps doing it.

In order to move into an intent to learn and set a loving boundary, Renee needs to be willing to feel the heartache when Donald doesn't care about her feelings. She needs to be compassionate with herself so she can be compassionate with him. Then she can approach the conflict with caring and curiosity—a compassionate intent to learn.

**Renee**: Honey, there must be a good reason why you keep grabbing my breasts when I've told you I don't like it. I'd like to understand it.

**Donald**: Oh, come on. I'm just doing it in fun. It's not hurting anything. (He is unwilling to open to learning about himself with her).

**Renee**: Why don't you hear me when I tell you that I don't like it?

**Donald**: Well, sometimes you let me do it, so it must not be that bad.

**Renee**: So because I give in to you sometimes, that makes you not believe me when I say I hate it?

**Donald**: Yeah. Besides, what's the big deal? (He is not asking a real question. Instead, he is discounting her feelings in an effort to have what he wants).

**Renee**: Donald, I have very good reasons for hating it, and I would be happy to tell you what they are when you are open to it. (Accepts her heartache and helplessness over his intent to protect and does not engage in exploration, because she knows that would only leave her feeling even worse, since Donald is clearly not open to learning right now.) Meanwhile, if you do this again, I will sleep in another room for a week. (Sets the boundary.)

**Donald**: (looks hurt and confused).

If Donald is open to exploring his hurt and confusion with Renee, she can assist him. If not, she would need to walk away and not take responsibility for his feelings, instead praying for him to open his heart and take responsibility for his own wounded self. She would not discuss this issue with him again unless he came to her with an intent to learn. When setting a boundary like this, it is not helpful for Renee to tell Donald *why* she doesn't like it when he grabs her breasts *unless he asks with an intent to learn*. If she explains herself to Donald when he is not open to learning, he may shame her for her reasons. She cannot force him to understand her feelings. Explaining herself when he is not open is hurtful to her inner child.

The next time Donald grabs her breasts, she can immediately turn around, look him in the eyes, and say calmly but firmly, "Stop. This feels awful," and then sleep in another room for a week. (Taking action on the boundary.) If he tries it again, she can respond in the same way. If she keeps respecting herself by setting a loving boundary, he will probably stop doing it and may learn to respect her feelings.

Simon and his live-in lover, Paul, are furnishing a vacation house. Paul has taken on most of the responsibility for decorating and does most of the shopping himself, using Simon's credit card. Simon wants Paul to have access to the credit card, since he does grocery shopping and takes care of other errands, but he does not want him abusing it. He is the only wage earner in the relationship (which he is not happy about), and although he makes a good living, he is fairly frugal. He has made it clear that he wants to be consulted before Paul spends his money on anything costly. Yet Simon came home one night to find that Paul had purchased a very expensive piece of furniture without consulting him. This was not the first time this had happened.

Simon has only two choices: to accept the piece of furniture or return it. If he accepts it, he must be willing to have Paul continue to buy expensive things without consulting him. If he sets a loving boundary and returns it, he must be willing to incur Paul's anger, disappointment, or rejection. It has to be more important to Simon to take good care of himself than it is to protect against the heartache he will feel if Paul rejects or blames him. Once Simon has done his own Inner Bonding process, he can move into an intent to learn with Paul:

**Simon**: Paul, there must be a good reason you didn't consult me before buying this. I'd like to understand.

**Paul**: I was afraid you would say no.

**Simon**: I might have, or I might not have; at least we could have discussed it. Do you believe that I shouldn't have a say in what we spend?

**Paul**: No, but I really wanted it.

**Simon**: Then we could have talked about it. But this way, I have no say, and that feels violating to me. I feel used when you don't respect what is important to me and spend money without discussing it with me. It looks to me like having the things you want is more important than respecting me. Since you chose not to consult me, I am going to have this returned. Do you want to handle it, or shall I?

If Paul gets angry and blames Simon, Simon can set a boundary by saying, "I'm not available for being blamed by you. I just want you to be a real partner and treat me with respect." Once Simon respects himself by setting an appropriate boundary and acting on it, he is much more likely to get Paul's respect. Paul is unlikely to buy expensive things again without talking to Simon about it, knowing that Simon will return them.

By treating himself with respect, Simon offers Paul an opportunity to become a more caring person. If Simon does nothing and accepts the piece of furniture, he supports Paul's uncaring behavior, which is not loving to either of them. Simon puts love into action in his life when he speaks his truth to Paul and treats himself with respect.

Andrea's husband, Sam, who can be very sweet, is also very jealous and has a violent temper. Andrea knows that he often listens in on her phone conversations and snoops through her purse. Many things can touch off Sam's jealousy, at which point he yells, threatens, even hits her and beats her up, sometimes in front of their children. He is always very sorry afterward and promises never to do it again, yet the next time his jealousy comes up, the same thing happens. Andrea has asked Sam to get help, but he comes up with all sorts of excuses why he can't or won't.

The difficult thing for Andrea to accept is that as long as she is there and available for this abuse, it will continue. Sam does not have the inner resources—a developed loving adult—to stop this behavior without help. His wounded self knows of no other way to deal with the extreme anxiety and fear at the root of his jealousy. Sam's jealousy comes from a deep fear of loss, which in turn comes from deeply ingrained core shame beliefs resulting from childhood abuse. These beliefs will not change on their own: Sam doesn't even know he has them.

The only boundary that Andrea can set that will protect her and their children is to leave until he gets the help he needs. As long as she *hopes* that Sam's behavior will change, she will probably stay. She will also stay as long as she believes that his behavior is in any way her fault.

Violent behavior is never caused by another. It is caused by one's own fears and resulting reactions. Until Andrea is willing to accept her helplessness over Sam's behavior, she will stay and try to manipulate him into changing. Until she is willing to feel the heartbreak and take responsibility for her feelings and safety, she will stay. She will also stay as long as she believes she deserves to be treated badly. Once she realizes that no one deserves to be abused no matter what, she can find a way to leave.

Sometimes people are unwilling to give up the belief that they deserve to be treated badly because they want to believe they have control. If Andrea believes, "I am *causing* Sam to be violent because I am not good enough, and when I do things right, he will change," she may be unwilling to give this belief up because it gives her a feeling of control. When she is willing to accept her helplessness over Sam, open to her spiritual guidance, and ask, "What is the loving action toward myself and my children?" she will begin the process of leaving.

Andrea may need to get some help before she can take this step. It is a hard step to take for many battered women, because their sense of self-worth is generally low, and they may be trauma-bonded as a result of childhood abuse. Without help, it is likely that nothing will change. If Andrea is staying for financial reasons, she needs to seek help for job training through community outreach centers. If she is staying because she fears being alone, she needs counseling to help her develop her own loving adult. In this way, she will be able to take loving action on her own behalf and on behalf of her children. A loving adult never allows the inner child, or actual children, to be abused.

If Andrea decides to leave, she should not discuss this with Sam. She needs to simply do it, then call him when she is in a safe place. Since he is a violent person, it is not safe for Andrea to tell him where she is. She can give him the phone number of a mutual friend for emergencies and tell him that she will not see him or communicate with him until he gets help—and then only with a counselor present.

Marina works as a freelance bookkeeper for a number of different attorneys. She likes her job, but one of her clients, Tom, is a very angry man. As soon as Marina comes in each week, he starts yelling at her about the bills, asking her in an accusatory tone about things he does not understand. He doesn't listen for her answer; he just orders her to fix the problem. Marina has been afraid to say anything to him for fear he will get even more angry. Instead, she tries to be "nice," acting as if it doesn't bother her, although she feels awful inside.

To set a loving boundary, Marina needs to accept her helplessness over Tom's behavior. She cannot make him be kind and respectful, even by being "nice." Next, she needs to be open to feeling her sadness at being treated this way. Finally, she has to decide if she is willing to lose her job with Tom, which could happen if she sets a boundary with him. If losing this work would cause her hardship, she needs to seek another client. Until then, the best she can do is let her inner child know that Tom's behavior is not personal. If she is willing to lose her work with him, she needs to ask her spiritual guidance about the loving action in this situation.

There is never only one loving way to handle a particular situation. Marina could say, "Tom, the way you speak to me feels very disrespectful. I'm not willing to discuss anything with you until you treat me with respect." If he continued attacking her, she would need to act on the boundary and leave the room, refusing to engage with him until he was respectful. If she has reached the point where she is totally unwilling to be around this treatment anymore and she can afford not to work for Tom, she can say, "Tom, if you continue to treat me this way, I will quit."

Sometimes people violate our boundaries without realizing it and are open to hearing our feelings about it, and sometimes they just don't care. It is important to know that in our personal relationships, we do not have to be around someone who violates us in some way and has no adult present with an intent to learn.

When you cannot leave a situation where you are being violated, such as when you are in a car, a work situation, or a marriage with children where you are financially dependent, stay open to learning with your spiritual guidance about how to best take care of yourself until you can find a way to leave.

Claudia is hurt and angry because her two close friends did not call her on her birthday. She had let them know that it was important to her, but still they didn't do it. When she told them she felt hurt, they grew defensive, and she ended up feeling even worse.

Claudia has been taught that sharing her feelings when she is hurt will be helpful, but she does not understand that her *intention* is also important. If her intention is to blame others and make them responsible for her hurt, then sharing her feelings is a way to control. In order to communicate lovingly with her friends, she would first need to do her own Inner Bonding process, exploring her part in creating the situation and identifying the false beliefs that caused her hurt and anger.

Part of the problem is that when Claudia let her friends know what she wanted, it was not a request but a demand. A request has no expectation attached to it, while a demand does. Claudia's hurt and disappointment were a result of her expectation. Had she made a request instead of a demand, she would have been curious about why her friends didn't call. She would have approached them with an intent to learn rather than with anger and blame. She would have wanted to know the good reasons they had for not calling. Perhaps they recognized Claudia's "request" as a demand and resisted her attempt to control them. Perhaps they were upset with her for past situations when she made them responsible for her feelings, so they unconsciously withheld from her. Or maybe they just don't care about things like birthdays, and it had nothing to do with Claudia. Whatever their reason, Claudia will not discover it until she intends to learn about herself as well as about them.

Estelle drinks three or four glasses of wine at dinner every night, then spends the evening spaced out in front of the TV. Sometimes she even drives in the evening after drinking. Her husband, Daniel, has told her many times that he worries about her when she drives and about the effect of drinking on her health, and he would like to spend time with her without wine and TV. That rarely happens. Daniel finds it difficult to carry on a meaningful conversation with Estelle and feels bored and frustrated with the relationship.

There are three ways of dealing with a situation like this:

- He can try to change her, which will likely result in power struggles and resistance.
- He can try to accept the situation, which, since it is unacceptable to him, will lead him to feel that he is giving himself up. Eventually he will get resentful and angry.
- He can leave. This is the only viable option for setting a boundary when someone is behaving in a way that is completely unacceptable to you.

People stay in unacceptable situations partly out of the hope that the other person will change. This is not realistic, since most people do not change until they are in pain. As long as Daniel stays with Estelle, she will not be in enough pain to motivate her to change. She may not be in enough pain even if he does leave. She might have to lose her job or injure herself or another while driving before she considers changing her behavior. Even then, she might not. Some people refuse to change when faced with the extreme consequences of illness or death, like the person with emphysema who keeps smoking or the person with heart disease who keeps eating poorly and refuses to exercise.

When people you love are unloving to themselves, it is unloving to support them in their self-destructive behavior. If they eat poorly, drink too much, take drugs or smoke cigarettes, or if they judge themselves harshly, are locked into resistance, are very negative or allow themselves to feel victimized, it is loving to do whatever you can to stop enabling them in their self-destructive behavior. This may mean setting boundaries in ways that take loving care of yourself rather than supporting them, or it might mean leaving the relationship. Setting boundaries for yourself is a learning process.

Often, in order to know how to set a boundary in a particular situation, I write out scenarios of situations where I have felt my boundaries were violated and practice what I would say or do next time. I've done this for each situation in which I haven't responded in a way that made my inner child feel loved and safe. With enough practice writing out scenarios until I find the words that feel right to me, and with enough rehearsal of these words, I've become better and better at setting loving boundaries in the moment the violation occurs. I can actually feel the rewiring in my brain!

When my deepest desire is to love rather than control, I respond to another's violation of my boundaries by moving into a compassionate intent to learn, giving comfort, speaking my truth, setting a loving boundary, or lovingly disengaging. In these cases, I feel terrific. It is gratifying to know that my feelings are always *my* responsibility, because then I can do something about feeling bad: I can continue to practice responding lovingly, *no matter what.*

I believe that responding lovingly, *no matter what*, is a soul lesson for all of us and one of the main reasons we are here on this planet. I used to find this very challenging. As soon as I was able to keep my heart open in one situation, I was challenged by a new one, and my guidance told me that this is a way our souls grow when we have opted for spiritual growth. This is the relationship path to Divine love. However, we are never given more than we can handle, and each time I respond lovingly in a new situation, I feel more and more loved, safe, and valued.

## Boundaries against Violating Others

Loving action in relationships is also about setting inner boundaries against violating others. It is the job of the loving adult to set boundaries against the wounded self's habitual way of responding to conflict.

Marshall's wife is screaming at him and yelling obscenities. He is enraged and wants to hit her. Instead, his loving adult recognizes what's happening and talks to his inner child: "I know you are very angry, and you really want to hit her, but I won't let you do that. It is not OK to hit people." Marshall decides to walk away from his wife and allow his inner child to discharge his rage through the Inner Bonding Anger Process. Then he explores his part in creating the present situation. When his feelings are resolved, he comes back and opens to learning with his wife, asking her why she is so angry. If she is not open, he sets a boundary, letting her know that he will not remain around her if she continues to scream at him. He can pray for her and send her love from his heart, but he cannot engage with her in a meaningful way while she is angry.

Most violence is the result of an out-of-control wounded self acting out the rage of not being taken care of by a loving adult. This seemingly bottomless well of anger dissipates once you learn from your anger rather than taking it out on others.

Aggie's husband, Allen, blames her for his not having enough time to play golf. Aggie's wounded self wants to defend herself, argue, explain, and debate, showing him how poorly he manages his time, proving that it is not her fault. Past experience, however, has shown her that when she does that, their interaction escalates into a shouting match where they each bring in all their old past hurts and blame each other for them. They both feel bad after one of these battles, wondering how they had such a huge fight over something minor.

Instead of engaging with Allen, Aggie needs to tell him that she doesn't want to talk about this now, then go off by herself and dialogue with her inner child, exploring why she feels the need to prove her innocence. What does this remind her of in her past? Was she unfairly blamed for things by her parents?

Is she making Allen responsible for validating her as a caring person?

Once Aggie understands what triggers her defensiveness, she can dialogue with her spiritual guidance and bring through the truth to her inner child: that Allen is the one responsible for his lack of golfing time. She can bring through Divine love and acceptance to her inner child, giving her inner child the acknowledgment Aggie has been trying to get from Allen. Once she is centered and open, she can go back to Allen and set a loving boundary by telling him she is no longer available for being blamed for his lack of time, and that when he does blame her, she will disengage from him. Then she can move into an intent to learn with him by telling him that if he wants to explore the time problem with her, she is available.

Mastering the art of staying open to learning, speaking your truth, lovingly disengaging, and setting boundaries with love and respect when you are in the middle of a conflict with someone is not easy. It takes focus to be aware of your intent. Every time you notice you are in a situation where you feel violated, you will need to be very conscious of your feelings and your intent in order to be able to stay in your loving adult. You may tend to set your boundary with harshness rather than with firmness until you have had some practice. But you will find that you are seen, heard, and respected far more readily when you can stay soft and open than when you are harsh and critical. When you've let things go on for a while without standing up for yourself, it is much more difficult to stay open and not get angry. When you feel angry at another, it is often a signal that you have not been taking care of yourself in some way.

Whatever the issue, your challenge is always the same: *to choose love instead of control*. When you take care of your boundaries in the moment, it gets easier and easier to stay open to learning and loving in the midst of conflict. Staying in compassion with yourself and others creates inner safety. If you have compassion only for yourself, you may feel angry and victimized by others. If you have compassion only for others, you may caretake and eventually end up feeling victimized as well. Only self-compassion *and* compassion for others will enable your inner child to feel safe, worthy, and loved.

# 14

# Rewards of the
# Inner Bonding Journey

Practicing Inner Bonding offers both immediate and long-term rewards. Noticing these rewards, or the absence of them (which indicates the need for further exploration and action), is the final step of Inner Bonding, Step Six: evaluating the results of our actions. This is where we go inward, as in Step One, to see how we are feeling, this time to discover whether what we are doing is working for us. Our feelings of peace and joy, among many other rewards of the healing journey, let us know that we have indeed taken a loving action.

With time and practice, we find that our inner growth no longer seems like hard work. At times it even seems like play, a delightful and exhilarating experience of discovery. We feel spirit, the grace of God, flowing through us, leading us toward wholeness. Rather than dreading the pain and difficulties of life, we meet them as opportunities to evolve our souls.

As we use the power of Inner Bonding to heal from our spiritual abuse, we have the deeply fulfilling experience of knowing that we are not alone: Divine love is always with us. Fear is replaced by faith as we experience grace through growth, and growth through grace. Moving out of fear and into faith is a sure sign that we are taking appropriate loving actions.

## Faith and Trust

Faith is one of the wonderful rewards of this sacred journey. Faith is a deep knowing that our higher guidance is always with us and that everything that happens is for the highest good of our souls. We feel faith when we move out of the earthly level onto the spiritual level, recognizing that all earthly challenges are opportunities to evolve. Experiencing Divine love teaches us the faith that is *knowing*, not just believing, and allows us to let go of control. Until you *know* you are being guided every step of the way, your wounded self cannot relax its vigilance.

I love this poem by Patrick Overton about faith:

### Faith

*When you walk to the edge of all the light you have*
*and take the first step into the darkness of the unknown,*
*you must believe that one of two things will happen:*
*There will be something solid to stand upon,*
*Or, you will be taught how to fly.*

As your faith grows, so does your trust in your spiritual guidance. Day by day, as you do your inner work, taking loving action based on the guidance you hear in Step Four, you come to trust that guidance far more than the guidance of your wounded self. You come to trust "the still, small voice within" (as the Quakers call it; see 1 Kings 19:12). Eventually, the clamoring of your wounded self fades into the background. Life becomes much easier, even in the face of difficulties, because you go with the flow, rowing your boat gently downstream instead of battling the current.

As your trust in your spiritual guidance grows, your trust issues with others gradually recede. You no longer need to depend on them to make you feel safe. You no longer need to put your faith and trust blindly in them: you now have faith and trust in your own loving adult and your spiritual guidance. Your guidance tells you whether or not others are trustworthy, whether or not they are lying or being truthful. You no longer feel betrayed, because you do not put yourself in a position to be betrayed. And you no longer betray yourself by abandoning yourself. When you put your trust in your spiritual guidance rather than in what others tell you, you will no longer be pulled into situations that are not in your highest good.

Many of my clients have deep trust issues. If their parents were untrustworthy, they may not trust that I care about them. They want a guarantee that I will never let them down. They want me to *prove* that I am trustworthy. I tell them that I cannot do that: I will undoubtedly let them down at times, since I am human and cannot live up to all their expectations. I tell them that they will trust that I have their highest good at heart only when they learn to trust themselves. As they learn to trust their own knowing, they will *know* that my intention is to support their highest good. I tell them they will also learn to trust their own knowing about when someone does *not* have their highest good at heart. When they have faith and trust in their spiritual guidance, they can truly take good care of their inner child.

Faith is a lot like a savings account: you have to add to it every day, so that when a need arises, you have enough to see you through. When you practice Inner Bonding, you are building up your faith—making deposits in your faith "savings account"—by putting Divine love into action.

## Gratitude for the Sacred Journey

Gratitude is another reward of the sacred healing journey. When we have faith that we are here on this planet in order to evolve and manifest our gifts, we can gratefully embrace our experience. Being here is a sacred opportunity. If you could remember your original determination to evolve in this embodiment, you would be in deep gratitude each moment for the challenges and opportunities presented to you. You would not be angry or depressed, even when you are heartbroken. You would know that managing the painful feelings of life and staying loving anyway is a major part of the curriculum on schoolhouse earth.

Since the painful feelings of life do not exist in the spiritual realm, we can learn about lovingly handling them only on earth. To do this, we need to stay connected to the spiritual perspective *in each moment*. It is easy to become addicted to the earthly perspective. On the earthly level, there is much existential pain, and it is easy to get stuck in protecting against it. When we see our loneliness, grief, heartbreak, and helplessness concerning others from a spiritual perspective, these feelings become challenges to stay open-hearted. In every moment, we can either be stuck in the painful feelings of life and trying to avoid them, or be in gratitude for the opportunity to move into love in the face of these challenges.

We need to learn to live *on* the earth without being *of* the earth. As soon as we are truly in gratitude for the journey, the painful feelings of life become part of the journey. When we are in gratitude, we do not judge another person for being rejecting or needy. Instead, we see that they are giving us an opportunity to move into love and compassion. On the earthly level, they may want to take something from us or hurt us, but on the spiritual level, they are presenting us with an opportunity to evolve our souls.

Remembering why we are here—to evolve in lovingness and manifest our gifts—helps us stay in faith and gratitude. However, it is not just a matter of remembering *why* we are here, but remembering *that* we are here. Gratitude for the privilege of being here goes a long way toward managing the inevitable pain of life.

When we stay loving, we will feel sorrow, but not the suffering of a victim. Sorrow is what we feel at the suffering of others.

Sorrow is what we feel at the death of a loved one when we are in faith that they have gone home and we will see them again. Sorrow and heartache are what we feel when we miss someone we love, or when we are in the presence of someone whose heart is closed. Suffering is what we might feel when we take a loss, or someone's decision to close their heart, personally. Suffering is often what the wounded self feels. The loving adult, in connection with our higher guidance, helps us move beyond suffering.

Often our addiction to the earthly level gets in the way of faith and gratitude. It is an addiction to what we can have and achieve. When we are attached to having and achieving, we are attached to the outcome of things. Embracing our journey in this life with gratitude does not mean that we stop wanting what we want—fame, fortune, relationship, family—but it does mean that our happiness does not depend on getting it. It means that we embrace the journey and make *how we travel* on the journey more important than any outcome.

Most people resist letting go of their cherished plans and embracing the journey. This always reminds me of the joke:

"Do you know how to make God laugh?"

"How?"

"Make plans!"

Embracing the spiritual journey does not mean we will not feel sadness or heartache. It means that those feelings will become manageable rather than something we have to protect against. And what makes them manageable is our connection with Divine love and our gratitude for the journey. Each moment we are truly loving and grateful, we are peaceful, even in sorrow, sadness, and grief.

True gratitude is much more than everyday thankfulness. It is an experience of deep joy that we feel towards Divine love in response to all we receive, perceive, and experience on earth. Part of our challenge is to feel gratitude even for the experiences that are difficult. Although they are often tragic on the earthly level, they give us opportunities to become our most loving selves and evolve our souls. In order to find the Divine lesson in a painful situation, we may need to spend some time contemplating and searching for the lesson, as we do in Step Four when we ask, "What would love do here?" The very act of seeking the loving action soothes the gnawing pain of loss and helps us see the same circumstance with new eyes. We discover blessings in most things, even illness and loss.

## Integration and Consciousness

Integration is another reward of the sacred healing journey. Separating our various aspects—our inner child, our wounded self, and our loving adult—and connecting with our spiritual guidance lead to integration and wholeness. It may seem like a contradiction to say that separation leads to wholeness, but it is only through healing the separate aspects that they can integrate into a healed, whole soul.

If individuals begin inner work before becoming parents, educators, therapists, and other professionals who work with children, they could raise children who are naturally more whole, loving, and spiritually connected. We can each do our part in changing the world into a loving and peaceful place by doing our own inner work. We will never change the world by trying to change others. Only by our own deep commitment to our own healing process will we become integrated and whole, beacons in the darkness to light the way to love.

After a few years of practicing Inner Bonding, you will find that you no longer need to consider the separate aspects of yourself, even in your dialoguing. Your feelings and thoughts will work in harmony. You will be conscious of your inner experience, your higher experience, and your experience of the world all at the same time. This is consciousness—another reward of practicing Inner Bonding.

# Forgiveness

We are often told to forgive others because forgiveness brings you closer to the love that is God. Sometimes we are even told to force ourselves to forgive. Yet this is never necessary. Forgiveness is a natural result of developing a loving adult and healing the core shame of our wounded self. As long as we are still rewounding ourselves with unloving behavior toward ourselves, our wounded self will feel angry at those who hurt us in the past and present. Once you learn to be compassionate toward your wounded self, maintain an intent to learn, and set loving boundaries, you will find that you are no longer angry at anyone, because you know that your guidance walks with you. Consequently, there is no reason to be angry. You move into compassion and forgiveness, recognizing that whoever harmed you is or was suffering from his or her fears, false beliefs, and disconnection from God. You learn to see beneath the hard shell of others' wounded selves and address the spark of love within them, no matter how unloving they were or are to you. When you have a loving adult who is able to stay consistently connected to your guidance, you no longer move into your own wounded self in reaction to their wounded self. You become more and more immune to darkness. We can move toward this enlightened state each day. I don't know if I will ever reach a fully enlightened state, but to me, getting there is not the point. The point is being devoted to the journey.

Forgiving and loving yourself leads to forgiving and loving others. Forgiving and loving others leads to forgiving and loving yourself. It's another one of those victorious circles. But never force yourself to forgive others. Your anger at them indicates that you are not yet taking care of yourself. If you force yourself to forgive others before learning how to take loving care of yourself, you can actually make your healing harder. Forcing forgiveness cuts you off from your feelings of anger and blame.

Since these projections are letting you know that you are not taking loving care of yourself, you do not want to cut them off. Allow forgiveness to be the natural consequence of loving yourself.

## Grace, Oneness, Peace, Joy

When we embrace the sacred privilege of healing and evolving our souls, we experience grace. Grace is the feeling of profound peace and well-being that comes when we surrender our individual will to a higher will. It is a joyous lightness of being and a feeling of oneness with all of life.

A sense of oneness is essential to our well-being. The sense of oneness creates within us feelings of safety, belonging, community, acceptance, love, power, hope, purpose, and peace. It is the result of inviting Divine love into our hearts and healing all that has kept us separate from the love that is God. Perhaps our most sacred privilege is this direct communion with our higher source of love and wisdom. It is our most powerful, most replenishing, and most gratifying state.

The first time I experienced grace, I didn't know what to call it. I was standing at my kitchen sink, doing the dishes (a task I am not fond of), when out of nowhere a wave of lightness came over my being. Suddenly I loved the soap bubbles, the warmth of the water, the sunlight coming through the window, and the birds singing outside. In fact, at that moment I loved *everything*. I felt a sense of oneness with everything, and I heard myself singing, in spite of the fact that I can't carry a tune. The song was a childhood nursery rhyme: *Mares eat oats, and does eat oats, and little lambs eat ivy. A kid will eat ivy, too. Wouldn't you?* (As a child I thought the words were: *Mersie dotes and dosie dotes and little lamsie divy. A kiddelie divy too, wouldn't you?*) I felt joyful to the core of my being, and I burst out laughing in the middle of my song at how off-key I sounded and how funny the words were! Nothing had ever felt so wonderful. The feeling lasted for about four hours, then gradually faded, but I knew I wanted more of it. Of course, I wanted control over it, and only later, when I talked with Erika and discovered that what I had experienced was called grace, did I learn that it is a great gift, the natural outcome of surrendering and opening my heart to Divine love.

"Grace," says Erika, "is a place where the soul rests, where God and soul touch as the soul expands."

To me, the experience of grace is the best feeling in the world. When we are in this state, we are in love with ourselves, others, life, and God. There are no barriers to our loving. Our love is expansive, encompassing everything, and it comes flowing out of us as joy.

Grace is a gift from spirit that enters our being when our hearts are completely open and free of fear. Grace is a natural outcome of growth. Likewise, true growth, which is the healing of our fears and false beliefs and moving into faith, love, and truth, is the result of grace. Grace through growth—and growth through grace—this is the astonishing power of Inner Bonding.

As I said earlier, grace, peace, and joy, like love, truth, creativity, and beauty, are gifts of spirit. We cannot generate them within our own being. They enter our hearts when our hearts are open to receiving the fullness of Divine love. We know that God is with us when we feel peace and joy in our hearts. These feelings let us know that we are taking loving care of ourselves.

God is the experience of love, peace, and joy that fills our being when we open our hearts. The spirit that is God is always waiting to enter our hearts. We don't even have to reach out to God, for God is always reaching out to us. We only have to open. Healing spiritual abuse leads us to the grace of God, offering us an ever-expanding, joyful, and creative experience of life. When we embrace the sacred privilege of taking loving action to express and evolve our souls, we will feel the grace and oneness we long for.

## Freedom

Freedom—to be all that we are, to manifest our dreams and follow our bliss, to live with peace in our hearts—is another sweet reward of embracing the sacred healing journey. The more deeply we surrender to the love and guidance that is God, the more freedom we experience. Just as loving parents support their children's freedom to explore and learn and evolve, so Divine love provides loving support for us to do the same. A young child reaches out to loving parents and receives their love and guidance; similarly, our higher power is here to love and guide us when we reach out to it.

As we heal the wounds that have kept us enslaved, we come to know that it is never a higher power that enslaves us: it is our fears and false beliefs. As we heal them, we are released from the prison of our addictions. The more we fill our hearts with the love that is God, the more freedom we have to share that love with others. We are no longer seek out others in order to *get* from them; we are free from being needy of others' time, attention, or approval. Now we seek out others to *give* to them, to share with them and learn with them, and we experience great joy in the act of giving, learning, and sharing. We leave behind controlling relationships and move into ones where we are free to truly share love. Older friendships may fall away, and new friends—friends who connect with us on a soul level, friends with whom we are free to be all that we can be—come into our lives.

Rather than losing our personal freedom by surrendering to our higher guidance, we discover that we have acquired a freedom beyond price: the freedom to love the spark of the Divine that is in us and others and to allow that love to spill out to everyone and everything.

Freedom, peace, joy, passion, wholeness, creativity, love, gratitude, forgiveness, faith, trust, and grace—these are the rewards of the sacred healing journey, the narrow road, the intent to learn about loving. We reenter the paradise we lost when we decided we could find our way without the love that is God and plucked the apple from the tree of knowledge. We heal our "original sin" of separation from Divine love. We heal our aloneness and discover our oneness.

# Epilogue

## A Prayer to Open the Heart

Sweet spirit of Divine love, we will to will thy will—to be thy will and do thy will and know thy will. We thank you for helping us to have the courage to look within, to heal all the dark places, all the shame and the anger and the guilt and the fear and the judgment. We thank you for the support and love and compassion that come through us as we support ourselves and one another in this healing journey, so that we may each become pure instruments of your love and your compassion, your peace and your patience, your truth and your wisdom, your joy and your freedom, your creativity and manifestation, and your healing and serenity.

We thank you for helping us see and be open to what we need to heal, and for helping us remember the compassionate intention to learn, each and every moment. We thank you for helping us remember who we are in our souls and why we are here, which is to become love and share love. We thank you for helping us to remember that we have a child within, our feeling self—our true soul self—that needs our care each and every moment. We thank you for helping us to remember that when we are in pain, we can open to learning about what we are doing or thinking that's causing that pain and do the healing work that we need to do.

We thank you for all opportunities that come our way to teach us, to help us to learn, and to heal and grow in love and compassion. We thank you for today, for the food, for the beauty of the flowers and the trees and the clouds, and for all learning opportunities that come our way today, no matter how challenging. We thank you for each other, and the love that we can share. We send love and blessings for the highest good to those we love, to the planet, and to all living things that share our planet, and we thank you for supporting our highest good and the highest good of all.

We are willing, sweet Spirit, to take full responsibility for our own feelings and needs. We invite you into our hearts to help us to learn about our fears and limiting beliefs and about love and truth. And we open to learning now with our inner child and our higher guidance, asking what they would like to talk with us about today. We will then take loving action based upon this dialogue, and we will consciously and continually pay attention to how we are feeling throughout the day and how our own thoughts and actions are affecting us. We breathe in the light, bringing with us a state of openness and readiness to learn.

# Afterword

by Erika J. Chopich, PhD

Shortly after Margaret and I met many years ago, I was standing in her kitchen. "I can teach you to cook!" I offered as we eagerly explored our budding friendship. "And I'll teach you to throw pots!" Margaret smiled. I thought to myself, "Gee, this woman really hates to cook!" A moment later I learned she is a master potter as well as a brilliant artist. We burst into screeching belly laughter, and so began the first step in exploration that would last into today.

We have spent all the days of our friendship in exploration. We talk endlessly, sharing our triumphs, our tragedies, our joys, and our frustrations, and have even summoned the courage to share our darkest natures. I have been Divinely blessed to have a kindred spirit to walk my journey with, step for step and side by side. We have explored who we are, and more importantly, the deeper nature of being. We have confronted and comforted and challenged and healed.

While I have been blessed with clarity and depth, Margaret has been gifted with vision and expression. The culmination of this process is *Lonely No More: The Astonishing Power of Inner Bonding*. I believe Margaret's exceptional work in this book is truly an inspiration, and I am grateful for the part I have had in helping her to bring another powerful, in-depth book about Inner Bonding to fruition.

Inner Bonding is like the graceful wings of a great sailplane: it will allow you to soar as high and as far as you wish. Margaret is a great designer. I hope your flight will be as exciting and freeing as ours.

# Resources

## Books by Margaret Paul

*How to Become Strong Enough to Love: Creating Loving Relationships through the Six-Step Pathway of Inner Bonding* (2022).
A powerful book for healing and transforming your relationships.

*Six Steps to Total Self-Healing: The Inner Bonding Process* (2021).
This is a transcription from an Inner Bonding workshop, including questions and answers and working with participants.

*The Inner Bonding Workbook: Six Steps to Healing Yourself and Connecting with Your Divine Guidance* (2019).
In this workbook, the Inner Bonding process is greatly updated with all new exercises. A powerful book that came straight from Dr. Margaret's guidance!

*Diet for Divine Connection: Beyond Junk Foods and Junk Thoughts to At-Will Spiritual Connection* (2018).
Learn to experience a consistent, at-will connection with your spiritual source of love and wisdom.

*Healing Your Aloneness* (1990).
The first book written on Inner Bonding. Takes you on a deep inner journey of healing. Helps you understand who the child is, who the loving adult is, and how to dialogue. With many examples.

*Inner Bonding* (1992).
Inner Bonding becomes a five-step process in this next book. This book presents role modeling for taking loving care of yourself in your relationships with your mate, friends, parents, children, and coworkers.

*The Healing Your Aloneness Workbook* (1993).
Teaches the Six Steps of Inner Bonding through many different exercises.

## WRITTEN WITH JORDAN PAUL, PHD

*Do I Have to Give Up Me to Be Loved by You?* (1983).
Describes how the intent to learn, as opposed to the intent to protect, leads to loving conflict resolution in committed relationships, and how conflict becomes the arena for creating learning, growth, and passion.

*Do I Have to Give Up Me to Be Loved by My Kids?* (1985).
Shows how to move beyond both authoritarian and permissive parenting into loving parenting.

*Do I Have to Give Up Me to Be Loved by You? Workbook* (1987).
Helps you to discover the ways you protect against the pain you fear, which actually creates your present pain.

# Digital Audio and Video
## AUDIO

*Beyond Fear and Addictions*

This two-hour audio presents an overview of Inner Bonding, bringing you through the Six Steps in a visualization, including contacting your spiritual guidance. I also demonstrate the process with a volunteer from the audience. Questions and answers follow.

*Anger and Inner Bonding*

In this tape, I give a one-hour overview of Inner Bonding where the Six Steps are acted out, along with the three-part anger process that is part of Step Two.

*Opening to Learning Meditation Tape*

This is the twenty-minute clearing and prayer that I do at the beginning of each day at an intensive. Each participant receives one of these recordings at the end of the intensive.

*Do I Have to Give Up Me to Be Loved by My Kids?*

This set of audios (two hours, twenty minutes long) explains how to parent children with an intent to learn and to role-play many different conflict situations, followed by questions and answers.

*From Conflict to Intimacy and Beyond*

This three-hour audio is exceptionally helpful in teaching the difference between the intent to protect and the intent to learn in relationship conflicts. Much role-playing of different conflict situations.

## VIDEO

*The Inner Bonding Introductory Lecture*
This is a one-hour, twenty-minute overview of Inner Bonding, along with the LifePaths charts. Extremely helpful in reminding you of the process and in introducing others to Inner Bonding.

*The Master Teacher Connection*
In this one-hour and forty-five-minute tape, Erika describes how she sees the spiritual Master Teachers and some of what she has learned from her Teacher. Erika is an excellent speaker, and this is a fascinating tape.

# Digital and Online Courses

*The Inner Bonding Workshop: Loving Yourself to Abundance, Freedom, and Vibrant Love*
The powerful eight-odule Inner Bonding Process for healing your aloneness

*SelfQuest*
An in-depth online membership program that teaches you Inner Bonding.

*Complete Self-Love*
A wonderful package that includes Dr. Margaret's new introductory Video, SelfQuest, the 30-Day Love Yourself program, and IBVillage membership.

*The Power to Heal Yourself*
A powerful package that includes SelfQuest, Love Yourself, IBVillage and many other programs.

*Love Yourself 30-Day Inner Bonding Program*
End anxiety, guilt, shame, toxic anger, depression, unhealthy addictions, and relationship failure with Dr. Margaret's Foundational 30-Day Inner Bonding Course.

*Attracting Your Beloved 30-Day Course*
End loneliness, isolation, or serial relationships that keep ending up the same way. Move beyond love addiction within yourself or within the people you attract. Heal the blocks that are keeping you from attracting a loving relationship.

*Passionate Purpose Vibrant Health*
Uncover the blueprint for what you came here to do—for what has heart and meaning for you. Enhance your creativity, unblock yourself from resistance and procrastination, and create a joyful, vibrantly healthy and fulfilling life with Dr. Margaret's 30-Day program.

*Wildly, Deeply, Joyously in Love*
Dr. Margaret's 30-Day course for creating loving relationships, and for healing your current relationships with your partner, parents, children, friends and coworkers.

*Unlocking Your Inner Wisdom*
Learn how to connect with your spiritual guidance, or deepen your connection, and manifest your dreams with Dr. Margaret's 30-Day course.

*The Intimate Relationship Toolbox*
Twelve-week online course with Dr. Margaret Paul, including videos, audios, and text.

*Dr. Margaret Paul's Permanent Weight Loss*
Twelve-week online course with Dr. Margaret Paul.

*Dr. Margaret Paul's free weekly podcast*
Dr. Margaret speaks about a different topic each week.

*The Inner Bonding Facilitator Training Program*
If you have a desire to be of help to others through Inner Bonding, this program is for you. It is the most deeply emersive program we offer, so even if you don't want to be a Certified Inner Bonding Facilitator, you can great accelerate your own healing through this in-depth course.

## Website

Visit our website, innerbonding.com, for events, workshops, support groups, events, and facilitator training. You can also book phone, Skype, or Zoom sessions with Dr. Margaret.

# About the Author

DR. MARGARET PAUL is the cocreator of Inner Bonding®, along with Dr. Erika Chopich, and is author/coauthor of several best-selling books, including *Do I Have to Give Up Me to Be Loved by You?*; *Do I Have to Give Up Me to Be Loved By You?: The Workbook*; *Inner Bonding*; *Healing Your Aloneness*; *The Healing Your Aloneness Workbook*; *Do I Have to Give Up Me to Be*  *Loved by My Kids?*; *Do I Have to Give Up Me to Be Loved by God?*; *Diet for Divine Connection: Beyond Junk Foods and Junk Thoughts to At-- Will Spiritual Connection*; *The Inner Bonding Workbook: Six Steps to Healing Yourself and Connecting with Your Divine Guidance*, and *Six Steps to Total Self-Healing: The Inner Bonding Process*.

Dr. Paul's books have been distributed around the world and have been translated into many languages. She holds a PhD in psychology and is a relationship expert, noted public speaker, workshop leader, educator, consultant, and artist. She has appeared on many radio and TV shows, including *The Oprah Show*. She has successfully worked with tens of thousands of individuals, couples, and business relationships and has taught classes and seminars since 1967.

Margaret continues to work with individuals, couples, and groups throughout the world on the phone, Zoom, and Skype. During her sessions, workshops, and Intensives, she is able to access her own and her clients' spiritual guidance, which enables her to work with people wherever they are in the world. She offers life-changing thirty-day courses, and she continues to conduct One-Day Inner Bonding Breakthroughs, Inner Bonding Workshops and Three-Day and Five-Day Inner Bonding intensives. She continues to develop content for www.innerbonding.com, and her passion is distributing SelfQuest®, the online program that teaches Inner Bonding. It is being offered to prisons and schools and sold to the general public.

In her spare time, Margaret loves to paint, make pottery, read, learn, grow, and spend time with her loved ones.